A guide to
the birds of Scotland

Frontispiece overleaf
Black-throated Diver, whose British nesting haunts are confined to the Scottish Highlands and Islands and southwestern lochs

Eric Hardy

A guide to
the birds of Scotland

Constable   London

First published in Great Britain 1978
by Constable and Company Ltd
10 Orange Street London WC2H 7EG
Copyright © 1978 Eric Hardy

ISBN 0 09 461170 X

Set in Monophoto Baskerville
Filmset and printed in Great Britain by
BAS Printers Limited, Wallop, Hampshire

Contents

Illustrations

Introduction

The noblest prospect of the English bird-watcher is the road to Scotland. Where Sassenachs stepped forth, properly harnessed in shooting gear for the 'Glorious Twelfth' by London's top tailors, 20,000 bird-watchers armed with binoculars and telephoto lenses now arrive annually in greater sartorial liberty, following press handouts and AA signs to ospreys at Nethybridge. The August visitor to the moors is less likely to be shot by a cabinet minister, though his way is restricted during the shooting season in some reserves like the Cairngorms.

Private 'bush telegraph' news of rare birds replaces the grouse-shooting prospects one formerly prepared for the newspapers and the Gamekeepers' Association's *Gazette*. Grouse research at Banchory field station turned our attention to ecology, rather than Burns's exaggerated 'carnage' from the thundering guns in his *Brigs of Ayr* and people who paraded their display of destruction. There is no legal ownership of wild birds. Everyone who does not harm them, or their haunts, has equal right to observe and study them.

The first county-by-county guide to bird haunts, with bird lists, was in my 1950 *Bird Lover's (Watcher's) Week-End Book*, developed from the 'Choosing a Bird Holiday' feature in *Wild Birds Magazine* (1946–7) which I edited. The present work succeeds Kenneth Richmond's 1968 *Regional Guide to the Birds of Scotland*, the first of its kind, and conforms to the new series of Regional Guides begun with David Saunders's 1974 *A Guide to the Birds of Wales*.

For convenience we have grouped the counties within the twelve new regional divisions, except for the isles of

Argyll, Ross and Inverness, listed with the Hebrides. Unlike their recorders, birds and bird-watchers are not divided by political boundaries. Ornithology should be considered on ecological divisions like watersheds, mountain ranges and islands. Botanical 'vice-counties' have never been accept-able. However, many good bird haunts overlie county boundaries, notably the Cairngorms, Hebrides and larger firths, bays and estuaries, or range outside the bounds of reserves like Balranald and Loch Garten.

Precise location of many rarities is withheld. The law has no exclusive bird-watching rights; but sometimes there are restrictions on access and penalties for wilfully disturbing breeding species. Here caution is advised. One of the modern field guides to birds, a pair of prismatic binoculars supplemented for long-distance views with a telescope of at least 30 × magnification (which doesn't require a stand, if used deerstalker's way), gumboots for estuaries and wet morning fields, 1 inch or new 1:50,000 Ordnance Survey maps, and the wild goose's vice of getting up early, all aid the energetic bird-watcher. Privileged circles in the 'bush telegraph' of current information, societies owning reserves available to members, and the Nature Conservancy Council which issues National Nature Reserve permits to *bona fide* ornithologists without charge, are further aids. The Automobile Association's 1975 *Tourists' Guide to Scotland* should be of assistance to motorists.

Improved access by motorway and car ferry, chair lifts, bird observatories, guided bird-watching weeks and private cruising among the islands enable many to see birds without the endless energy of the real bird-hunter with legs like a mountain goat, the many eyes of Argus and a mind like a card index of memories of places where he first found nests or migrants. This brought problems of pressure of people;

but practical ornithologists, skilled in fieldcraft, should not be blamed with the lemming-like horde who come to the country looking for toilets and teas, and tramp out vegetation in forest and hillside.

To avoid much repetition, I have made one check list of Scottish birds; the regional lists of breeding birds and visitors localise this, with their county bird haunts, without including every vagrant visitor. Scientific names and their classification are so frequently changed by the British Ornithologists' Union as to flood bird literature with synonyms and confusions. Modern standardisation of English names may be at variance with the *Oxford Dictionary*, like shoveler and wigeon, and vernacular names are often wide of the truth. Britain lacks an *Academie Française*, and not every ornithologist accepts the BOU's assumption of such powers.

I must apologise to those who find anything wrong with this book or my presentation, and gratefully thank all who have supplied information, my friend Dennis Green for kindly allowing me to include some of his Scottish photographs, my publisher for his cooperation and courtesy and my tolerant companions at Alltshellach, Loch Awe House, Altachorvie, and many less comfortable places. At least I cannot be blamed for the duplication of so many place names in Scotland, or the barbarous Gaelic names of the 'hills'. Four and six figure map references refer to the Ordnance Survey maps which are now replaced by a new 1:50,000 series. The latter mark Nature Reserves and Forest Walks.

I have never bought, sold or collected eggs or bird-skins, or shot birds except for food. I was an active member of the RSPB over 50 years ago, as its journal records in the early 1930s. We were prepared to 'bend over backwards' as life-long conservationists over how much information to leave out, despite criticism like 'lack of sufficient detail' or 'lacks proof' (*e.g.* Fisher's *The Fulmar*, 1952, p 235, when it was never asked for). There seems to be an unacceptable claim of privilege, rather than example, where exact locations have been permitted with rarities in several previous books on birds of The Highlands, Northern Britain, etc. Press handouts are issued for publicity when new sites are acquired, and keep public interest at a peak by regular repetitions, thus creating the demand to see more birds. The leading bird-protection magazine has carried many advertisements for holiday residences mentioning rare breeders in the precise areas. Without vetting, anyone upon subscription to a branch is taken on coach-trips to see winter haunts (*e.g.* harrier-roosts) and nesting season haunts of rarities. This, and numerous unvetted members of the 'grape vine' of immediate telephoned news of rarities, are privileged publicity within a 'closed shop' denied to many harmless bird-watchers who have equal right to study and enjoy birds without harming their haunts. No complaint was made of the earlier book of this title naming road and water of the Loch Ba black-throated divers. It is more alarming that many ex-collectors and bird-shooters have attained high office in bird-protection societies and privileged access to reserves denied to life-long conservationists unable to afford high subscriptions. As dead birds can't lay any more eggs, the tolerance of shooting magnificently plumaged duck which were specially protected by public funds in their arctic nesting haunts, seems illogical conservation, as Professor Owen, of Lund University, Sweden, expressed in *The Times* a few years ago. Nevertheless, we ask readers for caution, without disturbance, and have omitted many details of rarer birds.

Bird-watchers come north because more rare migrants drift to Shetland isles than anywhere else in Britain, and fifteen British breeding birds nest only in Scotland. Many nestings have been under-recorded for security or from incomplete coverage, notably ospreys in seven counties, dotterel and golden eagles on many, and snow-buntings on several, mountains, Highland hobbies and fieldfares, bitterns, goshawks and peregrines. Not everyone reports to the rarities' committee or the ornithological journals. After voluntary and friendly discussion at the Scottish HQ of the RSPB, it was agreed to delete over 340 locations, chiefly of Schedule 1 birds. This was agreed with many unpublished personal findings, even with information already existing in books on northern birds and in ornithological journals and, despite information in Nature Conservancy brochures for reserve visitors, in SWT reports on their nesting grebes and ospreys, and so many sites mapped in the recent *Atlas of Breeding Birds of Britain*. It was agreed despite the RSPB's magazine advertising accommodation which tempted unvetted customers to the presence of golden eagles, ospreys, choughs, harriers, crested tits, etc. (with all details available on arrival), and RSPB coach-parties guided to haunts of eagles, etc; despite a book by a former director (secretary) of the society being privileged without criticism to pinpoint dotterel haunts we have deleted, and a former reserve warden privileged without criticism to list breeding haunts of crossbills, dotterel, greenshank, snow-bunting, Highland peregrines, eagles, wood sandpipers and whimbrel, and island phalaropes. Despite, too, the 'grape vine' of instantly-telephoned rarity news to privileged circles. Locations already published in many books and journals were deleted in case foreign readers were not yet aware of this information.

Knowledge cannot be a closed book. Obviously for security a policy agreement is required to be accepted by all forms of publication, from the privileged grape vines to ornithological journals, books and the Press without the recent privileged exceptions. 'Publication with protection' is often fund-raising and recruitment publicity. In 1973, the RSPB's conservation planning officer admitted to me that its flood of press hand-outs and TV interviews increased public desire to see birds, while the veteran editor of a major bird club's annual Reports feared the increasing risk of bird-watching becoming 'a theoretical study with birds seen through telescopes at long-range in centrally heated hides behind barbed wire entanglements.' Except on Nature Conservancy reserves, access to rare bird-watching is too easily purchased by unvetted visitors and not otherwise available to seriously active ornithologists and conservationists in the area. This, and privileged exemptions from the Protection of Birds Act, such as a young golden eagle to a falconer in 1977, became an unfortunate challenge to trespass. Secrecy also encourages false monetary values on eggs and birds, leading to vandalism which will be stopped only by heavier penalties. But some people have assumed powers they do not possess in law. While the conservation of birds should be our prime concern, there is too often the case of 'Don't do as I do, but . . .'. Alas, *Avis dictatorius* is not a declining species.

Chapter 1

Scotland—a brief introduction

Climatically, Scotland may be divided between a wet, windy, mild west with barnacle flocks and overwintering waders, as well as American visitors, and a colder, drier east where November brings hordes of pinkfoot geese to farmlands, where spring's departures are later and easterly winds drift continental migrants. North of the Great Glen (Fort William to Inverness, where the Forestry Commission has large areas) or the Highland boundary fault one sees more western Scandinavian influence, dating from the land bridge whereby red deer, mountain foxes and alpine plants colonised ancient Scotland. Shetland and the Northern Isles are most Scandinavian in their bird life.

What is there to see? Five hundred and seventeen Scottish birds include 192 nesters and sixty-one escaped or introduced species ignored by serious ornithologists. Over 300 wild species are recorded annually. The attraction is that much cannot be seen elsewhere in Britain. Over 360 pairs of golden eagle nest in the Highlands and Islands. Sixty to eighty pairs of dotterel return annually to the mountains; snow buntings nest in three counties, and the shore lark bred once. Peregrines haunt 100 eyries. The Highlands of Argyll, Inverness, Perth, Aberdeen, Angus, Banff and mid-Perthshire are the main haunts of eagles, the high-pitched cry of the osprey, ptarmigan, crossbills, crested tits and slavonian grebes. The northwest mainland of Wester Ross, northwest Sutherland and western Inverness-shire are the main haunt of divers and greenshank. Temminck's stints nested in the Cairngorms. Ptarmigan and red grouse overlap at 2500–3000 feet (750–900 m); but the farther north one goes the lower is the altitude of birds, and ring ouzels breed at 400 feet (120 m) near Inverpolly, and ptarmigan at 600 feet (180 m) in the northwest.

Great island-strewn lochs, glittering in a bowl of black mountains, or featureless sheets of lowland water, provide over fifty nesting pairs of slavonian grebes at twenty-four sites in five counties, nineteen pairs of black-necked grebes on five waters in the central lowlands from Inverness-shire. Goldeneye and scoter in six counties, scaup in five, as well as between 500 and 1000 pairs of goosanders nesting, over 1000 pairs of red-breasted mergansers and some 10,000 pairs of eiders. Nearly sixty pairs of black-throated divers occupy islands in lochs, sixty-two pairs of red-throated divers also breed and sometimes great northerns. About a score of osprey eyries in seven counties are often in trees with a few on rocks. Eight pairs of wood sandpiper nest in the straths of two Highland counties; sometimes green sandpipers breed and there are 300–400 pairs of green-shank, mostly in Wester Ross and southwest Sutherland. Over thirty-five pairs of dainty approachable red-necked phalaropes nest in three counties, over thirty in Shetland. Inland colonies of cormorants breed at Wigtown's Castle Loch and North Uist's Loch an Tomain. Rich waterfowl reservoirs lie in the urbanised Lowlands and southern Uplands.

Over 200 forests covering nearly 809,400 ha (2,000,000 acres) are not all the gloomy, sunless conifers of their critics. They increased the haunts of raven, hen harrier, black grouse, capercaillie with voices like shoveler, golden eagle, coal tit and siskin, while nest-boxes assisted the breeding range of redstart and pied flycatcher to the Highlands in modern times. Nearly 500 pairs of crested tit breed in the forests; fifty pairs of redwing nest in five counties, and there are opportunities for seeing nesting fieldfares, Scottish crossbills and ospreys. Nearly half the British population of peregrines nest on Highland coastal and inland rocks, and a high percentage on Hoy in Orkney. Britain's biggest arctic terneries are on Westray and Papa Westray in Orkney.

The most rewarding bird-watching for rarities and listing new species is on Fair Isle, half way between Shetland and Orkney, followed by the Isle of May off the Firth of Forth. Then, much more accessible, comes the Spey Valley, stretching to the Cairngorm massif. Fourth and most accessible is Aberlady Bay, on Edinburgh's doorstep. Many lack legs to reach ptarmigan in the Cairngorms and eagles in Glencoe. Even tea-creepers may sit in the comfort of a car on the A975 watching masses of eiders and waders in the Ythan estuary. The more adventurous may work an army stint on St Kilda, for its seabirds.

Though migrant cock nightingales reach Shetland and Perth, they do not nest in Scotland. When lemming-like hordes of summer trippers go home to hibernate like the hedgehog, there are surf scoters, king and Steller's eiders, massive flocks of long-tailed duck, velvet scoters and 2000-strong flocks of snow buntings in the northern isles. Mile-long rafts of duck bring bird-watchers to the Firth of Forth and great gatherings of barnacles and grey geese lure coachloads from Manchester, Liverpool or London to north Solway and Islay. A few hundred Greenland whitefronts regularly visit southwest Scotland and there are annual arrivals of waxwings, great grey shrikes, European crossbills, flocks of little auks, great northern divers, snowy owls and 100 sightings of Scandinavian ospreys on passage. From August to October, northern isles and headlands offer rewarding sea watches for the great bird movements over the oceans: great and sooty shearwaters and long-tailed and pomarine skuas, if the wind is favourable. Great northern divers often summer there. Arctic races of auks are numerous off Shetland in winter. The wider entrance to the North Sea admits more oceanic shearwaters and skuas to the east coast than the Irish Sea admits to northwest England. As many as fifty-six yellow-browed warblers and twenty-two red-breasted flycatchers have been recorded on passage in a year.

The Hebrides and the Northern Isles offer the best prospects for seeing black-browed albatross, ivory and Ross's gulls, surf scoters, Steller's and king eiders and little auks. Arctic seabirds visit them. While American waders favour the Hebrides in autumn, rare passerines from northern Europe favour the Northern Isles. Corncrakes make the sound of summer on their poor farmland; several cliff heronries linger on their rocks, and Leach's petrels breed where the rocks have soil. Sooty shearwaters regularly pass the Outer Hebrides in autumn, while as many as thirty-five great northern divers flock in Shetland's Quendale Bay in April. American waders also make their landfall in Shetland, and Fair Isle, like the Isle of May, is a landfall for rare aquatic warblers. Foula's position receives less continental migration than Fair Isle and fewer snow buntings than the east coast.

The wetlands of most importance are Loch Leven (Kinross), Solway, the Firth of Tay, the Eden estuary and the lochs of Strath Eden, South Uist and east Aberdeenshire. The Firth of Forth, the area where most birdwatchers live (especially the south side), is the haunt of over 300 species, with important island nesting sites of five species of tern menaced by great black-backed and other predatory gulls, as well as of major winter flocks of great crested grebes, Britain's biggest duck masses, especially mallard, 85 per cent of scaup wintering in Britain and

Ireland (over 15 per cent of the European population) between Leith Docks and Musselburgh sewer (Seafield), over 1240 scoter, more than half the winter goldeneye counted in Britain and Scotland's major flocks of 62,000 waders. Temminck's stint and gull-billed tern are autumn passage migrants. The black-browed albatross brought a migration of bird-watchers to the firth, where arctic skuas and Manx shearwaters are regular autumn visitors. Flocks of up to 230 little gulls occur in August off Fife. Sooty shearwaters are regular autumn migrants off May. The firth is on the track of the continental drift of passerines. Radar shows overland movement of probably Icelandic waders from Aberlady Bay, etc., to Ayr and Solway, and another southeast over the Cheviots to Teesmouth.

The Moray Firth has Britain's greatest wintering gatherings of long-tailed duck and velvet scoters. Black guillemots and great northern divers winter regularly in Dornoch Firth and Beauly Firth.

Sailing down the Clyde on a wartime troopship bound for North Africa in the fast-fading dusk, my last sight of Scotland was its second largest gull roost, some 5800 common gulls and a white cloud of post-breeding black-headed gulls. Nearly 30,000 waders flock on the Inner Clyde. Here are big flocks of shelduck, nearly 2000 eiders in January, and nearly 200 mergansers in December. In 1968 the Inner Clyde attracted Scotland's first nesting little ringed plovers.

Scotland's major wader flocks, over 70,000 birds, roost along North Solway's October tides. Later come 5000 Spitzbergen barnacles to the Caerlaverock–Rockcliffe area, a major British attraction. Fifteen thousand barnacles are in western Scotland and the Isles early in April.

Contrary to many English views of the Scottish winter,

parts are sometimes sufficiently sheltered to overwinter chiffchaff, blackcap, greenshank, and a ring ouzel on Arran (and presumably another recorded in Lanark on 11 January and a wheatear on the shores of Forth on 2 January). A common tern reached the Forth estuary on 20 January and a ring ouzel on 1 February (with another on the coast at Ullapool on 12 February). The corncrake was in Midlothian on 3 February and in Orkney nesting haunts by 24 February. The osprey has returned to Speyside by 6 March, the dotterel in the Highlands by 12 March. A bluethroat was on Fair Isle by 22 March, a red-necked phalarope on passage in Dumfriesshire by 19 March and at Fetlar breeding haunts by 11 May. The spotted flycatcher reached Perth by 28 March and Angus by 8 April, the swift in Midlothian by 4 April and the honey buzzard in Fife by April, though a January Kirkcudbrightshire bird probably overwintered.

Bird lists are often inflated out of regional balance by the intensity of bird-watching where areas are most accessible, or wind-drifted casuals whose landfall might have occurred in many other places. However, much depends upon the ecology, like Speyside, or an isolated position concentrating birds, like Fair Isle. Foot-slogging over high Cairngorms for dotterel or bogged down seeking green sandpipers and greenshank on a Highland moor vies with joining a fishing boat off Rockall. But a seabird watch probably adds more new knowledge. Late one May, after passing through the Pentland Firth into the North Sea, an ornithological friend on a Liverpool ship reported to me the presence of four cock house sparrows, first seen when 137 miles (220 km) east of the nearest land, the English Farnes. On 15 December 1953 two cock eastern American cowbirds, brown-headed birds, flew aboard his ship off the Canadian Great Banks and remained aboard until 59 miles (95 km) off Rockall. After circling they left in a northeast direction at 0900 hours, in a west-southwest wind. Maybe they made the 215 miles (346 km) to St Kilda, 243 miles (391 km) to Barra Head, or even Tory Island, with no ornithologist there to record them. In January 1975 a gyr falcon rested on the Forties Field oil rig, 124 miles (200 km) northeast of Aberdeen.

Despite protection, bird life may be temporary and change with the age of forest trees like harriers, short-eared owls and warblers, with changing water levels at lochs and reservoirs, and the sudden drainage of black-headed gulleries. The presence of people brought feeding chaffinches to Glen Nevis car park. Conservationists may be in conflict over the preservation of rubbish tips whose presence brings the rarer arctic and American gulls, or sewage works, like Seafield, with their waders. Fish stocks influence shag and cormorant numbers, the summer seabirds off eastern Shetlands and autumn seabird watches. Shoals of brit and sand eels increase the Ythan estuary terns, but foxes and trippers deplete them. Fishery interests may destroy cormorant colonies, like Moan in Ayr. New barley crops changed the Tay Valley from greylag to pinkfoot country and the November flockings to mainly in the east and southwest of the country. Cessation of cattle grazing in Orkney increased willow scrub and with it breeding reed buntings and sedge warblers.

Gamekeeping, now extinct in Orkney, influences the destruction of eagles still condoned in the Western Isles. Ptarmigan shooting is less fashionable nowadays because 'guns' are less energetic than bird-watchers; but shooting influences bird life in Montrose Basin, the Eden estuary, and between Grangemouth and Tyninghame in the Forth. Birds would increase greatly in Aberlady Bay if it became a no-shooting reserve. Boating may ruin a waterfowl haunt; but, providing the ecology is not changed, birds recover from the sudden effects of severe winters, oil spills and other temporary destruction.

The future influence of North Sea oil production, with its shore base at Sullom Voe on Mainland Shetland, by Yell Sound, may have been exaggerated; but it will increase human populations and bring some risk to seabird colonies. Meanwhile, offshore oil-rig platforms brought new opportunities for fixed seabird studies of regular movements of Scottish birds, and recording exhausted birds settling in adverse weather. A six weeks (September–October) list sent to me by a graduate on a rig 207 nautical miles due east of Dundee comprised some 30 species. Snipe and redstart were common; others included fulmar, gannet, knot, great black-backed, common and herring gulls, collared dove, shore lark, swallow, song thrush, redwing, wheatear, robin, blackcap, goldcrest, great grey shrike, starling, chaffinch, siskin, brambling, meadow-pipit, little bunting, also undetermined species of owl, stint and crake and a possible merlin.

Climatic changes in modern times induced the nesting or summering of such birds as scaup, Steller's eider, long-tailed skua, sanderling, wood and green sandpipers, shore lark, waxwing, golden oriole, bluethroat, brambling and Lapland bunting, and an increase of breeding snow-buntings. Increased numbers of glaucous gulls were followed by hybridisation with the closely related herring gull.

Chapter 2

A brief history of Scottish ornithology

Archaeologists in recent years excavated from the *c.* AD 900 Viking age at Skara Brae in Orkney bones of great auk, gannet, shag, mallard, barnacle goose, curlew, great black-backed gull, sea eagle, peregrine, crow, crane, whooper, great northern diver, black and red grouse, greenshank, rockdove and pelican. Bones were often stained darkly, as if buried in ashes of peat fires. At Jarlshof, in south Shetland, forty-two species unearthed from Bronze Age and Iron Age deposits included great northern diver, gannet, cormorant, shag, heron, lapwing, white stork, eagle, falcon, herring gull, skuas, swans and geese. Later Iron Age deposits there, from the first to eighth centuries AD, included storm petrel, turnstone, curlew, great black-backed gull and great auk. More bones found in the Brochs of Caithness (Keiss) and Orkney's Broch of Ayre included great northern diver, shearwater, gannet, cormorant, shag, whooper, great auk and guillemot.

These are the raw material of history. Fife caves of the second century AD revealed red-throated diver, shag, geese and gulls. The buzzard was in a Romano-British site at Haddington, AD 43–400. Viking gannet, fulmar and puffin were found on St Kilda's Hirta.

No bird is peculiar to Scotland, but when Scotland became separated from the continent and the islands were isolated, non-migratory birds with more limited breeding stock sometimes evolved subspecies with geographical variations. The red grouse is an insular form of the continental willow grouse. Its white feather bases revert occasionally in the northeast to its ancestral plumage, which can be confused with an occasional albino grouse. Many have much white in their winter plumage, often the entire belly and legs; underwing coverts and breast or face may be white, occasionally wings, tail and back. Isolation in the Outer Hebrides and Ireland evolved a quieter subspecies, more skulking and approachable, the paler cocks with more pronounced barring. The Scottish ptarmigan evolved a paler, greyer plumage than its continental ancestor, the female more golden buff with more noticeable black bars.

Most change occurred with the island wrens. With local dialect songs, they produced the larger, longer-winged, more robust and stocky Shetland wren ('Robbie') with a wider bill; the darker Outer Hebridean wren with its sweeter, higher song adding more reeling notes; the greyer, slightly larger, more barred St Kilda wren with longer feet and bill, with its louder, shriller, higher song; and the usually paler, more barred Fair Isle wren, less dusky than the Shetland wren, with a whiter throat and more buffish underparts and its loud, clear song adding a chatty bar of variations. Darker plumages distinguish other changes in the Outer Hebrides, like the darker, less red Hebridean twite, and the darker Hebridean song thrush, Hebridean hedge sparrow and Hebridean rock pipit. This darkness may be because they haunt more vegetation than bleak island cliffs of greyer, barred St Kilda and Fair Isle wrens.

The Shetland starling is a darker race with slightly longer wings and thicker beak, more like the heavily built Faroe starling. The Scottish crossbill evolved in the Highlands a larger beak and larger wings (the claim that it is a paler subspecies of the parrot crossbill is not usually accepted). The Scottish crested tit also evolved there as a darker race, with a longer song period. Some ornithologists would have a Scottish linnet with darker, richer colour and a more striated mantle, in the north and western islands, Lanark and Renfrew, a southwestern Scottish chaffinch with darker ear coverts and throat, and a Shetland guillemot with darker streaking on its underwing and flanks. It is felt that such claims are too ambitious.

The welcome return of snowy owls to nest on Fetlar in 1967 was erroneously publicised as their first breeding in Scotland. I wrote in the *Sunday Times* in June 1974, and in previous articles in the *Aberdeen Press & Journal* and ornithological magazines, that, after examining the notes and catalogues of the Liverpool collector William Bullock, I had no reason to doubt his claim that they nested in Scotland at the beginning of last century—and probably continued to about 1856. Dr W. R. P. Bourne, Aberdeen University seabird authority, wrote to me: 'I agree about the snowy owls; I had to add a note to the proceedings of the Conservancy symposium on Shetland drawing attention to the old records, because the RSPB, who are supposed to be dealing with Shetland birds, left them out.'

Bullock, a wealthy Liverpool jeweller and accomplished collector, was a Fellow of the Linnaean Society, publishing information in their Transactions and the Supplement to Montagu's *Ornithological Dictionary* (1813). In 1807 his private museum contained a great snowy owl from Dr L. Edmonston, ancestor of the present laird, which inspired him to tour Orkney and Shetland in 1812, Bullock having moved his collection to Piccadilly where it became the London Museum. The 1830 *Companion* to his London Museum mentions watching from 40 yards (36·5 m), in July 1812, a male snowy owl on the rabbit warren on the Links in 'the Island of North Ronaldshaw', its mate having been killed a few months before. He mentions one on adjacent

'Isle Westra' and obtained a specimen on Unst, adding that from the testimony of Edmonston, who protected the owls, and other islanders, he had not the smallest doubt about it breeding and remaining the whole year there and on Yell. On two occasions birds were seen at the end of the summer in company with three or four brown young. He collected male and female. One wounded on Balta disgorged a young rabbit; another he obtained contained a sandpiper. He sent specimens to Edinburgh Museum and to private collectors. One crofter shot over thirty on Unst. From 1955 it became a regular visitor to Whalsay, Unst, and Fetlar after a modern abundance of Scandinavian lemmings brought a surplus of snowy owls. It breeds in Iceland.

Bullock obtained one of a pair of great auks, the last for a long time on Papa Westray. The female was killed just before his arrival. On the sale of his collection in 1819 this went to the British Museum. He shot Scotland's first collared pratincole at Baltasound, Unst, in 1812, and discovered Leach's petrel as a British bird at St Kilda in 1818. Towards the end of June he found a 'king duck' (king eider) with six yellowish-white eggs rather smaller than an eider's, on a rock impending the sea on Papa Westray. Shetland is notable for its nesting history of a number of northern European birds, rarely, if ever, breeding else-where in Scotland. The recent increase in its whimbrel, snowy owls, fieldfares and Icelandic black-tailed godwits inspired hopes of a return to breeding by turnstone, purple sandpiper, long-tailed duck, great northern diver and snow bunting.

Conservation now commands attention where museums and private collectors made rare birds rarer by killing them. Charles St John (1809–56), a wealthy London civil servant, a protégé of the *Edinburgh Review*, shot his way around the

Highlands, committing dreadful slaughter among ospreys and eagles. Lt. Col. Peter Hawker returned from the Peninsula War for his famous punt gun to strike terror among all the wildfowl on the Solway. At Crosby Library, on Merseyside, magnificently mounted bird corpses stare with sad glassy eyes out of glass coffins in their dying shame for the ambitious ignorance of a Victorian collector: Lt. Col. (purchased commission, late Indian Army) C. T. Echalaz (1844–1910). Lacking the fieldcraft of St John and his intrepid gillie, he paid gamekeepers to lead him to the nests of harriers on Barra in order to shoot one sprung off her nest 'with the intense satisfaction of seeing her come tumbling down into the water'. I quote from his book, published at the ratepayers' expense, relating at length his murder of rare birds on their nests, setting traps for buzzards, etc., to satisfy an ambition to leave a 'collection' for posterity to remember him. He went shooting great northern divers in the Sound of Barra. His gun ended the life of splendid specimens of fierce-eyed peregrine falcons nesting on Mull, and of inoffensive razorbills. He silenced the cuckoo in the farthest Hebrides, but knew nothing of its natural history, for his book on the birds (which begins with a chapter on 'How I Shot My First Tiger') quoted all their descriptions verbatim from Howard Saunders's manual of the day. When I was asked to write the foreword to the corporation's recent *Guide* to their idol's collection, the chairman preferred not to publish my criticism of such Blimpish characters who necessitated the 1880 Wild Birds Protection Act. Dead birds cannot lay any more eggs; but killing raptors, notably eagles, continues under game preservation, particularly in the Outer Hebrides.

Scotland has long been the venue for English egg collectors. That some recently convicted offenders belonged to leading bird protection societies reflects the need for better screening of appointments. I was called to examine 2000 eggs left by the late J. Veevers, a Lancashire collector honoured with Fellowship of the RSPB. These included gadwall, wigeon and pintail from Orkney and Shetland reserves, sixty guillemot eggs and those of slavonian grebe, red-necked phalarope and whole series of kittiwakes. In the 1930s the late C. H. Gowland, a convicted egg dealer (claimed to be the biggest in the world), catalogued Scottish crossbill eggs at 6s. 6d. each, Scottish crested tits at 1s. 6d., dotterel at 12s. 6d., greenshank at 10s., and golden eagle eggs at £1, with well-marked ones at £2. He showed me his cheque book counterfoils naming now eminent ornithologists who supplied him. In Liverpool Museum in 1931, the curator showed me such an eagle eggshell taken recently in Ross-shire. After annual press publicity hand-outs from the RSPB drawing attention to Loch Garten's ospreys, I received (and published) a correspondent's letter about osprey eggs which a Welsh collector brought back from Scotland. An enormous list sent to me by Rosenberg, the Edgware (London) dealer in 1938, offered British skins of: red-throated diver, summer plumage, 12s. 6d., great northern diver, winter, 27s., crossbill 4s., peregrine 15s., great skua 17s. 6d., arctic, immature 4s. 6d., snow bunting 1s. 9d., black guillemot 4s. 6d., and golden eagle £3. In previous years he offered me British short-eared owl skins for 10s. and osprey for 22s. 6d. I have never bought or sold bird skins or eggs.

In 1960, a Nature Conservancy survey of Highland birds stated that collectors were more of a nuisance than a lasting effect upon golden eagle, snow bunting and dotterel. I could not understand why so many ex egg collectors received privileged access at 'restricted' bird reserves for ospreys, snowy owls, etc., denied to us after life-long conservation.

However, more bird life is increasing than decreasing in Scotland's changing ecology and climate. Rintoul and Baxter's excellent 1953 two-volume *The Birds of Scotland*, a standard reference work, is now outdated. In 1933 I wrote in the scientific journal *Nature* of the increasing passage of Scandinavian ospreys, and that 'sufficient protection in suitable Scottish localities should induce the osprey to nest again'. In an article on the osprey in the *Aberdeen Press & Journal* that year, I wrote: 'There is absolutely no reason why the osprey should not nest again, providing suitable protection be afforded it.' The Scandinavian influence also increased nesting of tree pipit, wood and green sandpipers, Temminck's stint, spotted crake, slavonian grebe, blue-throat, fieldfare, redwing, and possibly long-tailed skua, and brought wrynecks to Speyside in the late 1960s. Several boreal birds extending south brought more snowy owls, king and Steller's eiders, etc. Increasing Nearctic birds (Greenland–North America) include scoter, goldeneye, scaup, great northern diver, Sabine's gull and the autumn drift of American waders to Western and Northern Isles. The Caspian influence is seen in the increase of black-necked grebes, Mediterranean black-headed gulls and collared doves.

Calm weather or storm controls the small boat visits to bird islets without landing piers for Caledonian Macbrayne's ships. Flooding in wet seasons often drowns nests of divers; but climatic changes like recent mild winters increased the range of great tit and spread the blue tit into Sutherland and Caithness, while cooler summers kept redwings and fieldfares back to breed. The king eider came back as a visitor with the recent climatic change.

Like a centre-forward scoring a goal at Ibrox Park, the bearded tit's dramatic arrival on the Scottish bird list in 1972 probably excited bird-watchers more than any other modern addition. No previous claim existed when seventeen appeared in five counties. However, the biological success stories are the arctic fulmar, which now saturates the cliffs, yet until 1878 it nested only on St Kilda, and the Mediterranean collared turtledove, which first nested, in Moray and Ayr, in 1957, in Lewis by 1962 and in more than a score of counties by 1965. The little ringed plover began nesting in 1968, in inner Clyde, the great northern diver in 1970, in Wester Ross. The lesser spotted woodpecker was a new species in 1968 and 1971 in Perthshire and Inverness. In 1975 the American spotted sandpiper made its first European nesting in the Highlands. Increasing herring and lesser black-backed gulls necessitated culls on May and other Forth islands, while the arrogant voice of the great black-backed gull increased inland. Increasing wild grey geese visiting Islay and northeast Scotland provoked requests by farmers for their control, while an overflow of increasing golden eagles, mergansers and goosanders spread into the English Lakeland. In the first half of this century winter pinkfoot geese increased from fourteen to twenty-five roosts in southeast Scotland, and greylags from five to twenty-nine. In 1976, the little ringed plover reached Shetland (Fetlar).

Other increases include black-throated diver, osprey, gannet, shag, great and arctic skuas, black and slavonian grebes, hen harrier, gadwall, pintail, shoveler, tufted duck, pochard, scoter, eider, shelduck, curlew, oystercatcher, carrion crow, wood warbler, goldcrest, great spotted woodpecker, redwing and fieldfare. Wild swans and glaucous, Iceland and little gulls increased as winter visitors. Great black-backed gulls became regular inland visitors. Nest boxes extended the forest range of pied flycatchers, redstarts, and certain duck.

Reports of pygmy owls nesting in Glen More, Speyside, have not been confirmed, though confusion may have arisen from hearing tape-recordings played to lure possible birds from the woods.

Changes in one species sometimes affected the population of others. The great black-backed gull's increase at Noss caused a decline in lesser black-backed gulls; increasing great skuas in Shetland kept down the great black-backed gull there where it is less numerous than in Orkney. Pressure of seaside trippers depleted many terneries and the cormorant colony on Balcarry Point (Kirkcudbrightshire), though ptarmigan were little affected, and more damage was caused to the turf, by the enormous increase in chair lift skiers and walkers in the Cairngorms. Modern research showed that generations of 'vermin' destruction in game preservation had less lasting effect upon red grouse than has the conservation and propagation of heather. Conservationists soon see how birds settle in unshot areas where visitors do not harm them.

Shipping dispersed rats to the destruction of island colonies of auks and terns. Abandoned cats preyed on Fair Isle birds and Island of Roan storm petrels, while great black-backed gulls ate young puffins on North Rona. Several bird haunts deteriorated in recent years, notably Loch Ken's bean geese and Ben Lomond, the southernmost haunt of ptarmigan. Increasing town rubbish tips increased inland gulls. Enormous colonies of Sandwich terns at Morrich More, in Easter Ross, and on Sands of Forvie, Aberdeen, were almost decimated by the modern increase of foxes as well as by public interference. Other birds have retreated before great skuas, great black-backed gulls and fulmars.

Declining birds include shearwater, merlin, ptarmigan, golden plover, dotterel, red-necked phalarope (especially in Orkney and Uist, though it tried to regain a foothold on the mainland of Caithness and Sutherland), terns, corn bunting and mistle thrush. Puffins declined dramatically on Clo Mor, St Kilda and the Shiants, though their virus infection seems to be more localised than publicity implied. It may be a natural, long-term population control. Corncrakes declined even in Shetland as they were less inclined than partridge to nest in hedge bottoms with the advent of closer, quicker mechanical hay cuttings. Peregrines are recovering slowly from the effects of pesticides which reduced Highland eyries from over 330 to 75 by the 1960s; but swallows are scarcer now in Shetland, the Outer Hebrides and the northwest. Flight lines of wild duck may change. Lochs Feochan, Melfort and Craignish, attracting hundreds of duck to the Argyll coast after the last war, were hardly worth a duck count in 1960.

Though Scotland's largest gamebird, the capercaillie, was brought back from the edge of extinction by introducing Scandinavian stock, sea eagles from Norway were introduced to Rhum in 1975, and the Western Isles and other places have been stocked with ptarmigan, game pheasants and Hungarian partridge; introductions are the modern recorder's headache. One thousand feral greylag and Canada geese breed in the southwest. Free-flying white and blue lesser snow geese from Birkhill, Cupar, Gaudry (Firth of Tay) and Ross's geese from elsewhere join wild pinkfeet and act as markers of Perthshire flocks wintering on Lancashire feeding grounds. Escapes from duck zoos, like the American wigeon at Auchlossan in March 1972, also include confusing hybrids, necessitating checking eye colour in 'ferruginous' ducks and bill tip in crossbred 'scaup', 'tufted duck' and 'pochard' types. Increasing importations by avicultural dealers, here and elsewhere in Britain, resulted in more aviary escapees like red-headed buntings, the painted bunting of limited migration appearing on Voe in Shetland, free-flying night herons from Edinburgh Zoo, a Manchester Zoo pelican on May, an American double-crested cormorant on Glasgow's Broomielaw wharves and exotic cranes and flamingoes.

Golden pheasants have been naturalised in Wigtown, Kirkcudbrightshire and Lothian, and Reeve's in Inverness-shire. Red-legged partridge liberated by their would-be shooters in parts of Buchan, Sutherland, Banff and Angus usually find the winter too wet to become permanently established on the fauna list. Fifty to eighty per cent of trained hawks and falcons are eventually lost or hacked back to the wild, making every free gos or gyr suspect, even if it has no jesses on its legs. Often different, distant geographical races are imported and such goshawks, or other birds, may breed with natives, producing a mongrel stock, thus disrupting the evolved adaptability of local races to the ecosystem, thereby endangering their existence. I have had rough-legged buzzard and Greenland falcon, brought exhausted on Liverpool ships from the North Atlantic, liberated later in Scotland where they are safer from gunners; but these are migratory visitors unable to stay and breed with local subspecies. Feral pigeons, of greyer-rumped Asiatic rockdove origin, inter-breed among native white-rumped rockdoves on many cliffs. The races of Canada geese and game pheasants are usually too interbred to determine.

Thus, from early hunting of birds for food, then destroying

predators upon his stock and game, man has progressed through shooting them for sport, or collecting them for prestige, to more intelligent conservation and observation in modern times. There was no 'Glorious Twelfth' until the Game Act of 1773 shortened the original grouse season from the previous Act of 1761, when it started on 26 July. The term red grouse came into the nineteenth century Game Books with mass driving for lazy Victorian guns, whose energetic ancestors walked up their 'moorfowl' and shot them over dogs, in a twelve-hour day on the moors. The blackcock was then their 'heathcock'.

When the Wild Birds Protection Bill was debated in Parliament in 1927, the late Jimmy Maxton, raven-haired member for the Bridgeton division of Glasgow, complained of its class distinction in protecting only a select few. He moved the rejection of the Bill because he considered that all birds should be protected, with certain exceptions. So did everyone else when the 1954–67 Act was passed. But the ambiguities of the Scottish Sabbath got into its bird laws. Ravens in Argyll must belong to the 'Wee Free'. Unprotected on weekdays, they may not be killed on Sundays or Christmas Day, whereas the apparently agnostic ravens of Skye may be shot any day. The law also treats wildfowl as Christians: they may not be shot in Scotland on Sundays or Christmas Day, as they may in England; and while the Game (Scotland) Act of 1932 allows gamebirds to be shot on Sunday or Christmas Day it is illegal to shoot wild birds on those days. Barnacle geese may be shot in the Hebrides in December and January, but not on Sunday or Christmas Day.

Goosanders, red-breasted mergansers and rockdoves, protected by law in England, are deprived of protection in Scotland where they cannot behave themselves.

Sanctuary Orders protect all birds and their eggs on Horse Island (Ayr), Lady Island off Troon (few if any terns now breed there), Loch Garten, Fetlar, Hamilton Low Parks and Glasgow's Possil Marsh. One would expect a state nature reserve to be a safe place for the gannet, emblem of the Scottish Zoological Society, to fly to. Not so on Sula Sgeir reserve, where the Act deprived the gannet of protection afforded it on Ailsa Craig, the Bass and elsewhere. A few tins of corned beef and some different Bass could have compensated the gannet hunters for their lost meat. The Nature Conservancy also issues permits for shooting barnacle geese at its Caerlaverock reserve.

Visitors should be aware of the British Protection of Birds Act 1954 & 1967 which includes penalties up to £100 or a month's imprisonment for killing, taking eggs, or 'wilfully disturbing on or near a nest with eggs or young,' birds in its Schedule 1, and up to three months' imprisonment for subsequent offences. Exceptions include privileged permits for photography and 'scientific and educational' purposes, obtained from the Nature Conservancy Council, and for taking young birds for falconry or eggs for aviary breeding, obtainable from the Home Office. Amendments are made by the Secretary of State for Scotland (consulting an advisory committee on the protection of birds for Scotland), Scottish Home and Health Department, 13 Carlington Terrace, Edinburgh EH7 5DG. In Forestry Commission land, the photography of any wild bird-nests and the use of hides require a permit. Schedule 1 comprises: Avocet, Bee-eaters, Bitterns, Bluethroat, Brambling, Snow-Bunting, Honey Buzzard, Chough, Corncrake, Spotted Crake, Crossbill, Divers, Dotterel, Eagles, Fieldfare, Firecrest, Garganey, Black-tailed Godwit, Goldeneye, Goshawk, Black-necked and Slavonian Grebes, Greenshank, Harriers, Hobby, Hoopoe, Kingfisher, Kite, Merlin, Long-tailed Duck, Golden Oriole, Osprey, Barn and Snowy Owls, Peregrine, Red-necked Phalarope, Kentish and Little Ringed Plovers, European Quail, Black Redstart, Redwing, Ruff and Reeve, Wood Sandpiper, Scaup, Common and Velvet Scoter, Serin, Red-backed Shrike, Sparrowhawk, Spoonbill, Black-winged Stilt, Temminck's Stint, Stone Curlew, Whooper Swan, Black, Little and Roseate Terns, Bearded and Crested Tits, Dartford, Marsh and Savi's Warblers, Woodlark, Whimbrel, St Kilda Wren and Wryneck. Apart from a limited number of predatory species, and some limited to authorised persons, other wild birds have legal protection under most circumstances.

Chapter 3

General information

Regional reserves, societies and local publications are noted under the respective counties, together with the Scottish Ornithologists' Club's local recorders. The following sources of information are on a more national coverage.

Avifaunas
More than two decades have not lessened the position of the 1953 *Birds of Scotland* (in two volumes) by the late Miss S. L. Baxter and Miss L. J. Rintoul as the standard reference work for the ornithologist as serious as an owl—updated by the annual *Scottish Bird Report* of the Scottish Ornithologists' Club. The modern bird-seeker, alert as a jay, his mind crammed with observations in a lifetime of excitement at each new discovery, finds each decade of changing ecology outdating the distribution notes in standard works, like D. A. Bannerman's lavishly illustrated twelve modern volumes on *The Birds of the British Isles*. Armed with modern *Field Guides* not only of British but of European and American birds which may be wind-drifted his way, even with more specialised tools of his craft like Cramp, Bourne and Saunders's *Seabirds of Britain & Ireland,* and Porter, Willis, Christensen and Nielsen's *Flight Identification of European Raptors,* he comes with a ready-for-anything look—less dangerous to Scottish birds than Charles St John's classic *Sportsman and Naturalist's Tour in Sutherland* (1891) or his *Notebooks* (1846–53), the best Scotland could offer after White's *Selborne.* Harvie-Brown's pioneering regional *Faunas* led the way to more serious recording, like D. Nethersole-Thompson's fresh and sunshiney *Highland Birds* (1971). The latter's erudite books

on *The Greenshank* (1951), *The Snow Bunting* (1966), *Pine
Crossbills* (1975) and *The Dotterel* (1971) have a specially
Scottish background, like Seton Gordon's and Gilbert
and Brook's books on the golden eagle, N. Rankin on *Haunts
of British Divers* (1947), even Eagle Clarke's 1912 *Studies in
Bird Migration*. The Nature Conservancy Council's *Nature
Reserves in Scotland* is a comprehensive resumé of more than
forty National Nature Reserves and the Forestry Commission *Records* include well-illustrated booklets on such birds
as *Crossbill* (No. 86), *Coal Tit* (No. 85), *Capercaillie* (No. 37),
Crested Tit (No. 41).

The BTO's recent *Atlas* of the breeding distribution of British birds is a cooperative work based on
occurrence in 10 km squares, while its Register of Ornithological Sites will be the Domesday Book of information
filed (not a book) for fieldworkers.

Reference Addresses
BTO (British Trust for Ornithology): Beech Grove, Tring,
   Hertfordshire, HP23 5NR.
CHA (Countrywide Holidays Association): guest-houses, Perth
   (Kinfauns Castle) Onich, etc., Birch Heys, Cromwell
   Range, Manchester M14 6HU.
Farm House Guide: (accommodation).
Forestry Commission: 231 Corstorphine Road, Edinburgh
   EH12 7AT; North: 21 Church Street, Inverness; East: 6
   Queens Gate, Aberdeen AB9 2NQ; South: Greystone
   Park, Moffat Road, Dumfries DF10 9ED; West:
   Portcullis House, 21 India Street, Glasgow G2 4PL.
HF (Holiday Fellowship): 142 Great North Way, London
   NW4 1EG; guest-houses: Alltshellach, Onich (West
   Loch Leven), Loch Awe House, Arran (Lamlash),
   Strathpeffer.

Nature Conservancy Council (National Nature Reserves): 12 Hope Terrace, Edinburgh EH9 2AS.

National Trust for Scotland: 5 Charlotte Square, Edinburgh EH2 4DU.

Royal Scottish Museum: 1 Chambers Street, Edinburgh EH1 1JF.

RSPB (Royal Society for the Protection of Birds): 17 Regent Terrace, Edinburgh EH7 5BN.

RAC: (Road conditions, etc.) 17 Rutland Square, Edinburgh EH1 2BQ.

Scottish Field Studies Association Ltd.: Kindrogan Field Centre, Enochdhu, Blairgowrie, Perthshire. PH10 7PG.

Scottish Mountaineering Club: Regional Guides.

Scottish Ornithologists' Club: (journal *Scottish Birds*) 21 Regent Terrace, Edinburgh EH7 5BT.

Scottish Tourist Board: 23 Ravelston Terrace, Edinburgh EH4 3EU.

Scottish Wildlife Trust: 8 Dublin Street, Edinburgh EH1 3PP.

Scottish YHA (Youth Hostels Association): 7 Glebe Crescent, Stirling FK8 2JB: over ninety hostels from Kirk Yetholm (Pennine Way) to Lerwick; see its *Handbook*.

Borders Region

FIRTH OF FORTH

▲ Lamb

▲● Fidra

Craigleith

▲ Eyebroughty

△▲ Bass Rock

* Gullane Pt.

■ North Berwick

Inchmickery ▲

Aberlady Bay ▲

Tyninghame

NORTH

SEA

Cramond I.

EAST

Linlithgow
Park WEST

LOTHIAN

Edinburgh

Leith

■ Musselburgh

LOTHIAN

St. Abb
Hea

MID-
LOTHIAN

*Duddingston
Loch* ▲

Lammermuirs

Eye

Pentland Hills

*Cobbinshaw
Res.*

*Watchwater
Res.*

⊙ Duns Castle
Woods

*Gladhouse
Res.*

△ Hule Moss

Lauderdale

B E R W I C K

Tweed

Portmore Res.

Moorfoot
Hills

⊡ The Hirsel

Tweed

Bemersyde

P E E B L E S

Hare Moss
△

■

⊙ *Junction Pool
Kelso*

⊙ *Yetholm Loch*

Ettrick Forest

St. Mary's L.

S E L K I R K

Hoselaw Loch

R O X B U R G H

Teviotdale

Wauchope
Forest

Cheviots

Border
Forest

▲ Reserves

━━━ Seabird colonies

* Seabird migration watching points

● Terneries

•••••• Tidal wader haunts

0   10   20   30 miles

10   40 km

Chapter 4

Borders Region

Berwickshire

Scotland starts at the sandstone cliffs of Megs Dub, on the North Sea. This southeastern border admits birds advancing their range from England, like still scarce turtle dove, green woodpecker and pied flycatcher (at Coldstream), and the marsh tit at Coldingham. Until stolen by the English King Edward IV, Berwick-on-Tweed was the capital of ancient Lothian; but the seabird citadel at St Abb's Head remains the major ornithological attraction on the Berwickshire coast. North Berwick is in East Lothian, despite the Nature Conservancy's monograph on British wildfowl confusingly using the term North Berwickshire.

The Southern Uplands forced the A1 and the railway to the limited lowland near the coast; thus many visitors are less familiar with the grass and heather moors to the west which share the ecology of the Northumbrian borderland. They may miss the Lauderdale valley of the River Leader, which shares much of the bird life of the lower Tweed valley (Merse of March), like breeding goosanders and pied flycatchers and visiting firecrests. However, up to 330 moulting goldeneye gather at the Tweed estuary. Other river valleys include the Eye, flowing from the northern border to the sea at Eyemouth (945641) and White Adder Water (Paradise Wood) coming out of the steep, drier Lammermuir Hills, and its tributary the Black Adder, both favoured by dipper and kingfisher, and joining the Tweed above Berwick, with the coppery flash of the redstart's tail.

Berwickshire's 118,435 ha (460 square miles) are still mostly not developed or industrialised. There are important autumn and winter grounds of farm-feeding Icelandic pinkfoot and greylag geese, with occasional Greenland and lesser whitefronts. These flocks depend upon available roosts, like the moorland reservoirs, where disturbance causes them to alter their haunts. Such haunts are: Todrig and Old Greenlaw, off the A6105 up the Black Adder Valley at 55° 43′ N, 2° 28′ W; Hule Moss, turning off the lane running north of the A6105 2 miles (3 km) north of Greenlaw (715460), a haunt of up to 4000 pinkfeet as well as of goldeneye; and Harelow Moss, turning off the Hollyburton lane northwest from Greenlaw and before that village. Hule and Gordon mosses in the southwest of the district are also good haunts of wild duck like winter teal, pintail, tufted duck, goldeneye and a few wigeon. Another of these inland mosslands, Bemerside Moss near B6356 from Earlston, east of Melrose in Tweeddale, has a black-headed gullery. Pinkfeet and Greenland whitefronts also feed farther down the Tweed Valley opposite Coldstream (850400). Hare and Hoselaw (a loch off a lane northeast from the B6352 Kelso–Kirk Yetholm road, beyond Moorhouse) are also visited by duck and 'aquatic' warblers. Hoselaw Loch, 30 acres, 1·3 ha, and adjoining Din Moss, 20 acres, 0·8 ha, now form an SWT reserve, 5 miles, 8 km, east of Kelso. It is a winter haunt of greylag and pinkfoot geese and of wigeon; also of shoveler, goldeneye, goosander, pochard and tufted duck.

The Scottish border and Southern Uplands are a natural border to the northward range of most garganey, marsh tits, nuthatches and yellow wagtails, though these range further north in continental Europe.

General woodland birds may be seen at White Adder Woods and Duns Castle, and in winter rooks roost at Foxcovey (Simprin) by the A6112 (south of Swinton) and at Hutton Castle, northeast of this; there are some 4000 at

Cock Pied Flycatcher, a summer immigrant increased by nest-boxes in wooded valleys

Allanshaw's Pinewood, Duns Castle (780542), Hoprig
Farm, Cockburnspath (755698); also at Redpath Farm,
Longformacus, northwest of Duns and Redpath Hill,
Bemerside. The Lammermuir Hills on the northern border
form part of the Southern Uplands, the nesting haunt of red
grouse and of golden plover, but mostly of ring ouzels,
woodcock, redpolls and siskins. They include White Adder
Water and Watchwater Reservoir above Longformicus, on
the road west from the B6355, northwest of Duns, the latter
a haunt of a few goldeneye, tufted duck and wigeon and
1000 or more roosting greylags. There is also Primrose Hill
Pond, near the A6112/B6355 junction in the White Adder
Valley beyond Duns, also visited by a few water birds. Hule
Moss, two miles north of Greenlaw is a 750 feet high bog
where up to 6000 pinkfeet roost and autumn brings spotted
redshank, knot and black-tailed godwit, among 80 species
of bird listed there. Permits from: Hollyburton Farm, three
miles northwest of Greenlaw off the A6105.

The mostly rocky coastline attracts some winter seaduck
and a few wigeon. Turnstones, purple sandpipers, etc.,
winter from the border to Bildfen Creek; but being more
exposed than the Lothian coast further in the Firth of Forth,
and with less intertidal flats, Berwickshire attracts fewer
wader flocks, grebes and divers, although there are falls of
continental migrants, like firecrests. Cormorants nest
occasionally on the cliffs near Cockburnspath, and
kittiwakes on the Burnmouth-Eyemouth cliffs and on Gull
Rock. House martins nest on the Cliffs at Dunstonwood.
Exceptions to the generally rocky coast are Whiterigg Bay,
north of St Abbs harbour, and Eyemouth. Eyemouth tides
are 20 minutes earlier than Leith, with 4·7 m springs. Duns
Castle reserve of the SWT has nest boxes sometimes with
pied flycatchers. Tufted duck nest on Hen Poo water.

St Abbs Head (912698): Nineteen km (12 miles) north of Berwick-on-Tweed, access to St Abbs Head is by the A1107 to Coldingham, then B6438 to the lane from Northfield. Rising 300–500 feet (90–150 m), its sandstone cliffs are from May to July the breeding haunt of fulmars, northern guillemots, razorbills, a few puffins, shags, kittiwakes, herring and lesser black-backed gulls, and feral rockdoves (pigeons) among its many caves. House martins also nest on the lighthouse cliff, and there are cormorants. It is now an SWT public reserve, including 240 acres (97 ha) of grass land, and some woodland. Mire Loch has winter goldeneye and pochard.

The Hirsel: This is at Coldstream Mains, off the A6112, with private woodlands. It has nesting pied flycatcher, and blackcaps bubbling over with song, also a lake visited mainly by mallard, wigeon and shoveler, also goldeneye, tufted, goosander, teal and a few pochard and pintail. Owner, Lord A. Douglas Home.

Information
Recorder: K. S. Macgregor, 16 Merchiston Avenue, Edinburgh EH10 4NY.

Society: Berwickshire Naturalists' Club.

Literature: Brady, F., *Birds of Berwick-on-Tweed and District,* 1974 (25 Tweed Close, Eastside, Berwick-on-Tweed.)

Peeblesshire (Tweeddale)
This is not a major bird county, though peregrines nest near Peebles in Tweedsmuir, kingfishers at Broughton and the American pectoral sandpiper has visited the small West-water Reservoir in October 1970, where duck, like teal (and

terns), are the more usual visitors. A nutcracker came in August 1971, and in the same year a stone curlew followed at West Linton in October. Its 92,000 ha (354 square miles) contain much high land in the Southern Uplands, Tweeddale and Teviotdale; this is mostly mountain, moor and bog, and about an eighth is farmed. Its southern lochs are too high on the moors to attract many waterfowl, but Westwater Reservoir has a pinkfoot roost with 6440 of these winter visitors in the county in November. A greylag roost is by the Fruid River, where great crested grebes nest. The latter also nest on Loch Hill at Portmore House in the northeast's moorfoot hills, off the A703 beyond Eddleston, north of Peebles. A major bird water is the upper Tweed and its tributaries, near Peebles and Broughton. Oystercatchers nest inland and four pairs of ringed plover nested at Portmore loch. Icelandic pinkfeet visit Portmore, Libberton and Dolphinton.

Broad Law, the highest hill, rises 2723 feet (817 m) near the south border. Dollar Law (2680 feet, 804 m) is another high south-western hill in the mountainous Ettrick Border Forest haunt of black grouse and long-eared owls. Glentress Forest has a 4½ mile (6 km) 'trail' (NT284396) 2 miles (3 km) east of Peebles on the north side of the A72 Peebles–Galashiels road. Winter roosts of up to 5000 rooks congregate in the pines at Felton Farm, Dolphinton, and Burnhead Farm, Eddleston (248472).

Nightjar and corncrake linger among declining nesters; tufted duck and grasshopper warbler also breed, while the alpine swift has been among wind-drifted vagrants in recent years. Golden pheasants breed in Cadrona Forest.

Information
Recorder: A. J. Smith, Glenview, Selkirk, TD7 4LX.

Roxburghshire

A minor, inland bird district, with much of its 172,000 ha (665 square miles) heather and sheep-grazing, this is mostly hill country with many good woodlands. It shares the northern slopes of the Cheviots, rising to over 2000 feet (800 m) on the Northumbrian border approached by the B6351 and the B6352 west of Kirknewton, to the breeding haunt of merlin, peregrine and buzzard. Here black grouse lek and the hills echo the raven's throaty croak. Redstart, pied flycatcher, siskin and redpoll nest in the woods, oystercatcher and dipper by the burns where snipe drum over marshy valleys and woodcock rode at dusk among scattered plantations and birch woods. Whistling golden plover, shy dunlin, short-eared and long-eared owls (the latter in old crow nests in oak and fir woods), dippers, grey wagtails, curlew and occasional dotterel also nest here.

Along the Cheviot and Dumfries border lies the Border Forest, 59,000 ha of fellside and spruce woods, the haunt of black grouse and hen harrier. It includes Newcastleton Forest in Liddesdale, the Wauchope Forest at Riccarton, south of Jedburgh, and border Peel Fell and Kirton Moss in the south west. This great national forest is best entered from Saughtree (NY562968) on the B6357 Jedburgh-Longton road. There is also mountainous Ettrick Forest on the Cheviot border, another haunt of black grouse and long-eared owls. Harthope Burn and College Valley, like the Cheviot summit, are on the English side of the border.

A most impressive entry into the Borders Region, and Scotland, is by the A68 from Corbridge, which enters Roxburghshire 1371 feet above sea level at Carter Bar. One's eye is held to the northeast by the long granite line of the Cheviots, below them the Merse of Berwickshire and beyond, the Tweed flowing like a silver serpent from its lair in the Lammermuirs. This is a listening land, where R. L. Stevenson might just as easily have heard his whaups crying as over the sea to Skye.

The road continues through the Teviot hills to Jedburgh. Here Teviotdale, a tributary of the Tweed, traverses the district, a haunt of goosander and goldeneye, winter wigeon and whoopers, near Kelso Bridge (Junction Water), Nisbet, Burnside (Jedburgh), etc. Mallard, goldeneye and goosander also visit the Tweed near Kelso where migrating ospreys sometimes visit the Junction Water; but the water level of the Tweed varies more than on most rivers according to the weather. Two thousand noisy pinkfeet feed in autumn and winter at Greenhead near Kelso. Jedburgh Forest is largely rough moorland and hill, with grass and farmland, and several large woods. Yetholm Loch, where corn buntings breed, is an interesting water 6 miles (9 km) south of Kelso. Other visiting places for waterfowl, with nesting great crested grebes, are Acreknowe Reservoir, Alemuir Loch and West Worden Loch. Horselaw Loch in the west has a greylag roost in March and its mossland is the haunt of breeding duck and the grasshopper warblers' sizzling song. Another interesting 'moss' is at Kirkton Birnie, Hawick. Auchopecairn is the highest hill at 2382 feet (715 m). Dotterel nest on the border occasionally.

Oystercatchers nest inland, as in much of Scotland; there are marsh tits at Gattonside and red-legged partridge have been introduced at Bowmount, but their stock requires regular replenishment to survive the wet northern winters. Black grouse are numerous in the south of the county, herons nest in Leithope Forest, and hoodie crows and their carrion crow hybrids occur. Among occasional visitors are lesser whitethroat in summer and great grey shrike in winter, with an alpine swift in April 1951 and a white stork in May 1972. Turtle dove, pied flycatcher, sometimes the corncrake and, often overlooked in woods, the hawfinch, are also here. Winter rook roosts are at Cogsmill Stobs, Hoselaw and Spittal Bedrule, Cogsmill, attracting between 1000 and 3000 clamorous birds and at Spittal 5000.

Information
Recorder: A. J. Smith, Glenview, Selkirk, TD7 4LX.
Society: Kelso and District Ornithological Society.

Selkirkshire
Still in the minor counties, though attracting black-necked grebes to nest in 1965, these 66,000 ha (257 square miles) are inland and mostly hilly sheep farming, up to 2000 feet (600 m), the haunt of numerous plaintive, tumbling lapwings and a few declining corncrakes and nightjars, with oystercatchers nesting at Yarrow and elsewhere. Wigeon and gadwall have nested, but the high moorland lochs have only limited waterfowl. Great crested grebes nest on Lindean Loch and likewise share Akermuir Loch in Ettrick Forest (400240) in the southeast with a bickering, black-headed gullery. Far west of Selkirk, St Mary's Loch is the best water, visited by geese and wild swans, the nesting haunt of certain duck, but chiefly visited by tufted duck, pochard, shoveler, teal, wigeon and mallard. A pair of mergansers added to its list in 1973. This water covers 266 ha (633 acres) and is 153 feet (47 m) deep. Nearby Loch of Lowes (a Perthshire water also has this name) is 39 ha (96 acres) in area and 58 feet (19 m) deep and attracts mainly mallard but also goosanders, goldeneye, pochard, teal, etc. A few mallard, wigeon and teal visit Cauldshiel and Faldonside lochs near Selkirk, with tufted duck and goldeneye. Headshaw Loch, 3 miles (5 km) south of Selkirk,

is visited by mallard, wigeon, tufted duck and pochard. Gulls roost on Portmore Loch in winter. Hare Moss, south of Selkirk, is another attraction. Winter rooks roost in the warm conifers at Sunderland Hall farm. One bleak and blasty December evening in 1950 I tried to boost more interest in the county's birds in a lecture in the public library at Galashiels. It was before the great surge in bird-watching. People now have the energy to get out of 'Galla' in spring and seek the ring ouzel on Cramalt Crag and on Broad Law on the northwest border, or the attractions of Ettrick Forest (an old name for the whole county) astride the Tweed.

Information
Recorder: A. J. Smith, Glenview, Selkirk, TD7 4LX.

Check list
Nesters: Great Crested Grebe, Black-necked Grebe, Little Grebe, Fulmar, Cormorant, Shag, Mallard, Teal, Gadwall, Wigeon, Shoveler, Tufted Duck, Pochard, Eider, Goosander, Shelduck, Greylag, Canada Goose, Mute Swan, Buzzard, Sparrowhawk, Peregrine, Merlin, Kestrel, Hen Harrier, Red Grouse, Black Grouse, Red-legged Partridge, Common Partridge, Quail, Pheasant, Golden Pheasant, Water Rail, Corncrake, Moorhen, Coot, Oystercatcher, Lapwing, Ringed Plover, Golden Plover, Dotterel, Snipe, Woodcock, Curlew, Sandpiper, Redshank, Dunlin, Lesser Black-backed Gull, Herring Gull, Common Gull, Black-headed Gull, Kittiwake, Razorbill, Guillemot, Puffin, Stockdove, Feral Rockdove, Woodpigeon, Turtle Dove, Collared Dove, Cuckoo, Barn Owl, Tawny Owl, Little Owl, Long-eared Owl, Short-eared Owl, Nightjar, Swift, Kingfisher, Green Woodpecker, Great Spotted Woodpecker,

Skylark, Swallow, House Martin, Sand Martin, Raven, Carrion Crow, Rook, Jackdaw, Magpie, Jay, Great Tit, Blue Tit, Coal Tit, Marsh Tit, Willow Tit, Long-tailed Tit, Tree Creeper, Wren, Dipper, Mistle Thrush, Song Thrush, Ring Ouzel, Blackbird, Wheatear, Stonechat, Whinchat, Redstart, Robin, Sedge Warbler, Grasshopper Warbler, Blackcap, Garden Warbler, Whitethroat, Willow Warbler, Chiffchaff, Wood Warbler, Goldcrest, Spotted Flycatcher, Pied Flycatcher, Hedge Sparrow, Meadow Pipit, Tree Pipit, Rock Pipit, Pied Wagtail, Grey Wagtail, Yellow Wagtail, Starling, Hawfinch, Greenfinch, Goldfinch, Siskin, Linnet, Twite, Redpoll, Bullfinch, Crossbill, Chaffinch, Corn Bunting, Yellowhammer, Reed Bunting, House Sparrow, Tree Sparrow.

Pintail, Merganser, Goshawk and Common Tern have probably nested.

Migratory and rarer visitors: Goldeneye, Teal and Wigeon flocks in winter, Pinkfoot, Whitefront, Greenland Whitefront, Lesser Whitefront and Greylag Geese, occasional Rough-legged Buzzard, Stone Curlew, American Pectoral Sandpiper, Great Grey Shrike, Alpine Swift, Nutcracker, Bluethroat, Lesser Whitethroat, Firecrest.

Central Region

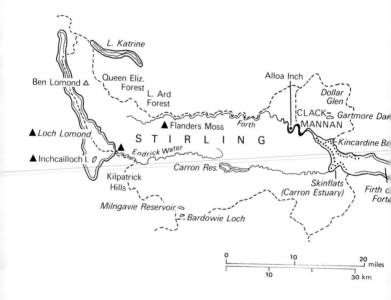

L. Katrine

Ben Lomond △ Queen Eliz. Forest

Alloa Inch

Dollar Glen

L. Ard Forest

CLACK MANNAN Gartmore Dam

▲ Flanders Moss Forth

S T I R L I N G Kincardine Ba

▲ Loch Lomond ▲ Endrick Water

▲ Inchcailloch I. ⬭ Carron Res.

Kilpatrick Hills

Skinflats (Carron Estuary)

Firth Fort

Milngavie Reservoir ⬭

⬭ Bardowie Loch

```
0              10              20
                                  ┘ miles
       10              30 km
```

Chapter 5

Central Region

Clackmannanshire

Scotland's smallest county, little more than 14,000 ha (54 square miles), is favourably sited for waterfowl on the north of the Forth (950890). To its north stretch the sheep-grazed Ochil hills with ring ouzels. The level lowlands have arable farms and 2 miles (3 km) northeast of Alloa, New Sauchie, by the A908, has nesting great crested grebes on mile-long Gartmorn Dam, a winter haunt of tufted duck, pochard, wigeon, teal, goldeneye, sometimes large herds of whoopers, a greylag roost and an autumn opportunity for seeing waders. Buzzards may sometimes be seen soaring over the woodland trail at Dollar Glen (950980), east of Dollar (962989) in the northeast. Among the county's nesting birds are green woodpecker, pintail, raven, willow tit, grasshopper warbler and tufted duck. Blackcock lek at Woodhill.

Lesser whitefronts have occasionally been claimed among geese on the River Devon, near the Firth at Cambus, where shelduck nest, and up to 133 whoopers have been counted at Alloa Inch, an island in the upper Forth. Shelduck also nest at Kennetpans in Kincardine Bay (not to be confused with Kincardineshire).

Ring ouzels breed in the hills and grasshopper warblers in the lowlands The Forth Road Bridge made access via the M90 quicker; but many bird-watchers pass it by as they speed to the rarities of Kinross or Inverness. Beside the Forth at Cambus, Tullibody and Kennetpans are autumn and winter wader haunts, while duck visit Peppermill Dam on the southeast border.

Information
Recorder: Dr C. J. Henty, 3 The Broich, Alva.

Stirlingshire
In the upper valley of the Forth, its 19,000 ha (447 square miles) range through such contrast as the industrialised southeast, north to Ben Lomond, parts of Loch Lomond, Loch Katrine, and the Queen Elizabeth Forest Park which includes Ben Lomond and Loch Ard. It has one of the first known haunts of the lesser spotted woodpecker on its Perthshire border. A few ptarmigan used to make Ben Lomond their southernmost breeding site, but their present whereabouts, like the dotterel's, are doubted. Probably the largest Scottish heronry with thirty-six nests is at Gartfairn, on the West Stirling/Perthshire border.

Ben Lomond is the highest of the southern Highlands, at 3192 feet (958 m), and the loch is Britain's largest inland water, 24 miles (38 km) long and $\frac{3}{4}$–5 miles (1–8 km) wide, with thirty wooded islands. Much of the best of the Lomond Nature Reserve is in the northwest of the county, where wigeon have bred and with the Endrick Marshes raising the rarity hopes of watchers making a short detour from the scenic A82 on their way north, or returning south.

Capercaillie nest at Mentieth Wood as well as on Inchcailloch island, pied flycatchers at Inversnaid, goosanders and pied flycatchers at Inversnaid, hawfinches and dippers at Bridge of Allan and still nightjars at Balmaha. Hen harriers breed in the west and there are nesting haunts of green woodpecker, corncrake, blackcap and whitethroat (west), grasshopper warbler, common gull and redwing. It is in the range of hoodie crows and their carrion crow hybrids. Great crested grebes breed on Antermony Loch by the A891, west of Kirkintilloch, Bardowie Loch, Carron

Dam and Carron Valley Reservoirs by the B818, Craigallian Loch, Edenkillan Loch and Mugdock Loch. Other waters include Loch Coulter in the east, by the A80, and Milngavie Loch and Bardowie Castle Loch on the southwestern border. The Carron Valley and Craigmeddie Reservoirs, 600–1000 feet (180–300 m) high, are a flyline linking Forth and Clyde, occasionally visited by bean geese, as is Lomond. Covering 374 ha (926 acres), they attract mallard and greylags from the nearby hills, but Loch Coulter's 74 ha (185 acres) a mile or two off are too exposed. The North Thirsk Reservoir of 56 ha (120 acres), 6 miles (9 km) from Alloa, has flocks of mallard and teal in winter. One hundred and eight whoopers have been counted at Menstrie on the Clackmannan border in February, while from Grangemouth (950820) to Kincardine Bridge of Bo'ness by the A905, waders like little stint may be seen, as well as high tide roosting knot at Longannel Point and Kincardine Bridge (Fife), visiting duck, including over 1000 winter shelduck, a greylag and pinkfoot roost, and all four visiting skuas on autumn east winds. West winds brought four grey phalaropes and seven American dowitchers in September 1975. A winter roost of 3000 rooks and jackdaws is at Stirling University, Airthrey.

The Queen Elizabeth Forest Park is more in Perthshire, but at Rowardennan in the west it includes 10 miles (16 km) of the east shore of Loch Lomond and Ben Lomond's summit. It can be reached 1½ miles (2·4 km) northwest of Balmaha, beyond the B837 Drymen–Balmaha road. Buchanan Forest walks in the western part of the Queen Elizabeth Forest Park start at NS380960, near Ross Wood, 4 miles (6 km) northeast of Balmaha, and at NS422912, north of Balmaha, near Lomond. In winter 10,000 rooks have been counted roosting in deciduous trees at Muiravonside

Common Gull at nest (overleaf)

(Lochcote), 5000–8000 in conifers near Drumgoyne Station
and 2000 at Dunmore House, Airth.

Campsie Fells in the southeast, the Kilpatrick Hills and
Ballaggan Glen have general bird interest. Black grouse
inhabit the Ochil and the Lomond Hills, and lek at
Sheriffmuir. Black-throated divers nest in the west; also
scoter, and there is a heronry at Gartfairn.

Loch Lomond Reserve (Nature Conservancy) (435880): Part of
this reserve is in Dunbarton, and the southeast is in
Stirlingshire. Comprising 252 ha (624 acres), 96 of them
oak and alder wooded, it requires a permit for some parts.
The reserve is reached via Drymen on the A809. Pied
flycatchers nest here as well as wigeon, buzzard, capercaillie, green woodpecker, wood warbler, redstart, tree pipit,
merganser, goosander, great and little grebes, common
gull, tree creeper, willow tit and ring ouzel. The Ben is
reached via Rowardennan in Queen Elizabeth Forest at the
end of the east lochside road, 2½ miles (4 km) northwest from
the B837 at Balmaha, from Drymen. It still has ravens, but
'Ptarmigan Spur' at 2398 feet (720 m) below the Ben
opposite Rowardennan youth hostel, and 'Ptarmigan
Shooting Lodge' a mile beyond Ardess, are mostly
memories of the past.

Permission is required to camp on the reserve (NS4089–
4190). There is a heronry at Buchanan Castle near Balmaha
on the southeast bank, with woodcock, long-eared owl,
redstart, grasshopper, wood and garden warblers, chiffchaff and redpoll nesting in the woods. Permits are
required to visit this, from the Factor, Montrose Estate,
Drymen. The loch has some thirty wooded islands. The
National Nature Reserve includes five in the southeast,
mostly with oak and alder, and visited by duck in winter

and passage waders in season—Inchcailloch (with capers), Torrinch (where capercaillie nested in 1971), Creinch, Clairinsh and Aber Isle. They lie along the Highland Boundary Fault and have unrestricted access. The reserve has three pairs of buzzards, great spotted woodpeckers, etc., and an interesting passage of passerines.

One of the reserve's most interesting bird haunts, the wader- and duck-frequented mouth of the slow-flowing Endrick Water (River) in the southeast suffers little if at all from the lemming-like weekend throng from Glasgow which fills the southern shore of Lomond. Fifty-five whoopers have been seen at this end of the reserve in March, odd bean geese sometimes visit it in January, a red-necked phalarope was on passage in June 1971 and an American long-billed dowitcher in May 1969. One thousand greylag are sometimes counted at this end of the loch, occasionally whitefronts (including Greenlanders) and pinkfeet. The duck are mainly wigeon, shoveler, pochard, tufted and mergansers, as well as the ubiquitous mallard. East winds one May brought a spoonbill. Scoter nested on the loch in 1971, and shoveler, gadwall, mergansers, shelduck, teal, tufted duck and pintail have also bred. Seventeen species nest on Crom Mhin, a 21 ha marshy bog on the southeast shore, on the reserve side of Endrick Water, including mallard, shoveler, teal, wigeon, water-rail, redshank, lapwing, snipe, curlew, oystercatcher, reed bunting, sedge warbler, pied wagtail and meadow pipit.

Elsewhere nest redshank, oystercatcher and snipe, and occasionally great crested grebes. Black-headed and lesser black-backed gulls bred in the past, when the loch had terneries, but the terns are now mostly visitors. Several spotted crakes, little gulls, black tern, wood sandpipers, green sandpipers, sometimes marsh and hen harriers, rock pipit and the American pectoral sandpiper visit the loch. Winter brings many wigeon, and other duck include odd longtails and smews, occasional Bewick's swans, though more whoopers. The osprey is now more often seen on spring or autumn passage than its occasional pre-war visits. *Warden:* 22 Muirpark Way, Drymen, by Glasgow G63 0DX.

Flanders Moss (630980): Extending across the Perthshire border, this great mossy peat bog is the nesting haunt of lesser black-backed, black-headed (west side) and herring gulls and the feeding ground, especially in late autumn and spring on its south and east sides, of grey geese. Pinkfeet roost on the open moss and at Loch Mahaick and Loch Rusky, and also feed on farms at Kippen and Thornhill, and as far as Buchlyvie. Whoopers also visit the moss. Bean geese still come occasionally. Greylags are also winter visitors, when there are short-eared owls, hen harriers, redpolls, siskins, sometimes a great grey shrike and at all times some black grouse. Gartmore, on the A811, is by bog and forestry. An SWT reserve of 640 acres is in the south-east.

East Moss: This is reached via East Polder Farm, kippen, by the A811 and B835 junction.

Skinflats: This is the Grangemouth, Carron estuary and tidal flats area along the eastern boundary on the west side of the upper Firth of Forth, a greylag and pinkfoot roost with a wader roost of knot, etc., and wintering duck, including a large flock of shelduck, as already mentioned. It extends upriver to the Kincardine Bridge into Fife. Yellow wagtail, stonechat and shoveler have nested in the area.

Ten thousand knot have been counted on January high tides, forty curlew sandpipers in August and 1000 winter shelduck. The seawall pools are particularly attractive to waders including little and Temminck's stints, green and wood sandpipers, black-tailed godwits and spotted redshank. Black terns visit them with easterly winds and a gull-billed tern was recorded in September 1969. A spoonbill was there in July 1973. Pintail and other duck are among winter visitors, and arctic, great, long-tailed and pomarine skuas have been recorded after favourable winds, chiefly arctic skuas, in autumn. It is an RSPB reserve.

Information
Recorders: West Stirlingshire: I. P. Gibson, Arcadia, The Glen, Howwood, Renfrewshire.
East Stirlingshire: Dr J. C. Henty, 3 The Broich, Alva, Clackmannanshire.
Society: Scottish Ornithologists' Club, Stirling Branch, Hon. Sec. Dr D. M. Bryant, Biology Dept., University of Stirling.
Literature: Bartholomew, J., Birds of Baldernol, West Stirling, *Glasgow & West Scotland Bird Bulletin*, **4** (1955).
Mitchell, J., (ed), *Loch Lomond Report* (annual).
Nature Conservancy, *Loch Lomond National Nature Reserve*, 14pp & map (Edinburgh 1964).
Tippet, R., *Natural History of Loch Lomond* (University of Glasgow Press, 1974).
Williamson, K., Oakland Breeding Bird Community in the Loch Lomond Nature Reserve, *Quarterly Journal of Forestry*, **68**, 9.

Check List
Nesters: (Black-throated Diver), Great Crested Grebe,

(Black-necked Grebe), Little Grebe, Heron, Mallard, Teal, Gadwall, Wigeon, Shoveler, Tufted Duck, Pochard, Merganser, Goosander, Shelduck, Mute Swan, Golden Eagle, Buzzard, Sparrowhawk, Peregrine, Merlin, Kestrel, Hen Harrier, Red Grouse, Black Grouse, Ptarmigan, Capercaillie, Partridge, Red-legged Partridge, Pheasant, Water Rail, Corncrake, Moorhen, Coot, Oystercatcher, Lapwing, Golden Plover, Snipe, Woodcock, Curlew, Sandpiper, Redshank, Dunlin, Lesser Black-backed Gull, Common Tern, Herring Gull, Common Gull, Black-headed Gull, Stockdove, Woodpigeon, Collared Dove, Cuckoo, Barn Owl, Tawny Owl, Long-eared Owl, Short-eared Owl, Nightjar, Swift, Kingfisher, Green Woodpecker, Great Spotted Woodpecker, Skylark, Swallow, House Martin, Sand Martin, Raven, Carrion Crow, Hoodie, Rook, Jackdaw, Magpie, Jay, Great Tit, Blue Tit, Coal Tit, Long-tailed Tit, Tree Creeper, Wren, Dipper, Mistle Thrush, Song Thrush, Ring Ouzel, Blackbird, Wheatear, Stonechat, Whinchat, Redstart, Robin, Sedge Warbler, Grasshopper Warbler, Blackcap, Garden Warbler, Whitethroat, Willow Warbler, Chiffchaff, Wood Warbler, Goldcrest, Spotted Flycatcher, Pied Flycatcher, Hedge Sparrow, Meadow Pipit, Tree Pipit, Pied Wagtail, Grey Wagtail, Yellow Wagtail, Starling, Greenfinch, Goldfinch, Siskin, Linnet, Twite, Redpoll, Bullfinch, Chaffinch, Corn Bunting, Yellow-hammer, Reed Bunting, House Sparrow, Tree Sparrow.

Migratory and rarer visitors: Winter flocks of Greylag, Pinkfoot, Whitefronted (including Greenland and Lesser) Geese, Whooper and Bewick's Swans, Longtail Duck, Gadwall, Smew, and other duck. Green and Wood Sandpipers, Curlew Sandpiper, Godwits, Knot, Little and

Temminck's Stints, Spotted Redshank, American Dowit-
cher and Pectoral Sandpiper, Red-necked Phalarope,
Dotterel, Little Gull, Black and Gull-billed Terns, Skuas,
Osprey, Goshawk, Marsh and Hen Harriers, Great Grey
Shrike, Rock Pipit.

Dumfries and Galloway Region

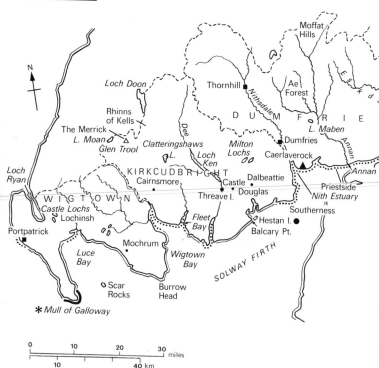

Moffat Hills

Loch Doon

Thornhill

Ae Forest

Rhinns of Kells

The Merrick
L. Moan
Glen Trool

Clatteringshaws

D U M F R I E

L. Maben

Dumfries

Caerlaverock

Dee

Milton Lochs

Loch Ryan

K I R K C U D B R I G H T

Cairnsmore

Loch Ken

Castle
Douglas

Dalbeattie

Annan

Priestside
Nith Estuary

Castle Lochs
Lochinsh

W I G T O W N

Threave I.

Southerness

Portpatrick

Fleet Bay

Hestan I.
Balcary Pt.

Luce Bay

Mochrum

Wigtown Bay

S O L W A Y   F I R T H

Scar Rocks

Burrow Head

✱ Mull of Galloway

0   10   20   30 miles
10   40 km

Chapter 6

Dumfries and Galloway Region

Dumfrieshire

The A74 bridge over the little trout river Sark, at Gretna, is the southwestern entry into Scotland. Here I have spent many happy days bird-watching along the Solway. The wide throat of the Solway is an arm of the Irish Sea famous throughout Britain for its wildfowl and waders, annually luring coachloads of winter bird-watching clubs, from England to Edinburgh, to see its geese, in particular Spitzbergen barnacles with a few albinos. Dumfriesshire's 275,000 ha (1062 square miles) also have much mountainous country to over 2000 feet (600 m) in the Moffat Hills where peregrines nest and extensive, lonely moorlands with black grouse along its northern borders. Falling away from these are the valleys, especially Nithsdale woods with their pied flycatchers (at Lime Cleugh and Sanguhar), green woodpeckers, willow tits, wood warblers, redstarts, tree pipits, blackcaps, goosanders and little grebe; the Annan whose floods lure many waterfowl and geese (A709 bridge), visited by a little egret in December 1972; and the wooded Esk. Mergansers nest along the Annan tributaries.

Seven peregrine eyries are known to me; spotted crakes occur; there are fourteen breeding sites of long-eared owls, five waters hold nesting great crested grebes, and dotterel are on the heights. It is one of the few Scottish haunts of Canada geese (at Wigton Merse, Kinmount and Loch-maben), and its breeding short-eared owls form roosts of more than forty at Eskdalemuir (255978) in July and August. Scottish crossbills come so far south in winter. Black-tailed godwits have bred on the Solway and goosanders breed right down to the border riverside trees at

Langholm. The hawfinch is a scarce nester, and the little owl (Moffat) is in its limited range.

The major Scottish wader flocks crowd the north Solway tideline to Priestside Bank and Caerlaverock Merse, or saltmarsh; but the firth extends over 276,900 ha (1100 square miles) westwards along the rest of the region. The Esk and Nith estuaries are good, with black-tailed godwit flocks at Glencapel. Heronries are at Whitcairn near St Mungo in the south and at West Skelton near Dunscore in the northwest. Tynron juniper wood is a national nature reserve between Thornhill and Moniave, an area with long-eared and short-eared owls, ravens and redstarts nesting. Drumlanrig Castle (Duke of Buccleuch) is a bird haunt by the A76 to the north. Ruehills, Lochwood oaks (owner, P. W. Hope-Johnstone) are visited by bird-watching parties in June, and Gilchristland, Closeburn (Sir A. B. Duncan) in May. Trails through Greskine and Ae Forest (NX985898) via a by-road 6 miles (10 km) from Locharbriggs, 3 miles (5 km) northeast of Dumfries on the A701, lead through nesting haunts of sparrowhawk, nightjar, crossbill and goldcrest. Border Forest Park adjoins the Roxburgh boundary. The Scottish Wildlife Trust has Fountainbleau and Lady Park. Winter rook roosts bring 10,000 birds to conifers at Dalgonar (Dunscore) and Halluchs (Lochmaben), and a thousand or two to Bankend (Locharwoods), Dunabie Farm, Mennoch (Braefoot), Mount Annan and Stenrieshill (Wamphray).

At inland waters, great crested grebes, shelduck, sedge warblers, etc., breed on the Castle and Hightae Lochs county reserve at Lochmaben, with unrestricted access to 137 ha (339 acres) at NY0881-0880, 7 miles (11 km) northeast of Dumfries by the A709 to the B7020 in the Annan Valley. Here shoveler, wigeon, teal and goosanders come in winter; it has a greylag roost and a purple heron visited Hae Tae in May 1973. The River Annan floods to Castle Loch's 85 ha (210 acres), attracting wigeon, shoveler, pochard and goosanders, and 1000 greylags with some whoopers. Grebes also nest on Mill Lochs at Lochmaben (078832), on Kirk Loch which also attracts black tern on passage, and on Glenkiln reservoir by the A75, 7 miles (11 km) west of Dumfries (848775). Loch Arthur (A711) often has smew among February duck. Common gulls nest at Loch Skene, off the A708 beneath Whitecombe Hill, and black-throated divers at their farthest south. Common crossbills nest in modern forests. Short-eared owls breed at Kelsholm. North American Wilson's phalarope has been among westerly visitors and the continental great grey shrike comes with easterlies. Langholm Moor is a summer watching haunt on the southern border. Red-breasted mergansers also breed along the River Annan's tributaries, like Water of Milk, and goosanders at Caple Burn, Mitchell Slacks and Closeburn.

Caerlaverock National Nature-Reserve (028658): These 2700 ha (13,514 acres) beside the Solway between the Lochar and Nith estuaries are bordered by 7 miles (11 km) of the B725 from Bankend, off the B724 Dumfries to Annan road, and encompass 6 miles (9.5 km) of the tidal East (Blacksaw) saltmarsh (607 ha—1500 acres), a restricted shooting area bulging into the Firth. Here common terns nest with four species of gull, redshank, dunlin, oystercatcher, occasional wigeon, and shelduck. It also includes the muddy Nith-Lochar foreshore. Black-tailed godwits have nested along the Solway in recent years and the Merse has many tidal waders; but its main attractions from September to April are its loud-voiced geese which roam the winter sky in

musical confusion. Some of its geese fly in from the Eden
valley of Cumbria. Five thousand Spitzbergen barnacles,
including some albinos, have been counted in recent
Octobers, arriving late in September, followed soon
afterwards by coachloads of British bird clubs. Also 10,000
to 15,000 pinkfeet roost here and some greylags. Brent are
rarer. It is the main Scottish pintail haunt with 800 in
October. Pintail and wigeon have bred. A Baikal teal in
February 1973 is more likely to have come from a duck zoo
than from Baikal. Six to seven thousand gabbling greylag
roost in winter, 2000 in spring. Access is restricted in parts
and on Sundays. *Warden:* Tadorna, Holland Farm Road,
Caerlaverock, via Dumfries (tel. Glencaple 275). The
Solway arouses nostalgic memories when its sky fills with
flights of geese and echoes their voices, with Gretna looming
grey along the coast, and flock after flock of golden plover
whistles its way overhead. Until the advent of modern
serious bird-watching, it was the monopoly of fowlers,
contemptuous   of   Shakespeare's   'winter   of   our
discontent'—summer was the season of their misery! Even
by the road at Isle Steps, a large herd of whoopers may now
be seen in winter. Carelaverock's 5,000 barnacles are seen
best from October to December. March and April provide
the closest views of pinkfeet near Glencaple.

Eastpark Farm (Wildfowl Trust): Complementary to and
partly overlapping the Caerlaverock reserve, and reached
from the T-junction signposted to Blackshaw, $2\frac{1}{2}$ miles (4
km) south of Bankend on the far side of the B725, it
comprises 94 ha (235 acres) of fields and 243 ha (600 acres)
of tidal, castle-dominated merse visited by up to 3000
barnacles and pinkfeet. Hides are behind the seawall, and
access to the conservancy's Saltcot observation tower. An

enclosure of pinioned birds. Admission charge and access restricted to holders of Nature Conservancy permits between 11 a.m. and 2 p.m. Closed Tuesday and Wednesday and 16 May to 31 August. *Manager:* tel. Glencaple 200. Kinmount (A75 Annan) has woodcock.

Solway Firth: Almost anywhere along the Solway tide is interesting. Whoopers visit the Nith at Glencaple (995688) where greylags graze, sometimes Greenland whitefronts, and fifteen curlew sandpipers have been together in September. Pinkfeet and greylags also rest on Priestside Bank with waders, west of Cummertrees; but there is a long

The Red-throated Diver seen on southern lochs and estuaries in winter, nests on mostly northern loch islands

shooting tradition at these places. Access is by the A75 and the B724 west of Annan, to track from Cummertrees. I have seen the Caerlaverock barnacles feeding on Rockcliffe marsh on the Cumbrian side in February or March, having eaten out their grazing below Blackshaw, when goldeneye, wigeon and mergansers flock off the Eden mouth, and I have seen the odd white pinkfoot. Geese and waders sometimes get up the Nith as near to Dumfries as Nettletown and Kelton. Odd bean geese visit the estuary. Mallard and Canada geese have been reared locally. Wildfowl use the mudflats in greatest numbers when hard frosts begin in January but 400 scaup were here in October 1960. Unlike the Cumbrian (south) shore, the Scottish Solway is a succession of estuaries, bays and promontories. When I reviewed, in a morning newspaper, Bill Powell's 1954 Solway fowling book, *My Wild Goose Chase*, he kindly invited me to Glencaple to try some haaf-net fishing, up to my neck in the Nith tide where drowning is imminent. The tide where waders flock at Annan Waterfront (191648) is 1 hour 53 minutes earlier than at Glasgow. Cracks Moss and Rocks Moss are interesting haunts inland and either side of the River Lochar. The North Solway, included in the Merseyside Naturalists' Association's shelduck census, had 982 adult birds and 542 young in July 1963. A lane from Cummertrees over Powfoot golf-course leads to good watching on the shore at Ridding Dyke.

Information
Recorders: D. Skilling, 86 Auchenkeld Avenue, Heathhall, Dumfries. R. T. Smith, Applegarthtown, Lockerbie.
Society: Dumfries Branch, Scottish Ornithologists' Club. Hon. Sec. W. Austin, 54 Albert Road, Dumfries.

Kirkcudbrightshire
Still much indented with small inlets, tidal firths and bays,
the Solway coast here becomes a little more precipitous
with cliffs. It attracts more duck and whitefronted geese
than neighbouring Dumfriesshire. Inland, its 23,000 ha
(582,982 acres) include extensive mountains with nesting
dotterel, and numerous lakes, of which Loch Ken is the
most important. Castle Douglas is the best centre. The old
province of Galloway extended from here through Wigtownshire.

Golden eagles breed in southwest Scotland, including the
2331 feet (699 m) Cairnsmore of Fleet and the Rhinns of

The Twite, a generally moorland nester wintering on the coast

Kells. In January an eagle flew each evening past the
Murray Monument at Castle Douglas. There are peregrine
eyries, twelve breeding pairs of great crested grebes,
nightjars in recent years at Brennan and the King Edward
Forest on the Wigtown border; there are also hen harriers
near the Gatehouse of Fleet, and goosanders (Glen Ken)
gadwall and pintail. Feral greylags breed on eleven lochs,
including near Castle Douglas. There are introduced
golden and hybrid Lady Amherst pheasants. Buzzards
breed here, goosanders mainly in the east, wigeon
occasionally, green woodpeckers at Lennox Castle; crossbills in the forests, pied flycatchers in Glen Trool and Glen
Ken, and herons at Agrennan, Carsphairn, Dalskairth
(Troqueer) and Machermore near Newton Stewart.

Cormorants nest with varying success, according to
disturbance, at Orroland Bay cliffs, via Dundrennan, on the
A711, Dookers' Rig at Portowarren, below the A710 at
Balcarry Point's fulmar and cormorant cliffs, and on
Hestan Island (839502), where arctic and Sandwich terns
sometimes nest with common gulls, oystercatchers, ringed
plover and rock pipits. About half a kilometre long,
Hestan has cliffs reaching nearly 200 feet (61 m), with
nesting greater and lesser black-backed and herring gulls,
and visiting guillemots and fulmars, as well as nesting
rockdoves. Great black-backed gulls nest on the Isle of
Fleet, cormorants and fulmars have been at Meikleroos,
and kittiwakes at Little Ross. Rough Island in Rough Firth,
below Dalbeattie, is an 8 ha (18 acre) reserve of the Scottish
National Trust, with terns, winter scaup and waders, a tidal
island via the A710, to White Loch, Rockcliffe or the side
road to Kingford, at low water when accessible on foot.
There is also the brackeny Jubilee coast path with chats at
nearby Rockcliffe and Kippford, with Muckle Land. Many

shelduck nest in Kirkconnel Merse.

Cairnsmore of Fleet with nesting eagles, harriers, peregrines, ravens, etc, is now a National Nature Reserve. Access is via Gatehouse of Fleet on the A75 west Kirkcudbright, then the B796. It includes the northern spur of Craignelder and covers 1329 ha (3285 acres).

Wildfowl are more scattered, with up to 900 Greenlanders and 1000 greylags among the geese and three black-necked grebes at Threave Island, Castle Douglas, in January 1972, as well as visiting lesser snow goose, beans, and odd lesser whitefronts. Seven thousand pinkfeet may be in the Nith estuary in February and 100 feeding in fields southeast of Dalbeattie. Greylags feed in Milton Loch (Bay). Flocks of scaup and waders favour the coast where occasional surf scoters are recorded. Thirty-two bean geese visited the Boreland of Balmaghie in February 1973 and sixty at Castle Douglas in December, the most for seven years. Over ninety whoopers have been counted in March, thirty at Loch Ken and seventy in the Nith estuary in February. The Dee valley, including Loch Ken, is the main inland haunt of duck and geese. One thousand crows use five roosts in the Ken valley, and up to 10,000 rooks roost in conifers át Meikle Auchenreoch (Crocketford), up to 5000 at Bridgend of Killoch and at Paddock Hall, Nether Corsock, and 3000 at Holehouse Farm, Dundrennan. Summer birds make the conifer plantations by the Dee interesting.

The 1972 influx of bearded tits reached here. Scottish crossbills and continental great grey shrikes are also visitors. There are occasional Montagu's and marsh harriers and three large winter roosts of ten to thirty hen harriers near Loch Stroan are famous. The North American Wilson's phalarope was at Kirkgunzeon, near the A711 north of

Dalbeattie, in August and September 1972, when a rose-coloured pastor visited Palnackie south of Dalbeattie. Greenshanks sometimes overwinter, as in other Solway counties. Mersehead Sands, between Southerness Point and Rough Forth at Southwick (not to be confused with Caerlaverock Merse) has pinkfeet and up to 1000 greylags in late winter, as well as waders. It is reached from the A710 near Lot's Wife pillar.

The Loch Stroan harrier roosts were used by ten to thirty birds in September to March in recent years, roosting on the ground over some 23 ha (59 acres) of low heather and rush moor. Two were 56 km (35 miles) apart. They were inland by sandhills and pinewood too, with an occasional short-eared owl hunting by day. Few ducks haunt the higher lochs.

The Galloway Hills, bordering Wigtownshire, are the nesting haunt of peregrines, merlins, etc.

In addition to Loch Ken, fresh waters include Auchen-reoch Loch (A75, south of the junction with the A712) and Milton Loch down the lane from Nine Mile Bar there, nesting haunt of great crested grebes and visited by duck, greylags and the 1972–3 influx of bearded tits. Grebes also breed on White Loch (A710, Colvend) near the south coast, Woodhall (A762), Arthur (A711 at Beeswing–New Abbey road) and Moan in the northwest, which has a black-headed gullery and great black-backed gulls. Loch Kindar (south), the large Clatteringshaws (and its woods) where ringed plover nest by the A712 west of New Galloway, and Lochtratten, are of some interest. Silver Flowe and Kirkconnel Flow (NX9769) form a National Nature Reserve of seven raised, undrained bogs of 191 ha (472 acres). On the coast, Kirkcudbright Bay and Fleet Bay to the west are visited by duck in winter, the former with a few greylags, the latter with nesting great black-backed gulls. In September spotted redshanks visit the Tarf estuary, Rough Firth, Carsethorn Creek (a winter haunt of scaup), large flocks of ringed plover visit the shores, etc., and there are wintering greenshank. American surf scoters wintered off Portowarren in recent years.

Woodlands include Bennan Wood (Cairnsmore), Caldons Wood (northwest), and The Merrick, the northwest border hill of 2764 feet (829 m).

Loch Ken and the Dee Valley (NX6375-6771): Castle Douglas (765623) is the centre for the Kelton Mains Farm Reserve of the Scottish National Trust, a wildfowl haunt of 525 ha (1300 acres), 1½ miles (2·4 km) southwest, with geese on the High Tae Drum (hill) and riverside meadows. The Dee Valley down the centre of the county to Kirkcudbright Bay is the main inland haunt of waterfowl with greylags and whitefronts, especially 10 miles (16 km) long Loch Ken from New Galloway to Crossmichael, with the A713 running close by, and on the west bank the A762 for part of it. Duck flocks and whitefronts are often above the Livingston viaduct, which divides the loch, while grass fields around nearby Parton attract grazing whoopers, greylags and up to ninety Greenland whitefronts together and occasional lesser whitefronts. Whitefronts feed in several fields, but the grey goose flocks are in relation to grass, and when this is ploughed their feeding flocks are fewer. Greenlaw Mains (moor) and Townshead of Greenlaw Dam, off the A713 north of Douglas, have had over ninety feeding whoopers. The river also has duck, including goosanders in winter. Threave Island (741625) marsh and Mains, in the river 3 miles (5 km) south of the loch, had 900 Greenlanders and three black-necked grebes in January

1972. Like other parts of the Dee valley, it was visited in January regularly for bean geese, usually with success until the last few years. Whoopers as well as pochard, tufted duck, goldeneye and smew also visit 60 ha (150 acres) shallow Carlingwark Loch (760612) beside the A75 out of Castle Douglas. Many wigeon come here and there have been 1000 greylags, 200 whitefronts and twenty-three whoopers.

Whoopers, divers and duck visit the Blackpark floods at the Kelton reserve, where there is a restricted observation hide.

As well as Loch Ken's important greylag and pinkfoot roosts in winter, there are visits of great grey shrike and occasional arctic skuas on windy days. Goosander and, in 1971, pintail are among its nesters. There are also in the Dee valley Loch Roan above Crossmichael, attracting whoopers in winter and grebes in summer, Woodhall Loch and Loch Stroan, etc. *Warden of the Kelton reserve:* Kelton Mill, Castle Douglas (tel. Bridge of Dee 242).

Knowetops Lochs, a 27·5 ha (68 acre) reserve of the SWT, 4 miles, (6·4 km) east of Balmaclellan on the A712 road north of Loch Ken, is a haunt of five species of duck, tree-pipit, garden and grasshopper warblers, etc. Permits are required from the owner, R. F. Steward, Knowetop, Corsock.

Southerness Point (978542): From the A710 southwest of Dumfries, or the A745 southeast of Dalbeattie, the flat fields end at this rocky point with its lighthouse on the mouth of the Nith estuary, a haunt of up to seventy whoopers, its tidal mudflats have a roost of pinkfeet and greylags from February to April. Whoopers feed in nearby fields. Flocks of seaduck, wigeon and sometimes in February the surf scoter favour the point; wintering greenshank, black-tailed godwits and lesser black-backed gulls favour the muddy Nith tidal marsh; purple sandpipers and turnstones feed on the seaweed beds. Two hundred scaup have been counted in January, occasionally with a tufted duck. Grebes winter offshore. The high tide wader roost is at 'Lot's Wife', by the A710 on Mersehead Sands. Carsethorn Creek, 4 or 5 miles (6–8 km) up the estuary, has flocks of knot and other waders (Carse Sands) and of scaup. Pintail have nested in the Nith estuary. It is good bird country from Preston Merse to Auchencairn Bay, and in bordering Wigtown Bay, described under the county of Wigtownshire. Loch Kindar near the A710 at the Nith estuary also attracts waterfowl.

Glen Trool (Galloway) National Forest Park (NX400790): This is at the west end of Loch Trool and also at NX415804 near the Bruce Memorial Stone on the A714 and Bargrennan 8 miles (13 km) northwest of Newton Stewart. The Rhinns of Kells, 2668 feet (800 m) (NX415804) and Merrick, 2764 feet (829 m), the highest hill in south Scotland, are in the park and the nesting haunts of golden eagle, peregrine, black grouse, golden plover, raven, short-eared owl, buzzard, hen harrier, red grouse, whinchat, stonechat, ring ouzel, grasshopper warbler, woodcock, dipper, pied flycatcher and redstart. There is a black-headed gullery at Loch Macaterick, with diving duck. The great grey shrike may be seen in winter and crossbills and pied flycatchers are found nesting in summer. This forest park of 526,721 ha (1,300,000 acres) with old oaks and younger pines includes Loch Trool and sixteen hill lochs, extending into Ayr. The main entry is from the A714 at Newton Stewart (241565). There is camping at Caldons Farm, southwest of Loch Trool.

Fleet Forest (NX606562): 1 mile (1·5 km) south of Gatehouse of Fleet (260557) by the road from the A75 Dumfries to Newton Stewart road (408650), Fleet Forest is a nesting haunt of black grouse and hen harrier, occasionally golden pheasant, with forest walks. South of it is Fleet Bay, off Wigtown Bay, with winter duck, and the Isle of Fleet with nesting great black-backed gulls. The Cairnsmore of Fleet National Nature Reserve covers 1315 ha (3288 acres) with nesting golden eagles, hen harriers, etc.

Kirrough-tree Forest Park (NX487717): This is half a mile (0·8 km) south of Murray's Monument (NX452646) near Palnure, and 3 miles (5 km) southeast of Newton Stewart on the A75 Gatehouse road. It has introduced golden and Lady Amherst's pheasants. Nightjars and crossbills nest at Cairn Edward Forest on the Wigtown border.

Solway Forest: There are walks at NX837602 on the A710 south of Dalbeattie, at NX843566 2 miles (3 km) further south, and at NX949712 on the by-road near Mabie, 1 mile (1·6 km) northwest of the A710.

Information
Recorder: A. D. Watson, Barone, Dalry, Castle Douglas.

Literature: Duncan, A. A., List of the Birds of the Stewartry of Kirkcudbright, *Trans. Dumfries & Galloway Natural History Society* (1947).
Guide to Glen Trool Forest Park (HMSO).

Wigtownshire
This southwestern extremity of Scotland covers 132,000 ha

(327,906 acres) and is only 25 miles (40 km) from Ireland. Its long coast has numerous deep, wide bays, but much of the countryside is poor grassland. It is the farthest south that hoodies and their hybrids breed regularly on the British mainland. Lesser whitefronts are seen occasionally among its winter geese and roosts of 1000 curlews and other waders occur in its bays, like Wigtown Merse and Bay. Here the tides at Garliestown are 1 hour 53 minutes earlier than at Glasgow, and at the Mull of Galloway, its senior seabird haunt, 1 hour 57 minutes earlier. One to five pairs of little tern nest and seven pairs of great crested grebe; jays are increasing westwards, and Britain's largest and Scotland's first inland freshwater colony of cormorants is on Castle Loch southeast of Glenluce. Herring gulls nest on some buildings in Stranraer (060608) the largest town; black guillemots nest in Portpatrick harbour (a seabird migration watch) and near the lighthouse, Mull of Galloway, and feral greylags on several waters. There are four merlin breeding sites, over fifteen pairs of breeding ravens, four or five pairs of golden eagle, and two pairs of hen harrier, as well as buzzards, peregrines, sparrowhawks, willow tits, teal, tufted duck, green woodpeckers, etc. Pochard bred at Loch Dornal in 1971. Sixteen pairs of golden eagle bred in Galloway in the past decade.

Feral greylags breed and flock at Loch Inch Castle Black Loch, east of Stranraer (A75), where great crested grebes nest (access by permit) and by the coastal road A747 at Monreith Park's White Loch, a nesting haunt of twite. Fifty to eighty cormorants breed on the coast at Piltanton estuary (a wader haunt), Meikle Ross and Mulberry. Herons nest at Machermore in the Cree Valley woods (Newton Stewart) on the Kirkcudbright border. A forest walk is at NX442486 in Bareagle Forest. off the Kirkinner–Sorbie road, 4 miles (6 km) south of Wigtown.

Greenshank sometimes winter in Skyreburn Bay, etc.,
and pinkfeet visit Whauphill saltings. Brent and bean geese
occasionally visit the coast at Loch Galloway, where eider
nest; several spotted redshanks visit the Carf estuary in
September. King eider and little egret are among visiting
rarities; a magnificent frigate bird was recorded in October
1969 and a little bustard in April 1964. Great grey shrikes
come in winter when up to 50,000 rooks roost at Outtle
Well, 11,000 at Stoneykirk and 5000 at Bladnoch Weir,
Dowalton Loch and White Loch of Milton (several White
Lochs are in the county). Cree valley woods above Newton
Stewart, Cree Firth below it, Rough Firth below Dalbeattie
and Auchencairn Bay are further bird haunts.

Scar Rocks, and Luce Bay (259333) : Big Scar, Scare or Great
Scaur, 6 miles (9 km) from the Mull of Galloway (159305),
is a site of special scientific interest (SSSI), 300 feet (90 m)
long and 60–70 feet (18–21 m) high, with semi-detached
Castle Rock on the west. Only seaweed and lichen grow on
it, but twenty-four recorded birds include twelve nesting
species: 1200 common guillemots, occasional black guillemots, and puffins (not now), 600–700 gannets, about sixty
razorbills, shags, cormorants, kittiwakes, greater and lesser
black-backed and herring gulls, and rockdoves. Birds do
not nest on six sea-swept Little Scar rocks. The islands were
formerly leased from the Crown Agents to the Scottish Bird
Protection Society, which has become less active in modern
times. See J. G. Young 'Birds of Scar Rock', *Scottish Birds
Magazine*, **5**, 4 (1968). Landings only in calm weather, from
Port William.

Luce Bay's more accessible bird haunts (excepting some
military restrictions) include shore waders at Torrs Warren

(Sands of Luce). Burrow Head cliffs at the east end, via the A746 from Wigtown to Whitehorn, then the A750, has nesting auks, kittiwakes, shags and cormorants. Little Ross lighthouse here is a good seawatch. The better known Mull of Galloway, at the west end, with nesting puffins and cormorants, guillemots and twite, is reached via the A75 Wigtown to Glenluce road, then A715 and A716 to Drummore harbour, for the B7041. Terns also nest in places and Scoter have bred.

Wigtown Bay: Wigtown Merse is occasionally visited by lesser whitefronts and other geese, 2000 scoter may be in the bay from late July, while the bay has 2000 wigeon in December and a roost of 1000 curlews. Wader flocks exceed 9000 on the Merse in October. Kittiwakes and four pairs of razorbills nest north of Cruggelton Castle, and cormorants in Rigg Bay, below the B7063 on the west side. On the east the A75 from Newton Stewart to Creetown is on the Kirkcudbright side, but 7 miles (11 km) from Spittal, above Creetown to Jultock Point, is sometimes visited by 2000 greylags and as many pinkfeet in March. Some Canadas and many duck are winter visitors here and on Wigtown Sands opposite, including 2000 scoter and many waders. Duck also visit the Moss of Cree inland. A little egret was at Garliestown Bay in September 1970. Terns also nest in places.

Loch Ryan: Few eiders breed in Wigtownshire, but moulting flocks reach 500 in July in this large shallow, sheltered sea loch in the northwest, skirted by the A77 and A718 from Stranraer. A drake king eider visited Kirkcolm in March 1970. Four thousand October wigeon, fifty goldeneye and as many mergansers have been off Stranraer in December.

Many herons winter here and the muddy shore at the head of the loch attracts greylags, duck and waders. Great crested grebes and greylags nest on Loch Inch Castle White Loch, by the A75 from Stranraer. From autumn to spring many grebes winter especially at The Wig, Sole Burn, Stranraer Harbour and between Innermessan and Leffnol Point, with up to 110 great crested in September, up to twenty-three black-necked, up to eight slavonians, and occasional red-necked. Tides are 20 minutes earlier than Greenock.

Castle Loch, Mochrum Loch (275547): These waters are reached on the by-road from Calshabben, off the B7005 west of Wigtown, and are the nesting haunt of great crested grebe and tufted duck; Britain's largest inland cormorant colony is on Castle Loch, with great black-backed gulls, and it is also visited by greylags. Greylags also nest on White Loch, Monreith Park, by the A714 from Port William, on the east shore of Luce Bay.

Mull of Galloway is an RSPB reserve for seabirds with nesting Puffins, etc.

Information
Recorder: A. D. Watson, Barone, Dalry, Castle Douglas, Kirkcudbrightshire.

Society: Wigtown Group, Scottish Ornithologists' Club. Hon. Sec. G. Shepherd, Bar House Restaurant, Gairnryan Road, Stranraer, Wigtownshire.
Dumfries and Galloway Natural History Society.

Check List
Nesters: Black-throated Diver, Great Crested Grebe, Little Grebe, Fulmar, Gannet, Cormorant, Shag, Heron,

Mallard, Teal, Gadwall, Wigeon, Pintail, Shoveler, Tufted Duck, Pochard, Scoter, Eider, Red-breasted Merganser, Goosander, Shelduck, Greylag, Canada Goose, Mute Swan, Golden Eagle, Buzzard, Sparrowhawk, Hen Harrier, Peregrine, Merlin, Kestrel, Red Grouse, Black Grouse, Red-legged Partridge, Common Partridge, Quail, Common Pheasant, Japanese Pheasant, Golden Pheasant, Lady Amherst Pheasant, Water Rail, Spotted Crake, Corncrake, Moorhen, Coot, Oystercatcher, Lapwing, Ringed Plover, Golden Plover, Dotterel, Snipe, Woodcock, Curlew, Black-tailed Godwit, Sandpiper, Redshank, Dunlin, Great Black-backed Gull, Lesser Black-backed Gull, Herring Gull, Common Gull, Black-headed Gull, Kittiwake, Common Tern, Arctic Tern, Little Tern, Sandwich Tern, Razorbill, Guillemot, Black Guillemot, Puffin, Stockdove, Rockdove, Woodpigeon, Collared Dove, Cuckoo, Barn Owl, Little Owl, Tawny Owl, Long-eared Owl, Short-eared Owl, Nightjar, Swift, Kingfisher, Green Woodpecker, Great Spotted Woodpecker, Skylark, Swallow, House Martin, Sand Martin, Raven, Carrion Crow, Rook, Jackdaw, Magpie, Jay, Great Tit, Blue Tit, Coal Tit, Willow Tit, Long-tailed Tit, Tree Creeper, Wren, Dipper, Mistle Thrush, Song Thrush, Ring Ouzel, Blackbird, Wheatear, Stonechat, Whinchat, Redstart, Robin, Grasshopper Warbler, Sedge Warbler, Blackcap, Garden Warbler, Whitethroat, Willow Warbler, Chiffchaff, Wood Warbler, Goldcrest, Spotted Flycatcher, Pied Flycatcher, Hedge Sparrow, Meadow Pipit, Tree Pipit, Rock Pipit, Pied Wagtail, Grey Wagtail, Yellow Wagtail, Starling, Hawfinch, Greenfinch, Goldfinch, Siskin, Linnet, Twite, Redpoll, Bullfinch, Crossbill, Chaffinch, Corn Bunting, Reed Bunting, Yellowhammer, House Sparrow, Tree Sparrow.

Migratory and rarer visitors: Greylag, Pinkfoot, Whitefront (occasionally Greenland and Lesser), Barnacle, Bean (occasionally Brent) Geese, many Duck, especially Wigeon, Shoveler, Pochard, Goosander, Scoter, Scaup, Surf Scoter, also King Eider, Smew, Whooper and occasional Bewick's Swans. Black-necked Grebe and Great Grey Shrike are fairly regular. Little Egret, Purple Heron, White-billed Diver, Bearded Tit, Frigate Petrel and Little Bustard are among stragglers. Many waders like Knot flock along the Solway shores, including Purple Sandpiper and Turnstone, some Spotted Redshanks and wind-drifted Americans like Wilson's Phalarope, as well as wintering Greenshank, and Black-tailed Godwits, along with wintering Lesser Black-backed Gulls. Scottish Crossbills are among winter visitors. Roller, Marsh Harrier and Turtle Dove are among uncommon summer visitors. Black Tern are occasional birds of passage on easterly winds. The Mull of Galloway, Portpatrick, Burrow Head and Corsewall Point have fair opportunities for skuas and shearwaters in a seabird watch with onshore winds.

Tayside and Fife Regions

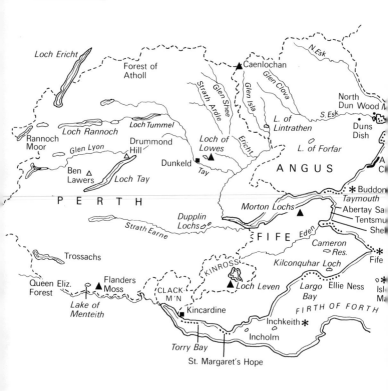

Loch Ericht

Forest of Atholl

N. Esk

Caenlochan

Glen Isla

Glen Clova

Strath Ardle

Glen Shee

Loch Tummel

Loch Rannoch

Rannoch Moor

Glen Lyon

Drummond Hill

Loch of Lowes

Ericht

L. of Lintrathen

North Dun Wood

Duns Dish

S. Esk

Ben Lawers

Loch Tay

Dunkeld

Tay

L. of Forfar

A N G U S

P E R T H

Buddo

Taymouth

Abertay Sa

Morton Lochs

Dupplin Lochs

Strath Earne

F I F E

Eden

Tentsmu

Shel

Cameron Res.

Trossachs

KINROSS

Kilconquhar Loch

Fife

Queen Eliz. Forest

Flanders Moss

CLACK M'N

Loch Leven

Largo Bay

Ellie Ness

Isl

Ma

Lake of Menteith

Kincardine

FIRTH OF FORTH

Inchkeith

Torry Bay

Incholm

St. Margaret's Hope

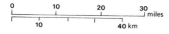

0   10   20   30 miles

10   40 km

Chapter 7

Fife Region

Fife

This great peninsula between the firths of Tay and Forth is a major landfall for continental migrants drifted across the North Sea on easterly winds. Its sandy foot in the sea at Tentsmuir is a good ternery and nesting reserve. Stretching 43 miles (69 km) east to west and 17 miles (27 km) north to south, its undulating countryside is broken by the ridge of the Ochil Hills in the north, with the sandstone lowland of the Hows of Fife (How Hollow or Stratheden, the Eden valley) between these and central hills. Its rocky northwestern moorland contrasts with the industrialised Dunfermline coalfield. Only 5½ miles (9 km) southeast of Crail, in the Firth of Forth, the Isle of May Bird Observatory is the second major migration haunt of rarities.

Its three terneries are declining and about five little tern pairs survive. Heronries are also decreasing in the Kincardine-on-Forth boundary and at Tentsmuir and Kinloch-on-Forth. Capercaillie occur, and nesting green woodpeckers and gadwall; shelduck breed at Culross, Tulliallan, Aberdour and other sandy places, bullfinches at Lethan and Cupar and eiders. As well the major freshwater haunt of Kilconquhar Loch (Nairn Estates, via Nairn Lodge), great crested grebes nest on Carriston Reservoir (56° 15′ N, 5° 06′ W) which is also visited by little gulls, etc., and on eleven other waters: Coul and Cullaloe Reservoirs, Loch Gelly, Lindores (where a little bittern was found in June 1970), Ore (visited by up to seventy-three whoopers), Tulliallan Castle (Kincardine-on-Forth), Dunfermline town loch, and on Raith Lake, Kirkcaldy. Shiresmill Pond in the west is a haunt of waders, and Cameron Reservoir, at the top of the Kenly River, by the A915, is a roost for up to 9000 greylags and pinkfeet. Here gadwall occasionally nest.

Scotland's second greatest wader flocks occur along the Forth tidelines between Fife Ness and Dunbar, the eighth largest along the Firth of Tay. East winds bring barred warblers, up to five yellow-browed warblers in a day, bluethroats, firecrests, etc., while Britain's major autumn flocks of little gulls total 325 at Methil (Largo Bay) in September, with others at Fife Ness, etc. It is a great nesting haunt of eiders, with winter flocks of 10,000 on the mussel-beds from Tayport to Broughton Ferry. These have regular seasonal movements with Aberdeenshire stocks. Flocks of up to 1500 velvet scoter, including the rare surf scoter, have been recorded in February. Travelling in winter along the south coast railway has enabled the great rafts of duck to be seen along the inshore waters of the Forth. One thousand goosanders may flock off Tayport and 220 mergansers off Culross marsh below Rosyth, Forth Bridge. Winter geese include a few brent, while 1000 roosting pinkfeet and greylags have visited Cameron Reservoir in the east.

The Scottish crossbill is among winter visitors, when waxwings and northern great spotted woodpeckers may come from the continent. East winds bring black terns. Parties of up to thirty curlew sandpipers and several spotted redshanks favour parts of the coast. Two hundred purple sandpipers have been counted in April; continental and Icelandic water rails have been recorded; a little bittern was at Largo Bay in June 1970, an American Bonaparte's gull at Cupar in February 1972, and Wilson's phalarope was first recognised as a British bird at pools between North Queensferry (135804) and Rosyth dockyard. There, at St Margaret's Hope (restricted by the Admiralty) and Hounds Foot, beneath the Forth Bridge, and reached from

Inverkeithing on the A823, the tides bring up to five spotted redshanks in a variety of waders. The black-browed albatross was at Elie Ness in 1969, and rarer shearwaters, skuas, divers and an occasional little auk reward seabird watches on the open coast. The modern irruption of bearded tits reached Fife.

The Scottish Wildlife Trust has a reserve at Bankhead Moss. Common terns have bred at Longannet Point up the Forth near Kincardine-on-Forth, roseates at Car Crag (south) and fulmars at Denarty cliffs. Inchkeith, an island in the Firth of Forth ecologically associated with islands on the Lothian side, is a breeding site of kittiwakes, razorbills,

American Wilson's Phalarope, first accepted as a British bird on pools by the Forth, September 1954

350 puffins and 400 pairs of fulmar. Shiresmill Pond (west) has attracted waders, and purple sandpipers, oystercatchers, ringed plover, knot, etc., winter in good numbers on rocky shores of the Forth estuary at Buckhaven–Pathead, Long Craig–Pettycur and Burntisland–Aberdour. Loch Fitty (northeast), Lindores reservoir and Peppermill Dam (southwest border) attract waterfowl. The Forth at Kincardine Bridge, by the sea wall below the old station level crossing, provides pochard, tufted duck, goldeneye, mergansers, waders and sometimes whoopers at high tide. Golden orioles nested for the first time known in Scotland in Fife in 1974.

Morton Lochs and Tentsmuir Reserves (454261 and NO498243): These are adjacent National Nature Reserves, and I travelled through one to reach the other, conveniently visited (with permits from the Nature Conservancy Council in Edinburgh) at the same time, from the B945 from Tayport, down a dusty lane 7 miles (11 km) or so on the left, signposted to Morton Lochs. Here, amidst chattering sedge warblers nesting in the rustling reeds, I looked out of the wooden hide upon the watery world of the shallow, marshy, north lochs rampant with fragrant meadowsweet, where great crested grebes and little grebes fed their piping young, a distant pair of shelduck sat in piebald splendour and a tufted duck began diving. The resort of nesting birds in summer, the twin lochs become the winter resort of wild duck and swans. Six of their 23 ha (59 acres) are woodland, mostly Corsican pine. Little gulls come in spring; they were visited by bearded tits in 1972, and there is a passage of waders. Shoveler, tufted duck, pochard, Canada geese and mallard nest here, among forty-five nesting species and a list of 136 birds, from willow

tit to bullfinch. Wigeon nested in 1953 and gadwall have
bred here. Barnacle and Canada geese have hybridised, as
in other places. Winter flocks of 200 teal and 150 tufted
duck have been counted, with pintail and wigeon, together
with black-headed gulls from Earlshall gullery to the south,
near Leuchars RAF base, where there are some restrictions.

Continuing with Dundee bird-watchers coastwise along
a rougher road through Tentsmuir pine forest I paused to
watch a hen capercaillie, said to be the first seen here, then a
timid roe, before emerging among the sandhills sanctuary
where guardians of the ternery have turned wartime
military posts into an observation tower and study centre.
Shore nests of common and arctic terns are subject to
destruction by spring tides, but the birds relay with the
oystercatchers in the dunes. Sandwich and little terns prefer
to be below the RAF station at Leuchars and Shelly Point in
the Eden estuary. Migratory waders choose the Abertay
sands (which are restricted in winter). Here pinkfeet and
greylags roost in the Tay mouth in sight of Dundee.

Of 192 species listed in 2550 ha (6301 acres) at
Tentsmuir, sixty-nine were resident, twenty summer
visitors, twenty-four winter visitors, thirty-one passage
migrants and forty-eight casuals. Nesters include little
grebe, heron, teal, shoveler, tufted duck, shelduck (130
pairs), ringed plover, woodcock, curlew, redshank, black-
headed gull, declining common, arctic and Sandwich terns,
stockdove, long-eared owl, goldcrest and occasionally
short-eared owl, spotted flycatcher and stonechat. Scoter
nested in 1947. Here is a junction of passage migration
southwards along the coast and inland via Tay and Forth to
the Clyde. Three hundred pairs of common tern have
nested here. Long-tailed duck come in spring and many
snow buntings in autumn. Moulting flocks of eider and

scoter summer offshore. Five thousand eiders flock in April.
This flat, sandy coast is increasing as the sea recedes at its
greatest rate in Britain. Red grouse and heather have been
introduced to the dunes. Eiders sometimes nest inland in the
forest. Roseate and little tern are in a more precarious
position as nesters. Great black-backed gulls began nesting
in 1972, and there are lesser black-backed gulls. Two
thousand one hundred bar-tailed godwits visited Tentsmuir Point on August tides, where up to 300 grey plover
winter.

Earlshall Moor (475215): Restricted and private, this
forms the third adjacent reserve in the Eden estuary, the
nesting haunt of herons, long-tailed tits, eider, shelduck
and black-headed gulls. The Eden estuary's Shelly Point
and Guardsbridge are regular passage haunts of 50–100
black-tailed godwits, with over thirty curlew sandpipers
flocking in August and September tides. They are also
visited by ruff, flocks of scoter, 2000 shelduck and other duck
and of little gulls. The estuary is 2 miles (3 km) north of St
Andrews, and at Shelly Point attracts the sixth largest
Scottish wader flocks.

St Andrew's Bay and Harbour: Visited by purple sandpipers,
terns, eiders, long-tailed duck, velvet scoter and up to 1000
common scoter, in January, this southern side of the Eden
mouth is always worth attention in autumn and winter,
even the golf course. The rocky coast to Ruddons Point
attracts many winter oystercatchers, purple sandpipers,
ringed plover, knot, etc.

Firth of Tay: Via Newburgh on the A913, or the A92 to
Newport and the A914 New Tay Bridge Road. Greylags

roost on Mugdrum island, and 8240 pinkfeet have been at
Abertay. Little gulls are regular in spring and autumn,
10,000 to 15,000 eiders flock on winter tides and 21,000 in
September; waders favour flats west of Tentsmuir; little
terns come in summer. *Warden:* M. Smith, Chesterfield,
Newport-on-Tay.

Fife Ness and East Neuk: This eastern headland is a good
migration watch. It had 900 velvet scoter in August; black
redstart and red-breasted flycatcher are among passing
visitors. Balearic shearwater and Sabine's gull have been
recorded. East Neuk is the faunal boundary 'No Man's
Land' between Tay and Forth. Elie Ness by the A917 some
10 miles (16 km) south, like Fife Ness and Shell Bay by
Ruddons' Point also has passage divers, skuas and
shearwaters. Nearby Kilconquhar Loch (489019) (Elie
Estates), 1½ miles (2·4 km) north of Elie, has nesting tufted
duck, pochard, shoveler, gadwall, great crested, little
grebe, etc., and sedge warbler, in its reedy northeast end.
This 40 ha (100 acres) of shallow water is visited by winter
duck and by greylags in March, summer black tern and up
to 500 little gulls in September and October. A great reed
warbler was recorded in June 1970. A firing range is
sometimes used near Ruddons Point.

Largo Bay: To the south, a nesting place of common
sandpiper and autumn haunt of little gulls, this area has
had 1500 velvet scoter in February and in spring and
autumn is visited by flocks of scoter, long-tailed and other
duck, as well as by divers in winter and white (*Sterna*) terns
and black (*Chlidonias*) terns in autumn. Greylag and
various waders come, including a long-billed dowitcher
record. Lundin Links by the A915 at Lower Largo are

interesting too. Pochard and grasshopper warbler have been noted in summer. Purple sandpipers and other waders winter in good numbers on its rocky shore. Many wildfowl including longtails winter off Methil.

Isle of May (655991): This 56 ha (140 acres) National Nature Reserve is a rocky island slammed by the stormy sea in the mouth of the Firth of Forth, an important seabird colony and migration observatory, via boat from Anstruther, with permits from the Nature Conservancy, Edinburgh. Two hundred and thirty-four birds listed include among nesters over ninety pairs of fulmar, 900 to 1700 shags, up to 3450 kittiwakes (Mill Dow and Maiden Rocks), 15,000 herring gulls and 2500 lesser black-backed gulls necessitating culling in recent years, 500 pairs of razorbill (Mill Bow), 3000 to 4000 puffins (Colms Hole-Burrain, West Rona and South End), 3700–4300 pairs of guillemot, 100 of eider, fifteen pairs of oystercatcher, odd pairs of shelduck, starlings (cliffs), common tern, swallow, song thrush, wheatear, forty-three pairs of rock pipits, meadow pipits, blackbird, hedge sparrow, linnet and feral rock pigeons (caves), occasionally pied wagtail, arctic tern and carrion crow. In recent years no cormorants, black guillemots, peregrines, arctic, common (except 1973) roseate or Sandwich terns bred. Here may be seen something of the great bird movements down eastern Britain. Migration is best with east winds in September and May. Its lengthy list of visitors include duck, especially longtails, velvet scoters and mergansers, skuas, great and sooty shearwaters, osprey, peregrine, Iceland and glaucous gulls, dotterel, northern great spotted woodpecker, continental great tit, black redstart, bluethroat, nightingale, northern chiffchaff, a Siberian thrush in 1954, three divers, four grebes, continental and Icelandic water rails, pine-grosbeak, rustic, yellow-breasted and little buntings, many warblers from Siberian lesser whitethroat to Raddes, greenish and icterine warblers, and waders including 400 purple sandpipers in November. Cormorants roost on its sheltered west cliffs in winter.

Inchkeith Island (295828): See under Midlothian.

Inchcolm (190828): This small island in Forth, off Aberdour is visited by waders and duck. Its occasional terns are wardened by the SWT.

Information
Recorders:
D. W. Oliver, East Cottage, Balass, Cupar. (Isle of May) J. M. S. Arnott, East Redford House, Redford Road, Edinburgh EH13 0AS.
Society:
St Andrews Branch, Scottish Ornithologists' Club, Hon. Sec. Miss M. M. Spires, Greenacre, Hepburn Gardens, St Andrews.
Literature:
Eggeling, W. J. (ed.), *Isle of May* (Edinburgh, 1960), and revised list as supplement to *Scottish Birds* **8** (1974).
Arnott, J., *et al.* Isle of May Bird Report, *Scottish Birds* (magazine) annual.
Laverock and Blackler, *Fauna and Flora of St Andrew's Bay* (Edinburgh, 1975).
Grierson, J., *Check List of the Birds of Tentsmuir*, Supplement to *Scottish Birds*, **2** (1962).
Nature Conservancy, *Morton Lochs and Tentsmuir Point National Nature Reserves*, 5 pp. and map (Edinburgh, 1964).

Check list

Nesters: Great Crested Grebe, Black-necked Grebe, Little Grebe, Fulmar, Cormorant, Shag, Heron, Mallard, Teal, Gadwall, Wigeon, Pintail, Shoveler, Tufted Duck, Pochard, Scoter, Eider, Merganser, Shelduck, Greylag, Canada Goose, Mute Swan, Sparrowhawk, Kestrel, Red Grouse, (Capercaillie), Partridge, Pheasant, Water Rail, Moorhen, Coot, Oystercatcher, Lapwing, Ringed Plover, Snipe, Woodcock, Curlew, Sandpiper, Redshank, Great Black-backed Gull, Lesser Black-backed Gull, Herring Gull, Black-headed Gull, Kittiwake, Common Tern, Arctic Tern, Roseate Tern, Little Tern, Sandwich Tern, Razorbill, Guillemot, Puffin, Stockdove, Rockdove, Woodpigeon, Collared Dove, Cuckoo, Barn Owl, Tawny Owl, Long-eared Owl, Short-eared Owl, Swift, Kingfisher, Green Woodpecker, Great Spotted Woodpecker, Skylark, Swallow, House Martin, Sand Martin, Carrion Crow, Rook, Jackdaw, Magpie, Jay, Great Tit, Blue Tit, Coal Tit, (Marsh Tit, Willow Tit), Long-tailed Tit, Tree Creeper, Wren, Dipper, Mistle Thrush, Song Thrush, Ring Ouzel, Blackbird, Wheatear, Stonechat, Whinchat, Redstart, Robin, Grasshopper Warbler, Sedge Warbler, Blackcap, Garden Warbler, Whitethroat, Willow Warbler, Chiffchaff, (Wood Warbler), Goldcrest, Spotted Flycatcher, Hedge Sparrow, Meadow Pipit, Tree Pipit, Rock Pipit, Pied Wagtail, Grey Wagtail, Starling, (Hawfinch), Greenfinch, Goldfinch, Siskin, Linnet, Redpoll, Bullfinch, Chaffinch, Corn Bunting, Yellowhammer, Reed Bunting, House Sparrow, Tree Sparrow.

Migratory and Rarer Visitors: Wader and Duck flocks, Eider, Surf and Velvet Scoters, Longtail, Pinkfeet and Greylag Geese, Whoopers, White-billed Diver, Grebes, Skuas,

Sooty, Great, Manx and Balearic Shearwaters, Curlew
Sandpiper, Ruff, Godwits, Purple Sandpiper, Dowitchers,
occasional Semi-palmated Sandpiper in autumn, Icelandic
Black-tailed Godwit, Turnstones, flocks of Little Gulls,
Glaucous and Iceland Gulls, Bonaparte's Gull, Black
Guillemot, Black-browed Albatross, Little Bittern, Spoon-
bill, Yellow-browed Warbler, Bluethroat, Firecrest, Great
Reed Warbler, Bearded Tit, Black Redstart, Red-throated
Pipit, Lesser Whitethroat, Scarlet Rosefinch, Scottish
Crossbill, Waxwing, Siberian Thrush, etc.

Grampian Region

NORTH SEA

Culbin Sands
Findhorn Bay
Lossiemouth
L. Spynie
Speymouth
Melrose Head
*Troup Head
*Pennan Head
*Kinnairds Head
Darnaway Forest
MORAY
BANFF
L. of Strathbeg ▲
*Ra... He...
Rora Moss △
B...
Grantown-on-Spey
ABERDEEN
Bu... of Bu...
Sand...
Spey
Glen Avon
Newburgh ▲
●▲ Fo...
Cairngorms
△ Carn Mor
Donside
Ythan Estuary
Ben Avon ▲
L. Skene
Aberdeen
Ben Macdhui ▲
Balmoral
Deeside
Girdle Ness
Kingcaussie Heronry
Mar Forest
Lochnagar
●Crathies
Banchory
Grampians
KINCARDINE
Fowlsheugh
▲● St. Cyrus

0   10   20   30 miles
10   40 km

Chapter 8

Grampian Region

Aberdeenshire

Separated from the mountains further west by the great glen, Glenmore, the Highlands reach the sea between Aberdeen and Stonehaven, leaving only a low coastal plain between Spey and Dee until the land rises to the seabird colonies of Buchan Ness and the Bullers of Buchan. Hilly and mountainous in the southwest, the district includes Ben Macdhui at 4295 feet (1289m), Cairn Toul at 4245 feet (1274 m) and Cairn Gorm at 4090 feet (1227 m) (005041), well known to dotterel and greenshank, and with the densest population of ptarmigan. The Highland Line is where the Dee meets the Burn of Dinnett. Many quarries scar the area, but flooded fields of the Dee and Don valleys, meeting at Aberdeen, attract whoopers. The great coastal Loch of Strathbeg is Britain's second major inland haunt of mallard and the River Ythan attracts important flocks of autumn waders and summer terneries. Many pairs of golden eagles nested on Deeside in recent years; Britain's largest rookery and rook-roost, 90,000 birds with 4000–5000 nests, extend 1½ miles (2·4 km) at Crow Wood, Hatton Castle, Turriff (NJ7564). There are three little tern colonies. Fieldfares nest at times in central and southern woods and crested tits on Deeside; inland there are nesting haunts of arctic terns and lesser black-backed and herring gulls, and at Auchmithie there are cliff-nesting house martins. Slavonian grebes, handsomest of waterfowl, are here; there are inland and coastal breeding peregrines, pintail, capercaillie (Strath Don) and occasional nesting grasshopper warblers and hawfinches. Bluethroats have summered in a glen. Winter duck like longtails, grebes, divers, etc., favour Peterhead Bay (south) breakwater. Magpies nest in Aberdeen suburbs and oystercatchers used Fosterhill College roof. Winter flocks of purple sandpipers, turnstones and other waders favour the breakwater to Kincardine. Herons nest at Parkhill, near Dyce.

Gulls favour Aberdeen, Fraserburgh and Peterhead when the fishing fleets are in port. Many purple sandpipers, turnstones, etc., winter on Peterhead–Rockend shore. Over sixty arctic skuas were at Peterhead one September day. The boats afford opportunity for sea trips. Aberdeen tides are 2 hours 16 minutes earlier than Leith's, Fraserburgh's 2 hours 16 minutes. Shoals of brit (young herring) and sand eels attract terns to the estuaries. Eiders feed on mussel beds upriver. Peaks of 14,750 greylag in January and 8900 pinkfeet in November include a few Greenland whitefronts as winter visitors to the estuaries and lochs. Apart from the Western Isles, this coast has most of the winter wildfowl in north Scotland. Three hundred and fifty whoopers were on Loch Davan in January. Good sea watches produce divers, autumn skuas, shearwaters, auks and terns. Cory's shearwater, less common on the east coast, was at Collieston in August 1970. Gyr falcon, waxwing and the recent invasion of bearded tits, lesser grey shrike, bittern, alpine swift, king eider, surf scoter (Murcar, September 1975) and brent goose are among visiting birds. A gyr was recovered one recent January on Forties Field oil rig, 124 miles (200 km) northeast of Aberdeen.

Cold springs and long, dry summers mark its 506,000 ha (1,251,000 acres) abutting the North Sea. Endless energy and legs like a mountain goat find nesting ptarmigan in the Cairngorms (Mar and Invercauld), the Grampians (003018), (Carn Ealor and An Sgarsoch in the west, Glen Ey-Carnwell, Glas Maol, Glen Callater), Lochnagar

(250855) above Braemar, Broad Cairn and Mount Keen-Braid Cairn in the east, Culardoch (north of Braemar), Morven (North Dinnet) and Ballater. These birds nest up to 5000 feet (1500 m) on the 100 square miles (25,900 ha) of the Cairngorm range, feeding on lichens and other food. Forest walks for crossbills, siskins, etc., include Bennachie (NJ66246) with a car park 1½ miles (2·4 km) south of the A979, 8 miles (13 km) west of Turriff near Mill of Delgaty, and at NJ957513 with a car park 2½ miles (4 km) southeast of Strichen. Kirkhill Forest is near Blacktop (NJ870045/868043 and 869039) 5 miles (8 km) west of Aberdeen, between the A93 and the A944; Midmar is near the Kincardine border at Tillygarmond Hill, 3 miles (5 km) southeast of Potard Bridge on the A93, the north Deeside road, west of Banchory. Blackhall Forest is attractive in May. Long-tailed skuas summering recently in the Grampians may nest. Snow buntings and spotted crakes also breed.

Scotland's first Bewick's swans arrive with their bugle voices here in autumn. Great crested grebes breed on Loch Davan, Loch Kinood, Sand Loch and Meikle Loch (A975) which also attracts geese and ruffs. Shallow Loch of Skene, amidst pines, by the A944 8 miles (13 km) west of Aberdeen, has the main winter flocks of up to 6000 whistling wigeon; many goldeneye, pochard and 830 tufted duck have been here in October. Pinkfeet also visit it. Loch Dinnert's oakwoods and Glentai are worth a June visit. Kemnay floods and Philorth attract waders. St Fergus Moss and Rora Moss, a site of special scientific interest (SSSI), have lesser black-backed and herring gulls nesting with common gulls 4 miles (6 km) inland from Peterhead. These gulls also nest 30 miles (48 km) inland on the Correen hills at 1700 feet (510 m), above Alford and Rhynie in the Don valley

Dotterel at nest, Cairngorms (overleaf)

where, more surprising, are several nesting pairs of arctic tern. This inland breeding habit of lesser black-backed and herring gulls is not so recent as might be inferred; I found them nesting 12 miles (19 km) inland fifty years ago, the bane of gamekeepers and poultry farmers. The old Scots pines at Ballochbuie, Glentanar and Mar are worth visiting. In winter, Hatton Castle with 65,000–90,000 birds and Straloch House (Old Meldrum) with 49,000 are Scotland's largest rook and jackdaw roosts. Over 21,000 roost at Arnage, Ellon.

Rattray Head and Loch of Strathbeg (088578) : The A952 from Peterhead to Fraserburgh gives access to both these bird haunts by the right-hand road between Blackhill and Crimond (405857), and via St Mary's Chapel, south end. Though it is also a nesting site of little terns, Rattray Head offers most as a seabird watch with northwest winds, or onshore northeast-southeast wind. There are movements of passerines, gannets, sooty, great and (in August 1970) Cory's shearwaters, especially in autumn, but not in anticyclones. A shag movement passes from November to January; skuas pass northwards in autumn, and there is an autumn auk and shearwater movement north to pass around north Scotland. Divers occur in headwinds, auks at dawn and evening, including little auk and black guillemot in winter. Skuas, terns, fulmars (1700 an hour in April) and, in winter, long-tailed ducks occur. Steller's eider was here in November 1970. Alpine swift and black redstart are also visitors. Kinnaird's Head, north of Fraserburgh Bay, is another suitable seabird-watching point.

Separated from the sea by a bar, the 441 ha (1200 acres) large, shallow dune loch is 2 miles (3 km) long and includes a 222 ha (500 acres) RSPB reserve. Four thousand six hundred pinkfeet have been counted here (3000 in April) and 4500 greylags, 8000 mallard, 2500 wigeon, 2764 pintail, 1580 tufted duck, 518 goldeneye, 354 mute swans, 400 autumn whoopers and autumn Bewick's swans (also at Pittenheath Pools). Ten species of duck winter here and in autumn Strathbeg is visited by terns and waders and sometimes a marsh harrier and a little egret. The 1972 bearded tit influx reached it. There are occasional bean geese and Caspian tern. Probably the northernmost nesting site of goldfinches (1974), it also has breeding great crested grebes, mute swans, sedge warblers, reed buntings, eider and tufted duck. There is a marshy area with

Nesting in Moray, Inverness and Caithness, the Slavonian Grebe is an increasing species

redshank. See Bourne *et al.*, 'Loch of Strathbeg', *Nature*, **242**, 93 (1973). A Caspian tern visited it in August 1974.

Buchan Ness (135423): Four miles (6 km) south of Peterhead near the A952, the cliffs and rocky lighthouse-island of this windy plateau are the most easterly part of the Scottish mainland, with 9 miles (14 km) of granite cliffs to the south, up to 200 feet (61 m), it has a few sandy bays and deeper water on the west. Peterhead tides are 1 hour 36 minutes earlier than Leith, with 3·8 m springs. Nesting kittiwakes, herring gulls, fulmars, guillemots (up to 10 per cent bridled), razorbills and shags are the summer attraction, while the August-November sea watch includes a passage of shags as well as divers, great, Cory's and sooty shearwaters with north winds. Peterhead Bay also repays a seabird watch.

Bullers of Buchan: These North Haven rocks south of Buchan Ness, below the A975 railway bridge have auks (puffins, guillemots), kittiwakes, etc.

Ythan Estuary, Newburgh and Forvie Sands, Slains (999253/009269): This National Nature Reserve, 758 ha (1774 acres) in extent, is 13 miles (21 km) north from Aberdeen. Reached by the A975 on the north side of estuary, there are 4½ miles (7 km) of tidal flats to Logie, Buchan Bridge, and dunes north to Collieston on the B9003, with Loch Cotehill and Sand Loch. Varying in adverse relation to foxes, spring tides, public disturbance, etc., nest 50–2000 Sandwich terns, 325–500 common terns, 80–125 arctics, down to one pair of little terns. Other nesters include ringed plover, oystercatcher, a black-headed gullery, stonechat, great crested grebe (Collieston), shelduck, sedge warbler (estuary reeds), short-eared owl, red grouse (border) and occasional, quail, shoveler, wigeon and goldeneye. In October–May there are up to 1000 greylags and 4000 pinkfeet. From September to November, up to 1000 tidal waders of seventeen to twenty species include ruffs, forty-two curlew sandpipers in September, a stilt sandpiper in September 1970, also occasional brent geese, and on lochs whoopers, grebes, wigeon, tufted duck, etc. Divers, scaup, longtail, goldeneye, wigeon and scoter, including velvet, are offshore and water rails in the river reeds. Seabird-watchers from Collieston see skuas, auks, fulmars, Manx, sooty, great and Cory's (August 1970) shearwaters, and gannets. Black tern and in 1973 white-winged black tern and winter snow buntings are visitors. *Warden:* Bridgefoot by Ellon (tel. Collieston 230). Permits are needed in the nesting and shooting seasons. Kittiwakes also nest at Cove Bay south of Aberdeen; duck and waders visit Nigg Bay. Newburgh eiders moult at sea off Murcar, a haunt of scoters with 300 velvets, also a surf scoter June–August 1971 (and at Courdon). Aberdeen University has a field station at Culterty, Newburgh. Much can be seen at high tide from cars on the A975, including waders in the fields. Newburgh tides are 50 minutes later than Leith.

Four miles (6 km) north of Collieston, turning off the A975 at Kiplaw to The Scares for the south side of Cruden Bay (095358), there are nesting kittiwakes. Just south of this on Whinnyfold cliff a few guillemots nest with kittiwakes. Meikle Loch is a waterfowl haunt on the north side of the A975, beyond Collieston. Also Sand Loch by the coast, and Cotehill. Kittiwakes and a few lesser black-backed gulls are on the rocky coast near Collieston and Slains Castle (048301). The Don estuary at Old Aberdeen is visited by waders, seaduck, grebes and up to 150 snow buntings in February. Kinnairds Head at Fraserburgh (999675) has good seabird-watching in autumn. Dinnert Lochs in June also attract bird-watchers. The oil base at Cruden Bay has some disturbing effect on the birds.

Upper Deeside: Glen Muick (1300 feet—390 m), from Ballater on the A973 to Loch Muick (325785), and Lochnagar (3786 feet—1136 m) are a 2566 ha (6350 acres) reserve of the Scottish Wildlife Trust; access is from Ballater on the A973 then the Spittal of Glen Muick. There are nesting ptarmigan, golden eagle, wood warbler, spotted flycatcher, siskin and redstart in Balmoral Forest. Upper Deeside includes golden eagle, nesting capercaillie, crested tit, raven, five pairs of merlin, goosander and buzzard, with 72,964 ha (183,297 acres) of Crathie (265949) and Braemar Forest (151913). Here are dotterel haunts. The border Cairngorms are described under Inverness-shire. Green woodpeckers are also at Crathie, Bieldsider, etc., and Scottish crossbills breed in old Deeside pinewoods.

Information
Recorders: W. Murray, Culterty Field Station, Newburgh, AB4 0AA. A. Knox, Zoology Department, Aberdeen University, AB9 2TN.
Society: Aberdeen Branch, Scottish Ornithologists Club. Hon. Sec. Miss F. J. Greig, 22 Loanhead Terrace, Aberdeen AB2 4SY.
Aberdeen University Bird Club, Department of Zoology, Tillydrone Avenue, Aberdeen AB9 2TN.

Literature: Watson, A., Hill Birds of the Cairngorms, *Scottish Birds,* 4, 2 (1966).
North-East Scottish Bird Report (Aberdeen).

Banffshire
The mountainous south of its 166,842 ha (410,112 acres) shares with Aberdeenshire the Cairngorms, the best haunt of mountain birds, contrasting with comparatively low northern farmlands. The valleys of Spey and Deveron flowing through this narrow county are major bird haunts and its fishing boats afford sea watch trips. There are inland and coastal peregrine eyries, ptarmigan, eagles and dotterel in the Cairngorms and Grampians, capercaillie at Rothiemay and summer goldeneye. Red-legged partridges have been introduced at Cullen (514670). Two hundred purple sandpipers may be found at Portessie in December, others at Buckpool and Banff. Ptarmigan nest on Cairngorm, Ben Macdhui (Aberdeenshire border) and Brynack Mor–Ben Avon, and a few on Creag Mhor, Ben Rinnes (Dufftown); they may also be seen on Ladder Hills (Lecht) and in Glen Fiddich, Bridge of Alvah, Tomintoul, etc. There is a heronry at Ballindalloch (Arne). Scottish crossbills nest at Huntly. Firecrest and bluethroat have summered in certain woods. An alpine swift was at Buckie in 1972. Waders resort to the Deveron estuary. Troup and Pennan Heads (see under Morayshire) are notable border haunts. A winter roost of over 15,000 rooks and jackdaws is at Birkenbog (Cullen) and up to 30,000 at Carron House. Over 1000 nests are in Tarryblake North's rookery. Crested tits occur in the north. Redwings, crossbills and snow buntings also breed.

Troup Head: Ten miles (16 km) east of Macduff, via Gardenstown off the B9123. Its 350 feet (105 m) cliffs are the nesting haunt of 8000 guillemots (with an albino in 1973), razorbills, puffins, fulmars, kittiwakes, herring gulls, house martins and occasional cormorants. Black guillemots

sometimes summer here. Guillemots also nest at Melrose
Head, 2 miles (3 km) east of Macduff, while 350 feet high
Pennan Head, 2 miles (3 km) east of Troup on the B9031
from Fraserburgh, then cliff-path from Pennan, has nesting
guillemots, razorbills, puffins, kittiwakes, fulmars, house
martins and other species. The rocky shore from Craigan
Roan to the Aberdeenshire border attracts winter flocks of
purple sandpipers, knot, turnstones and other waders.

Information
Recorder: J. Edelsten, 14 South High Street, Portsoy
AB4 2NT.

Kincardineshire
These 110,519 ha (248,284 acres) on the south of
Aberdeenshire are traversed by the Grampians from
northeast to southwest, rising to 2555 feet (767 m) and are
the haunt of ptarmigan, especially Mount Battock at
Banchory (370795). Also by the valleys of North Esk,
Bervie, Carron, Cowie and Dee. There is the fertile Howe
(or hollow) of the Mearns, between the Grampians and the
low coastal hills. Black guillemots bred in 1950. Fieldfares
nest on lower Deeside, capercaillie at Black Hill, Dum-
tochty, buzzards at Glaisal in the north, cliff house martins
at Muchalls and Montrose, and there is a colony of sixty
little terns and a heronry at Kingcaussie near Maryculter.
On the A943 Aberdeenshire (northeast) border, Craithe
Castle Woods and lochs have a nature trail (NO7396) near
Banchory. Bluethroat and nightingale are among its
visitors. Waders visit Pepper Mill Dam and 3000 eiders
flock to moult in July and August off the coast between
Johnshaven and Gourdon. Forest walks are at Mearns
(NO967798) 5 miles (8 km) northeast of Fettercairn, 3

miles (5 km) east of the B974, and also at Fetteresso and Drumtochty Forests. A broad-billed sandpiper visited the North Esk estuary, May 1974. The rough-legged buzzard is an occasional visitor which sometimes overwinters. Puffins nest at Findon Ness. Common crossbills breed occasionally after Continental invasions.

Fowlsheugh Cliffs: Three miles (5 km) south of Stonehaven, off the A92 between Dunottar Castle and Crawton, north of Henry's Scorth, this is a mile of nesting guillemots (many bridled) in the northeast's biggest concentration of these auks and of razorbills, with puffins, kittiwakes, fulmars and house martins, also shags and eiders. An RSPB reserve with cliffs to 200 ft.

St Cyrus: This 112 ha (227 acres) National Nature Reserve, the shore (750648) between Gourdon and Johnshaven, by the A92 north of the village of St Cyrus, is mainly botanical but with 3 to 104 pairs of nesting little terns at times. It is 5 miles (8 km) north of Montrose. Many purple sandpipers, turnstones and other waders favour the breakwater in winter.

Banchory (695955): On the Aberdeenshire border, with a Nature Conservancy research station at the Hill of Brathens, Blackhall, Banchory is the nesting haunt of capercaillie, siskin, jay, ptarmigan, goosander, merganser, green woodpecker, oystercatcher, black grouse, etc., with a forest walk at NJ645005, 4 miles (6 km) west of Banchory and 1 mile (1·6 km) north of the B976. It is the gateway to the Valley of the Feugh. There is a forest walk (NO648940) 3 miles (5 km) by road southeast from Potarch Bridge on the

A93. Crested tits may be seen. Kerloch Moor and Glen Dye Estate (Sir Wm. Gladstone) are red grouse study areas with a carrion/hoodie crow roost in pines.

Information

Recorders: (North) W. Murray, Culterty Field Station, Newburgh, Aberdeenshire, AB4 2NT, and A. Knox, Zoology Department, Aberdeen University. (South) G. M. Crighton, 23 Church Street, Brechin, Angus.

Moray (Elgin)

This mild, dry, northern part of the region has the largest Scottish firth, many quarries and forests, the bird-rich valleys of Spey and Findhorn, and over 30 miles (48 km) of flat, coastal land running to hilly inland areas. The tidal mudflats of the Findhorn (040645) attract up to 5000 waders and as many winter scoter offshore. Five or six slavonian grebes nest at one site, 400–500 common terns bred in 1974, also 162–450 arctics and five little terns. Herring gulls occasionally nest on buildings in Lossiemouth (238705), an area visited occasionally by crested tits in winter. Bluethroats nested in the Moray Basin (Easterness) in 1968, and there are two pairs of golden eagles, Scottish crossbills, crested tits nesting at Rosieble, and the north-east, wigeon and redwings. Two thousand three hundred long-tailed ducks were at two sites in January 1972 when pomarines were seen. Greylag geese visit fields and shores, velvet scoter are among the common scoter flocks, while the fourth largest Scottish wader flocks have included 22,000 on April floods. Little stints are especially common on the autumn floods, and twenty-six curlew sandpipers have been at Kinloss in August. Culbin Sands are notable Nairn border haurts. Darnaway Forest (via side road from the A96 on west side of Spey Bridge), Loch Buckie and Pools (with a black-headed gullery) and Lochindorb are also worth visiting. Scottish crossbills nest in some forests.

Moray Firth: Scotland's largest firth is shared with Nairn, Inverness-shire and Cromarty, attracting some 20,000 winter duck, including 12,000 common scoter, 2000 velvet scoter, 1300 longtails (April), up to 598 mergansers (September) and wigeon, chiefly in the inner firth (Inverness Firth) at Longman Point, Melton and Munlochy Bay (Easter Ross). However, Burghead Bay and Findhorn Bay attract winter watchers. Wintering greylag and Greenland whitefronted geese roost with over 1400 great black-backed gulls at Loch Eye, by the B9166 in Easter Ross. There are visiting glaucous gulls and skuas including pomarines, and up to 22,000 waders, chiefly in February and April. A modern decline in the fish stocks caused some decline in seabird visitors. The major seaduck haunts are off Easter Ross shores, the Moray share being some 4500.

Findhorn Valley: Access from Forres (034588) on the A96 and the A940. There are golden eagle, crested tit, crossbill, siskin, capercaillie, etc., and herring gulls in the bay near Kinloss. Black guillemots visit Burgh Head in summer, where black rafts of scoter occur in winter and up to 1600 longtails in February. On the tidal mudflats below Kinloss on the B9011 from Forres waders flock, including little stints, knot, godwits and fifteen curlew sandpipers in September, also up to 5000 wigeon and other duck. Three thousand longtails were off Findhorn, at the end of the B9011, in December 1972, and 12,000 scoter blackened the sea. Two thousand velvets and 600 longtails have been there in April and flocks of 400 scaup in January and February. Woodchat, firecrest, and other continental passerines occur. Darnaway Forest and Pools, above Forres, are worth visiting (black-headed gullery).

Culbin Sands, Bar and Forest (030629): On the Nairn border, on the left bank of Findhorn Bay, with a by-lane to Binsness, on the north side of the River Findhorn bridge, or 3 miles (5 km) from Nairn, 3232 ha (8000 acres) including dunes and 4 miles (6 km) long sandbar. Nesting eider, little, arctic, Sandwich, common tern and visiting duck, waders (avocet, April), swans, skuas and osprey. Includes lochs Long and Cran visited by duck among the pines near Nairn on the west, and 6 miles of pine forest with nesting crested tit, crossbill, capercaillie, siskin, goldcrest, nightjar (occasional), long-eared owl, (fieldfare) coal tit, redstart, tree creeper, tree pipit, sparrowhawk, whitethroat, wheatear, great spotted woodpecker and bullfinch. Forest access (permits from Head Forester) (NJ002612) via Brodie on the A96, Nairn–Forres road, then by-road to Kintessack. Autumn waders and skuas are noteworthy.

Speymouth and Fochabers Pinewoods (356650 and 336564): $1\frac{1}{2}$ miles (2·4 km) river walks from the A98 Elgin Road. 1 mile (1·6 km) east and $1\frac{1}{2}$ miles (2·4 km) south of Fochabers. By the B9015 from the A96, west of river, to Kingston at mouth, with up to 500 pairs common terns and arctics. Tidal winter flocks of longtail, goldeneye, merganser; also autumn waders, osprey, etc. A heronry is here and a winter roost of up to twenty thousand rooks in Balnacoul Wood.

Lossiemouth: Grey geese favour fields and shore, at Branderburgh ringed plover, herring gull and fulmar nest;

visitors include up to 114 purple sandpipers in March, and the estuary loch has little stints, wigeon, longtail, shoveler, goldeneye, eider, divers, etc. Crested tits are sometimes seen in the woods in winter. There is a heronry at Oakenhead (Lochside near the B9103). Collared doves nest at Coversea, while 2 miles (3·2 km) south of Lossiemouth, 80 acres, reedy Loch Spynie has a black-headed gullery, grebes, pochard, tufted duck, etc., and is visited in winter by greylag and pinkfeet, and by duck. Permits from Pitgaveney House. Four miles (6 km) southwest of Elgin the Laigh of Moray forest walk starts at NJ164587. Tides are 2 hours 58 minutes earlier than Leith, with 3·7 m springs. Purple sandpipers, turnstones, knot, etc., winter on the rocky shore to Burghead.

Information
Recorder: J. Edelsten, 14 South High Street, Portsoy, Banffshire, AB4 2NT.

Check list
Nesters: Great Crested Grebe, Slavonian Grebe, Little Grebe, Fulmar, Cormorant, Shag, Heron, Mallard, Teal, Wigeon, Pintail, Shoveler, Tufted Duck, Pochard, Eider, Red-breasted Merganser, Goosander, Shelduck, Greylag, Mute Swan, Golden Eagle, Buzzard, Sparrowhawk, Hen Harrier, Osprey, Peregrine, Merlin, Kestrel, Red Grouse, Ptarmigan, Black Grouse, Capercaillie, Red-legged Partridge, Common Partridge, Pheasant, Quail, Water Rail, Spotted Crake, Corncrake (occasional), Moorhen, Coot, Oystercatcher, Lapwing, Ringed Plover, Golden Plover, Dotterel, Snipe, Woodcock, Curlew, Common Sandpiper, Redshank, Greenshank, Dunlin, Great Black-backed Gull, Lesser Black-backed Gull,

Herring Gull, Common Gull, Black-headed Gull, Kittiwake, Common Tern, Arctic Tern, Little Tern, Sandwich Tern, Razorbill, Guillemot, Black Guillemot (1950), Puffin, Stockdove, Feral Rockdove, Woodpigeon, Collared Dove, Cuckoo, Barn Owl, Tawny Owl, Long-eared Owl, Short-eared Owl, Nightjar (occasional), Swift, Kingfisher, Green Woodpecker, Great Spotted Woodpecker, Skylark, Swallow. House Martin, Sand Martin, Raven, Carrion Crow, Hoodie, Rook, Jackdaw, Magpie, Jay, Great Tit, Blue Tit, Coal Tit, Crested Tit, Long-tailed Tit, Tree Creeper, Wren, Dipper, Mistle Thrush, Fieldfare, Song Thrush, Redwing, Ring Ouzel, Blackbird, Wheatear, Stonechat, Whinchat, Redstart, (Bluethroat), Robin, Grasshopper Warbler, Sedge Warbler, Blackcap (occasional), Garden Warbler, Whitethroat, Willow Warbler, Chiffchaff, Wood Warbler, Goldcrest, Spotted Flycatcher, (Pied Flycatcher), Hedge Sparrow, Meadow Pipit, Tree Pipit, Rock Pipit, Pied Wagtail, Grey Wagtail, Starling, Hawfinch, Greenfinch, Goldfinch, Siskin, Linnet, Twite, Redpoll, Bullfinch, Scottish Crossbill, Chaffinch, Corn Bunting, Yellowhammer, Reed Bunting, Snow Bunting, House Sparrow, Tree Sparrow, Goshawks have probably nested.

Migratory and rarer visitors: Gyr Falcon, Osprey, Cory's Shearwater, Pomarine Skuas, Greylag, Whitefront, Brent and Pinkfoot geese, Whooper and Bewick's Swans, Red-necked Grebe and White-billed Diver. Many duck including King Eider, Steller's Eider, Surf Scoter, American Wigeon (1972), flocks of Longtails, Velvet Scoters, many waders including Little Stint, flocks of Purple Sandpipers, Broad-billed and Curlew Sandpipers, godwits, Long-billed Dowitcher, Avocet, summering Green Sandpiper, etc., winter White-billed Divers, Little

Auks, Great Grey Shrike, Woodchat, Bittern, Caspian Tern, Roller, Red-breasted Flycatcher, Bluethroat, Rose-coloured Starling, Lapland and Snow Buntings.

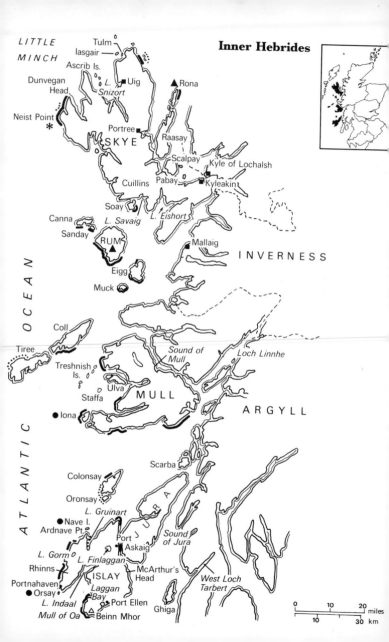

Inner Hebrides

LITTLE MINCH

Tulm
Iasgair
Ascrib Is.
Dunvegan Head
L. Snizort
Uig
Rona
Neist Point
Portree
SKYE
Raasay
Scalpay
Kyle of Lochalsh
Pabay
Kyleakin
Cuillins
Soay
L. Eishort
L. Savaig
Canna
Sanday
RUM
Mallaig
Eigg
INVERNESS
Muck

O C E A N

Coll
Tiree
Sound of Mull
Loch Linnhe
Treshnish Is.
Ulva
Staffa
MULL
ARGYLL
Iona

A T L A N T I C

Scarba
Colonsay
Oronsay
L. Gruinart
Nave I.
Ardnave Pt.
Port Askaig
Sound of Jura
L. Gorm
L. Finlaggan
Rhinns
McArthur's Head
West Loch Tarbert
Portnahaven
ISLAY
Orsay
Laggan Bay
L. Indaal
Port Ellen
Ghiga
Mull of Oa
Beinn Mhor

0   10   20 miles
0   10   30 km

Chapter 9

Inner Hebrides

Scotland has 787 islands. Some 400 west of the Mull of Kintyre, though not an official region, form an ecological unit better known as The Hebrides than as parts of Argyll, Inverness-shire, Ross and Sutherland. All are very windy in winter, the Inner Isles being more scattered but more accessible than the Western Isles or the Outer Hebrides, beyond the Minch. Most are mountainous, often with eagle, some with ptarmigan, all mild and wet with moss and moor, the haunt of harriers and poor sheep farms where the comb rasping cry of corncrakes survives. Cliffs are rich in seabirds, including puffins, black guillemots, some shearwaters, rockdoves, peregrines, storm petrels and some cliff heronries. Eleven pairs of declining choughs linger on southwestern islands, but summer holidaymakers often overlook the winter attractions with barnacle and Greenland whitefronted geese, great northern divers, etc., and their sea watches for autumn migration, including great shearwaters. Visitors range from ivory gull to golden oriole. These inner isles cover some 7,291,000 ha (2800 square miles) and are ideal for cruising. Feral Canada geese are on Colonsay. Ten per cent of guillemots are bridled. Gales often influence the site of heronries and nesting shags, etc., as well as boat landings.

Canna (278052): This 6 miles (10 km) long narrow island of 1010 ha (2500 acres) southwest of Skye, has two 500 feet (150 m) plateaux and a narrow grassy strip between. Sheltered, with earliest spring; it is a privately owned sanctuary with harbour, a rocky coast with many caves and a few sandy bays. Unlike most of the Hebrides, it lies east to west. Access by sea from Mallaig. Nesters: storm petrel, fulmar, Manx shearwater, sparrowhawk, peregrine, buzzard, mallard, eider, shelduck, guillemot (fifty pairs under boulders), black guillemot, puffin, razorbill (north), shag, oystercatcher, ringed plover, sandpiper, snipe, great black-backed gull, lesser black-backed gull, herring gull, common gull, kittiwake (north), arctic tern, corncrake, rockdove, hoodie (south cliffs), wren, wheatear, stonechat, whinchat, robin, song thrush, blackbird, sedge warbler, whitethroat, willow warbler, goldcrest, spotted flycatcher, hedge sparrow, rock and meadow pipits, pied wagtail, starling, greenfinch, twite, chaffinch, reed bunting, tree and house sparrow. Golden eagles are visitors. Sheltered by Canna on the southeast and joined to it by a footbridge, the 202-ha (500-acre) Isle of Sanday has a 200 feet (60 m) hill and nesting kittiwakes, razorbills, black guillemots (north), puffins (Dun Mor), rockdove, corncrake, lapwing, oystercatcher, ringed plover and skylark. Sanday is mainly flat and with nearby Hykseir, a seabird haunt.

Coll (228569): Flattest of the Inner Hebrides, Coll is 7 miles (11 km) west of Mull, near Tiree and Gunna, with access from Oban by steamer or air from Glasgow. Twelve miles (19 km) long, its average width is 4 miles (6 km), undulating to 339 feet (102 m). It has a rocky coast with a grassy, peatland top with arctic terns. An hotel is at Arinagour. Seventy-nine nesting species include arctic skua and red-throated diver but no longer its former choughs and red-necked phalaropes. There are also fulmar, shag, heron, black guillemot, teal, shelduck, eider, greylag, kestrel, peregrine, buzzard, short-eared owl, corncrake, oystercatcher, ringed plover, lapwing, snipe, sandpiper, redshank, arctic skua, common, herring and black-backed gulls, two pairs of little terns, common and arctic terns, rockdove, hoodie, robin, sedge warbler, pied wagtail and corn and reed buntings. Greylag geese have been introduced.

Colonsay (397941): West of Jura, access to this island is by boat from West Tarbert and Islay's Port Askaig. An accommodation list can be obtained from the Islay Tourist Association, Bowmore. *Owner:* Lord Strathcona, Vale of Kiloran (a sheltered area with sandy bay and 'tropical' garden, feral Canada geese and waterfowl). Inland and sea lochs, a rugged west coast and rocky heather hills. There is a hotel at Scalasaig. Central Loch Fada with a snipe bog has a winter roost of 300–400 greylags. Also lochs Sgoltaire and Cholla. There are visiting eagles and terns, kittiwakes, eider, fulmars, red grouse and pheasants (no partridge) among breeders and winter duck; sometimes barnacles, greylag and Greenland whitefronts, once (January 1897) a frigate petrel. The numbers of duck are small. Oronsay (134688) is linked at low tide across the short Strand, or by boat from Tarbert. A private landing strip belongs to Lord Strathcona. Greenland whitefronts visit the southeast Skerries and 230 barnacles are on Oronsay in April.

Eigg (485838): Southwest of Skye, the 2064 ha (5000 acres) island of Eigg can be reached by sea from Mallaig. There are two plateaux, of 1000 feet (300 m), a central col and the 1339 feet Scuir of Eigg, a lofty promontory to the south, and nesting shearwaters (declining from rats), fulmars (possibly storm petrels), red-throated divers, little grebes, shags, black guillemots, puffins, arctic tern, greater and lesser black-backed, herring and common gulls, mallard, eider, merganser, long-eared and occasionally short-eared owls, water rail, dunlin, kestrel, golden eagles (irregular), buzzard, peregrine, raven, hoodie, jackdaw, swallow, wren, great, coal and occasional blue tits, tree creeper, mistle and song thrushes, blackbird, wheatear, stonechat, whinchat, robin, sedge warbler, whitethroat, willow warbler, goldcrest, spotted flycatcher, hedge sparrow, meadow and rock pipits, pied and grey wagtails, starling, greenfinch, twite, chaffinch, reed bunting and house sparrow. Jackdaws have increased where once they were seldom seen.

Gigha (652488): This small rocky island, 6 miles (9 km) long, off Kintyre, has black-throated diver, kittiwakes, ravens, fulmars, eiders (southwest Eun Eilean Bay), shelduck, terns, mergansers, occasional storm petrels, heronry (Mill Loch), guillemots (Garth Eilean), golden plover, hoodies, oystercatchers, peregrines, many jackdaws, curlew, etc. It is visited by many divers, three species, and Greenland whitefronts; there are flocks of 300 eiders off the north. Rooks have a winter roost at Achamore House and whitefronted geese visit the banks opposite Gigha. Access is by boat from West Tarbert. Longtailed duck are frequent from here to Jura.

Gunna: Situated between Tiree and Coll, west of Mull, this tiny island has common and arctic terns, and 426 barnacles in February. Access is by boat from Oban, three days a week.

Iona (285240): West of Mull across the $\frac{1}{4}$ mile (2·5 km) Sound, Iona is reached by ferry from Fionnphort. This tourists' island, 3 miles by $1\frac{1}{2}$ (5 by 2·5 km), has nesting golden eagle, arctic tern, rooks (Manse) and seabird colonies. There are barnacle geese in winter, and there was

Red-throated Diver on nest

a golden oriole in May 1965, but no choughs are here now. The golden eagle here has nested on the ground.

Islay (365452): Twenty-five by 20 miles (40 by 32 km), covering 24,240 often treeless hectares (60,000 acres), except for a small, often southwest gale-wrecked, western forest, Islay's bird attractions are a little exaggerated by tourist publicity, but its bold, rocky coast is the best chance in Scotland to see choughs by the southwest Mull of Oa monument (NR2641), beyond the kittiwake colony and below Beinn Mhor, in sight and flight of their Irish colony on Rathlin. A peregrine eyrie is here. Energetic list-tickers can see eighty or ninety species in a week in May. Its increasing winter flocks of geese by south Loch Gruinart are a major cause of farmers' complaints over crop damage from November to a February peak. One year I found a pair of choughs nesting among very closely approached nesting black and common guillemots, razorbills, shags and chanting kittiwakes at the bottom of a gully easily climbed down between Lossit Farm (southwest Rhinns) north boundary fence and the trig point below Cnoc Breac. Auks and guillemots also nest south of this fence, and fulmars at Lossit Point. Dipper and marsh tit favour the burn by Lossit Bay. Choughs have also nested in the coves, and among kittiwakes and fulmars. In 1961 and 1965 exceptional inland nestings were at an old farm, Storakaig, near the blackcock's haunt, Cochlaidh Mhor, south of Kilmeny. Jura's eagles cross the sound to hunt on Islay, but birds have bred on Mull of Oa coast. Jackdaws are more frequent than on many Hebridean isles, and woodcock nest in the willow scrub on the Rhinns. Peregrine eyries are at four sites. A few merlins and buzzards (Beinn Bheigeir) nest, but raptors have often been destroyed in game preservation. From the

Nest and eggs of Red-throated Diver

pier at Port Askaig (431682) I watched black guillemots
flying from the Sound to their annual nest in rocks a little to
the north. They also nest further south at Am Meall, west of
Kintra farm on the north side of the Oa, and at Nave Island
and Rhuvaal lighthouse in the north. Single and sometimes
nesting hen harriers favour the nesting haunts of common
gulls, dunlin and teal on low peatlands between the A846
and the B8016, Port Ellen and Bridge House, towards
Ballygwent north of the airstrip, and in the Rhinns fields at
Craigens and Coullabus in the Gruinart winter goose
country. Short-eared owls hunt the forestry south of
Kilchoman, great crested grebes and possibly water rails
have bred in the north and kingfishers on the River Laggan.

Arctic skuas from Jura hunt over the Sound. A few arctic
terns nest on shore rocks between Bowmore and Bridgend,
Claggan Bay, Nave Island, Orsay, Eilean Mhic Coinnich
off Rhinns Point, and Killimellon shore. I found red-
throated divers nesting, and there are golden plover and
blackcock haunts at Staoisha Eararach and moors
northwest of Askaig, as well as 2 miles (3 km) inland of
Portnahaven (Rhinns). Slavonian grebes and divers had
other haunts; mergansers are numerous and nest on Lochs
Finlaggan and Bharradail in the middle of the island.
Islay's small heronries are at the Kildalton woods in the
south and the swampy villows near Foreland House, above
Kilchoman. Tufted duck and little grebe nest at Ardnave
and Loch Skerrols, behind Islay House, woodcock, redstarts and spotted flycatchers in the Bridgend woods. Occasionally ptarmigan stray from Jura. Eider are numerous
and I photographed an albino in the flocks daily attracted
to the discharge from Bowmore distillery. Puffins share
Nave Island with black guillemots and terns, and a few
breed on the Mull of Oa and in Sainmore rocks. Water rail,

scoter, barn owl and goldfinch also breed.

Black grouse are by the forest north of Diall (Bridgend),
Killaron and Staoisha Eararach (northeast). Odd puffins
may be seen at Sanaig rocks among the northwest auk
colonies beyond the end of the B8018. Partridge, tawny owl,
mute swan and nightjar also breed on Islay and rockdoves
occupy many cliffs. Scotland's first little shearwater visited
Frenchman's Rocks off the south-west Rhinns in June 1974,
and the first American laughing gull visited Loch Skerrols
(Bridgend) in April.

In winter a sixth of the world's barnacles, 17,000, come to
Loch Laggan from November to March, 3900 Greenland
whitefronts in November to Loch Gruinart, with 500
greylags; occasionally even wild small Canadas are claimed
true migrants. Flocks of 1100 scaup range from Bowmore to
Braichladdich; 300 eider, etc., arrive with wigeon, great
northern divers, glaucous gulls, whoopers, sanderling in
Laggan Bay and passage ospreys. Cory's shearwater was
recorded in August 1973, an American buff-breasted
sandpiper in Kilchoman Bay in September 1971 and a
little egret in July 1970. Seventy-three breeding species also
include goosander, wigeon, scoter, four pairs of little tern,
100 common tern, black grouse chiefly in Cachlaidh Mor
Forest (Kilmeny) and Staorch a' Carar, seven raptors,
collared doves, red grouse, shag, cormorant (west of
Rhuvaal lighthouse), great crested grebe (Loch Ardnave),
blackcap, wood warbler, tree pipit, etc. A winter roost of
100 ravens was near Bridgend. Storm petrels possibly breed.

Access is by air from Glasgow, or by boat from West
Tarbert. The sea passage may reveal great northern divers,
black guillemots, velvet scoters, long-tailed duck, slavonian
grebes, skuas, gannets and shearwaters according to season
including a little shearwater in 1974. White, sandy beaches

mark the west coast and the great sea lochs of Indaal and
Gruinart nearly divide the island into three rhinns.
Bonaparte's gull visited Loch Indaal in June 1975. 224
species including 110 nesters have been recorded by Booth.

Jura (488638): This rugged island between the mainland
and Islay, 20 miles (32 km) long with three peaks (Paps) to
2509 feet (753 m), is reached by steamer from West Loch
Tarbert to Craighouse, by ferry from Islay's Port Askaig, or
by air. It is nearly split into two by Loch Tarbert, and the
whirlpool of Corryvreckan separates it from Scarba at the
north. With sands, bogs and few inhabitants, it is organised
chiefly for sport, with the only road along the south from the
ferry to the north and east coasts. Nesting birds include ten
pairs of arctic skua, herons at Inver (southwest), woodcock,
ptarmigan, peregrine, raven, buzzard, golden eagle,
rockdoves, eider (Ardlussa Bay, etc., on east), merganser,
etc. The Sound of Jura has up to fifty great northern divers
in winter. Choughs have nested irregularly, also greenshank, and there is a cliff heronry. Eagles nest on Garvelloch
Island to the north off Scarba.

Muck (423794): This island of 647 ha (1606 acres), mostly
low, in the Sound of Eigg, only 5 miles (8 km) from
Ardnamurchan, is visited by sea from Mallaig. It has
nesting razorbills and kittiwakes (Eagamol), guillemots,
black guillemots, puffins, greater and lesser blackbacks,
herring and common gulls, arctic tern, fulmar, shag, herons
(middle plantation), buzzard, kestrel, mallard, eider,
shelduck, corncrake, oystercatcher, lapwing, ringed plover,
snipe, sandpiper, long-eared owl, rockdove, skylark,
swallow, raven, hoodie, song thrush, blackbird, wheatear,
whinchat, robin, willow warbler, hedge sparrow, meadow

and rock pipits, pied wagtail, starling, greenfinch, twite, reed bunting and house sparrow. Horse Islands, off the northwest, have nesting puffins, kittiwakes and ravens.

Mull (700280): The second largest island of the Inner Hebrides, 32 miles (51 km) by 29 miles (43 km), Mull is at the end of Loch Linnhe, 1½ miles (2·4 km) from the mainland. Access is by car ferry from Oban to Tobermory, or by Loganair from Glasgow. Mountainous, with fresh-water lochs, with ptarmigan, nesting eagles, short-eared owls and a few ring-ouzels. Birdlife is varied with peregrines, heronries at Loch Spelvie (east), The Burgh,

An Albino Eider swims with a normal duck off Islay's Bowmore distillery, an eider feeding haunt

Coillessan and Calgary Bay (northwest) and the islet of Ulva, hen harrier, raven, hoodie, rook, jackdaw, kittiwakes (The Burgh), puffins (west), razorbills, black- and red-throated divers, black grouse, great spotted woodpecker, curlew, corncrake, sedge and wood warblers, stonechat, swallow, redstart, rockdove (Tobermory–Salen), wood-pigeon, kingfisher, tree creeper and robin. Buzzard, fulmar and cormorant nest at Treshnish Point cliffs, sparrowhawks at the A848 conifer plantation 2 miles (3 km) south of Tobermory, and there are cliff heronries. Red-throated divers and mergansers nest, buzzards are common and, though usually inland breeders, common sandpipers nest on and close to the northern shores. The seabird cliffs of Calgary Bay (west) and some cliff nesting herons are also interesting, but choughs seldom visit Torosay now. Whoopers visit Loch Buie, barnacles the western islets, while long-tailed skuas and great northern divers are winter sea watch attractions. West Ardmore Bay attracts passage waders. Ulva, Staffa and the Treshnish Isles are seabird haunts in its western waters, and Iona off the southwest. Rough northern moors, a hilly centre and sandy machar at Ross of Mull make its landscape. Collared doves have for long occupied Calgary.

Oronsay: See Colonsay.

Raasay: See Skye.

Rhum (403988) (Rum): Seven miles (11 km) southwest of Skye, reached by sea from Mallaig (15 miles–24 km), this rocky, hilly National Nature Reserve island is the largest of the 'Small Islands'. It is 10,690 ha (26,400 acres) in area, some 20 miles (32 km) in circumference, and rises to 2553 feet (766 m). It is mostly uncultivated sheep and deer grazing. Mountainous, except for three glens, Kinloch Castle Woods are the best haunt of woodland birds. It has seabird cliffs. Though generally spelt Rhum, the island's name should be Rum, as purists point out. A Nature Conservancy permit is required to visit away from the only landing, on the east coast at Loch Scresort. *Warden:* White House, Kinloch (tel. Rhum 6), and Lyon House, Kinloch (Rhum 5). Canna and Sanday are to the west. Britain's biggest colony of Manx shearwaters, estimated at over 7500, is on the southern hilltops of Askival 2120 feet (636 m), Hallival, Ainshval and Trollaval. There are nesting fulmars, probably storm petrels, but no proof of Leach's. Also red-throated divers (high lochans), two to four pairs of golden eagle, peregrines, merlins, sometimes sparrowhawks, long-eared and short-eared owls (Kilmory Glen), puffins (100 pairs Camas Pliasgaig), razorbills (in the south), black guillemots, common guillemots, kittiwakes (in the north-east), greater and lesser blackbacks, herring and common gulls, common and arctic terns, rockdoves, red grouse, corncrakes, eiders, ravens, hoodies, stonechats, whinchats, wheatears, robins, redstarts (occasionally), ring-ouzels, sandpipers, lapwings, snipe, oystercatchers, woodcock, goldcrests (Kinloch Castle woods), wrens, tree creepers, sedge, willow and wood warblers, whitethroats (Kinloch), chiffchaffs, meadow and rock pipits, pied and grey wagtails, spotted flycatchers, house martins (occasional), skylarks, blue, long-tailed and coal tits, mistle and song thrushes, blackbirds, hedge sparrows, greenfinches, twites, siskins (occasional), chaffinches, redpolls, starlings and house sparrows. Ptarmigan are visitors. In 1975 the Nature Conservancy began an experimental introduction of Norwegian sea eagles. Few beaches are on its rocky coast.

Autumn passerine migration included a rustic bunting in 1975.

Sanday: See Canna.

Skye (495435): Northernmost of the Inner Hebrides, largest of these inner isles and nearest to the mainland, Skye is reached by car ferry from Kyle of Lochalsh (762272) including Sundays, and by Loganair from Glasgow. It is 50 miles (80 km) long, lying northwest–southeast, comprising forests, bogs, mountainous moorland and sheep farms, but few trees outside the forestry. It is mountainous except near the coast and northeast to Trotternish. The Cuillin hills, via Sligachan (A850) in the southwest, are among its haunts of eagles, greenshanks and ptarmigan (445231), while many sea lochs on the west and bays attract black guillemots, divers, terns and eiders. Close to the east is the Isle of Raasay (545364), 15 miles (24 km) long and 1 mile (1·6 km) wide, a breeding haunt of arctic skuas, black guillemots and rockdoves. North of this is the Island of Rona (618543) with storm petrels. South of Raasay is Scalpay, while off southwest Skye is the small, flat isle of Soay, 3 miles by 1 mile (4 by 1·6 km), with a natural harbour, and puffins. Arctic terns are on the Ascrib isles in Loch Snizort in the north, Skinider, Colbost island, Portree Loch (482425) and Loch Coruisk, and kittiwakes at Neist Point Lighthouse (a seabird watch), Iasgair, etc.

Over 120 breeding birds on Skye were an added interest on our way to the Uists, crossing from Kyle of Lochalsh to the car ferry from Uig. In the quiet morning one may see one's first golden eagle by the Dunvegan road near Portree, or circling near the jagged skyline of the Cuillins. Eiders breed on the east coast between Broadford and Portree.

Among twites nesting on the eagle's moors at Sligachan (A850) one disturbs the noisy greenshank and looks for black-throated divers. From cliff caves at Tarskavaig one disturbs wild rockdoves. One may visit seabird colonies at Hoe in the west and the northernmost cliffs from the A855 and Dunreg. Dipper and grey wagtail nest up the burns of the River Leasgeary, near Portree. A few redpolls nest. Broad-winged buzzard, croaking raven and ubiquitous hoodie soon make themselves evident. One visits Iasgair and Tulm for puffins; they share Fladda Chuain with guillemots, fulmars and kittiwakes, in the northwest. Flodigarry in the northeast has kittiwakes. Shags breed in the Sgathlan caves of the northwest coast and on the isles of Ascrib, Wiay and Raasay. On the west, Dunvegan Head, Ramasaig, Milovaig and Talisker, Tulm Island and Am t'Iasgair reveal black guillemots. Ring ouzel, golden plover and, on Ben na Cailleach and above Loch na Beiste, ptarmigan breed on high moors and mountains. Black-throated divers, grasshopper warblers, mergansers, tufted duck and sometimes pintail nest on certain waters; little grebes on Loch Fada and Mealt; woodcock are at Sleat, Broadford, Armadale and Dunvegan. Fulmars breed at Flodigarry in the north, Hoe in the west and to the south of Dunvegan Head. Loch na Beiste cliffs at Kyleakin, above the Loch Alsh (755264), have a small heronry. Other heronries are at Orbost, Kylerhea (Lochalsh), Armadale Castle, Loch Dunvegan, Raasay, Rona and Portree's Radcliffe House and Viewfield. Razorbills nest along the cliffs from Lorgill to Ramasaig and share with black guillemots and puffins the Ascribs in Loch Snizort. Cliff heronries are on Skye and Raasay. Whoopers visit twin lochs bisected by the causeway road from Dunvegan to Claggan beach.

Skye is largely forestry and sheep farming, making excellent golden eagle country, with four or five pairs nesting. Wigeon nest on one or two waters and ring ouzels on the northern peninsula of Trotternish. Buzzards breed at Sligachan and Dunvegan, eiders inland on Loch Dunvegan. There are Hebridean song thrushes, black grouse, peregrines, magpies (Braes), stonechats, siskins and corncrakes. Southern forests have redpolls, etc., nesting near Armadale, etc. Puffins breed also on Iasgair, a northern isle with kittiwakes, which are also at Rudha Hunish and Ramasaig. Greenshank may be found at Marsca and fulmars at Iarigill Point (west). Autumn brings shearwaters and gannets past sea watch points like Elgol, the western end of the A881. Winter brings whitefronts to Snizort, Beag and Dunvegan lochs, small flocks of barnacles to the northern isles of Iasgair, Ascrib, Isay (Loch Dunvegan), to Soay and the northeast isles, with 1000 in April, while flocks of 140 twite are seen at Pabay.

Staffa (325354): This island is 28 ha (70 acres) in area, with basalt cliffs and caves, 7 miles (11 km) west of Mull. Access is by steamer from Oban. Auks and, with Erisgeir, there are 150 barnacles in April. Kittiwakes also nest.

Tiree (048465): Furthest out of these Inner Isles, Tiree is 20 miles (32 km) west of Mull. Situated near Coll, it is accessible from Oban by steamer, also by air from Glasgow. It is 12 miles (19 km) long and its width varies from $\frac{1}{2}$ to 6 miles (7770 ha–19,199 acres); it is very flat. Ceann a'Mhara in the southwest has nesting kittiwakes, razorbills, black guillemots, shags, fulmars, rockdoves, ravens and wheatears. Sixty-one breeding species also include 500 pairs of fulmar, including the dark phase, mute swans, greylags, teal, mallard, pintail, shoveler, tufted, eider, goosander, merganser, peregrines, buzzards, arctic, common and thirteen pairs of little terns (airfield), oystercatchers, ringed plovers, snipe, dunlin, formerly red-necked phalaropes, red-throated divers and storm petrels, greater and lesser black-backed, herring, common and black-headed gulls, short-eared owls, rock and meadow pipits, stonechats, whinchats, twites, ravens, etc. Sandy and treeless, Tiree has a good passage migration of waders including Icelandic black-tailed godwit, and winter visiting barnacles (Balephetrish Bay), Greenland whitefronts (the marshy central reef and airfield), great northern divers and duck (Loch a' Phuill and Loch Barrapoll). A magnificent frigate bird was recorded in July 1953, a dowitcher at Loch Phuill in October 1969 and a gyr falcon in December 1973. Choughs seldom visit it now. There is a hotel at Scarnish.

Treshnish Isles (278415): Between Tiree and Mull (NM3044-2337) with cliff birds, especially at Lunga (storm petrels) and Dutchman's Cap (shearwaters), these have nesting kittiwakes, thick-necked razorbills, thin-necked guillemots and almost neckless fulmars, puffins (Harp Rock off Lunga), eider, terns and formerly cormorants. Barnacles come in October to Cairn a'Burg Mor, and 644 have been counted early in April. Shags nest at Lunga, a haunt of arctic skuas.

Information
Recorder: M. J. P. Gregory, Duiletter, Kilmory Road, Lochgilphead, Argyllshire, PA31 8NL.

Literature: Blatchford, J. G., Breeding Birds of Coll, *Scottish Birds*, **65**, 271 (1971).

Evans and Flower, Birds of the Small Isles (Muck, Eigg, Rhum, Canna), *Scottish Birds*, **4,** 404 (1967).

Boyd and Williamson, *A Mosaic of Islands* (Edinburgh, 1963).

Hardy, E., Bird-Watching on Islay, *Birds Illustrated* (magazine) (1967).

Booth, C. Gordon, *Birds of Islay* (Argyll Promotions, 1975).

Islay Tourist Association, *Isle of Islay for the Ornithologist*.

Gillam and Jacobs, Breeding Birds of Tiree, *Scottish Birds*, **6,** 5 (1971).

Boyd, J. M., Birds of Tiree and Coll, *British Birds* (Magazine), **51**, 41, 103 (1958).

Hardy, E., Over the Sea to Skye, *Birds Illustrated* (1965).

Bourne, W. R. P., Birds of the Island of Rhum, *Scottish Naturalist* (Magazine), **69** (1957).

Access: Loganair (Glasgow 041-889 3181) has flights to Skye and to Oban, Mull and Coll, and to Tiree and Barra.

Check list

Nesters: Great Crested Grebe, Black-throated Diver, Red-throated Diver, Little Grebe, Fulmar (dark phase), Manx Shearwater, Storm Petrel, Cormorant, Shag, Heron, Mallard, Teal, Wigeon, Shoveler, Tufted Duck, Eider, Scoter, Red-breasted Merganser, Goosander, Shelduck, Greylag, Canada Goose, Mute Swan, Golden Eagle, Buzzard, Sparrowhawk, Hen Harrier, Peregrine, Merlin, Kestrel, Red Grouse (Irish race), Ptarmigan, Black Grouse, Pheasant, Partridge, Water Rail, Corncrake, Moorhen, Coot, Oystercatcher, Lapwing, Ringed Plover, Golden Plover, Snipe, Woodcock, Curlew, Sandpiper, Redshank, Greenshank, Dunlin, (Red-necked Phalarope), Arctic Skua, Great Black-backed Gull, Lesser Black-backed Gull, Herring Gull, Common Gull, Black-headed Gull, Kittiwake, Common Tern, Arctic Tern, Little Tern, Razorbill, Guillemot (northern race), Black Guillemot, Puffin, Rockdove, Woodpigeon, Collared Dove, Cuckoo, Barn Owl, Tawny Owl, Long-eared Owl, Short-eared Owl, (Nightjar), Swift, Great Spotted Woodpecker, Skylark, Swallow, House Martin, (Sand Martin), Raven, Hoodie Crow, Rook, Jackdaw, Magpie, Chough, Great Tit, Blue Tit, Coal Tit, Long-tailed Tit, Tree Creeper, Wren, Dipper, Mistle Thrush, Song Thrush (Hebridean), Ring Ouzel, Blackbird, Wheatear, Stonechat (Hebridean), Whinchat, Redstart, Robin, Grasshopper Warbler, Sedge Warbler, (Blackcap), Whitethroat, Willow Warbler, Chiffchaff, Wood Warbler, Goldcrest, Spotted Flycatcher, Hedge Sparrow (Hebridean), Meadow Pipit, Rock Pipit, Tree Pipit, Pied Wagtail, Grey Wagtail, Starling, Greenfinch, Goldfinch, Siskin, Linnet, Twite, Redpoll, Bullfinch, Chaffinch, Corn Bunting, Yellowhammer, Reed Bunting, House Sparrow, Tree Sparrow.

Migratory and rarer visitors: Great Northern Diver, Great Shearwater, Frigate Bird and Magnificent Frigate Bird, Greenland White-fronted Goose, Barnacle Goose, Greylag, a few Bean Geese, Osprey; flocks of Scaup; Dowitcher, Gyr Falcon, Red-necked Phalarope, Grey Phalarope; Iceland-ringed Redshank, Snipe and Golden Plover; Golden Oriole, Skuas, Gannets, Ivory Gull, Yellow-billed Cuckoo.

Highland Region

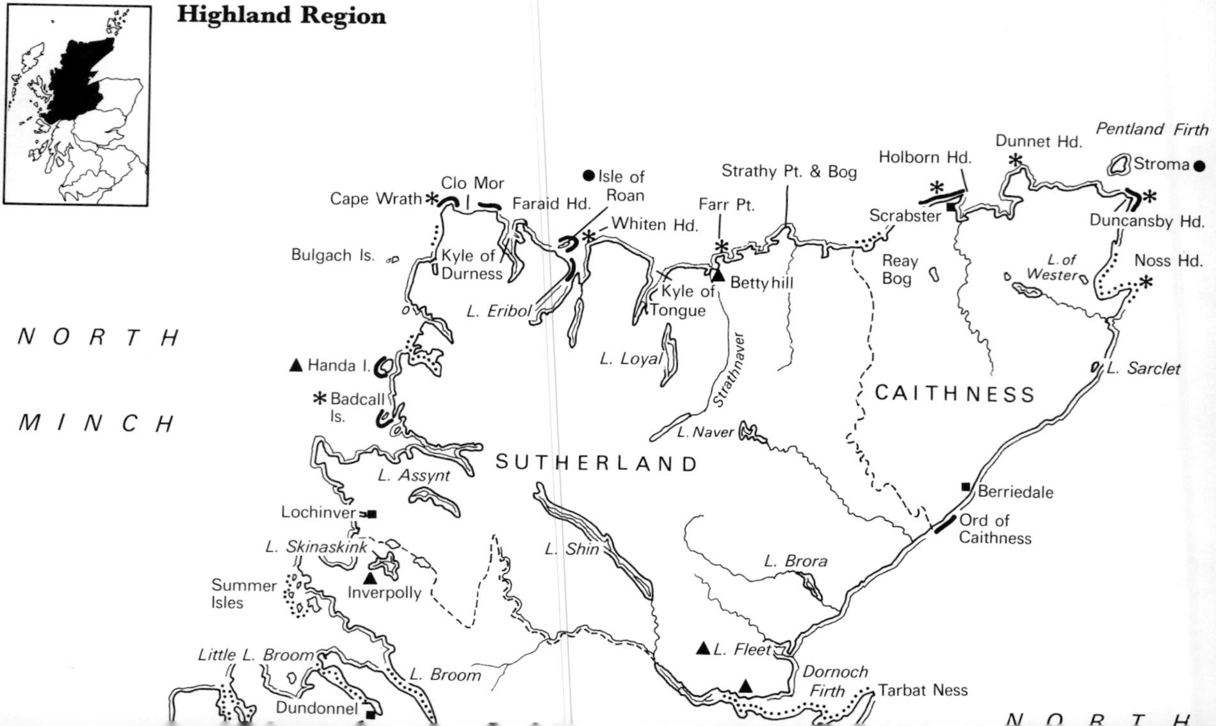

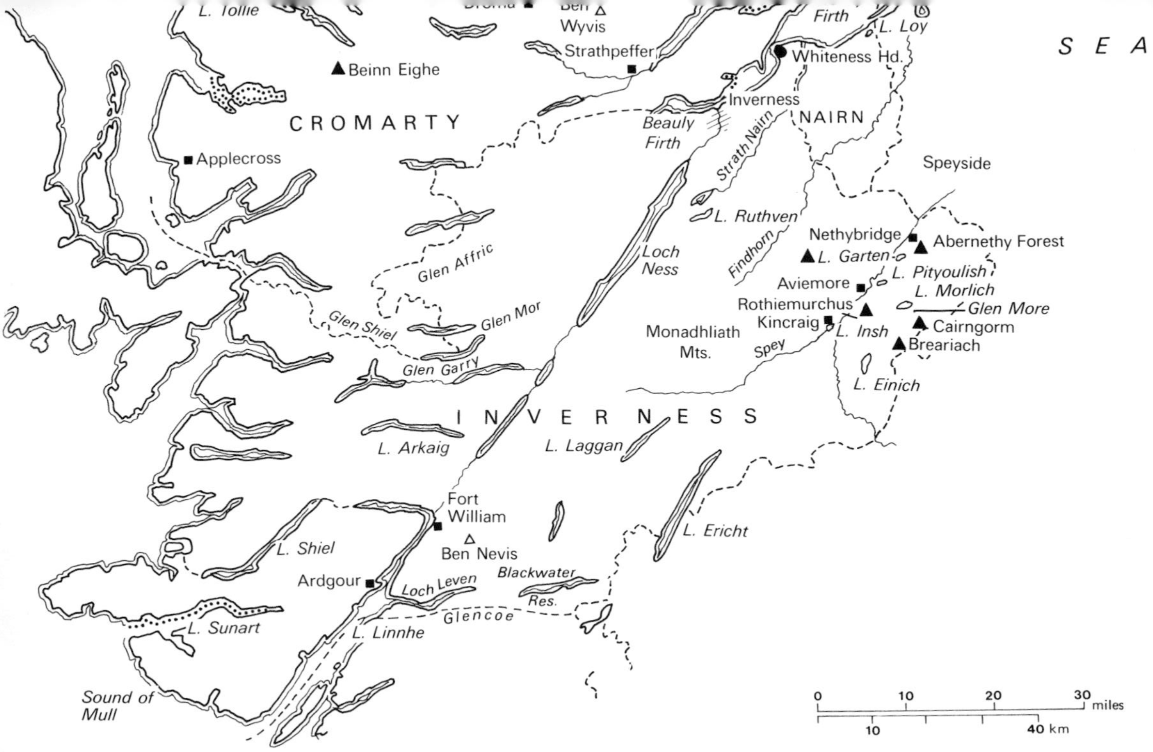

L. Tollie
Wyvis
Strathpeffer
Firth
L. Loy
SEA
Whiteness Hd.
Beinn Eighe
Inverness
CROMARTY
Beauly Firth
NAIRN
Applecross
Strath Nairn
Speyside
L. Ruthven
Nethybridge
Abernethy Forest
Loch Ness
Findhorn
L. Garten
L. Pityoulish
Glen Affric
Aviemore
L. Morlich
Rothiemurchus
Glen More
Glen Shiel
Glen Mor
Monadhliath Mts.
Kincraig
L. Insh
Cairngorm
Spey
Braeriach
Glen Garry
L. Einich
INVERNESS
L. Arkaig
L. Laggan
Fort William
L. Ericht
Ben Nevis
L. Shiel
Ardgour
Blackwater Res.
Loch Leven
Glencoe
L. Sunart
L. Linnhe
Sound of Mull
0
10
20
30 miles
10
40 km

Chapter 10

Highland Region

Comprising the four northern mainland counties and Skye (see under Inner Hebrides, Chapter 9) this region extends beyond the ecological Highlands and excludes the Argyll and Aberdeenshire highlands. A feature of its central-southern region is its great quantity of lakes: almost every glen has its loch, every mountain hollow is brilliant with its stream. Outstanding new nestings like the breeding of American spotted sandpipers in 1975 for the first time in Europe, and previously shore larks, Temminck's stints, green and wood sandpipers, as well as snow buntings, goshawks, bluethroats and large numbers of golden eagles, ospreys, peregrines, dotterel and ptarmigan give the higher lands a special attraction. Long-tailed skuas often summer, as in Easter Ross in 1975, though reports of their nesting were not confirmed. Sanderling in pairs have summered in Inverness-shire, Cairngorms and northwest Sutherland; a few hobbies have possibly bred too, and honey-buzzards have been summer visitors.

Caithness
This flat, undulating, sandstone northeastern plain of 177,680 ha (438,878 acres), with flattened hills, peaty, windy bogs and moors like Knockfin Heights, with increasing birchwoods, approaches tundra landscape in contrast to the central highlands. Its rocky coast has great cliffs and bays with promontories, attracting nesting and migrating seabirds to Dunnet Head, the most northern part of the Scottish mainland, beyond John O'Groats. Populated with more birds than people, it has Scotland's largest cormorant colony, the southernmost regularly nesting

black guillemots on Britain's east coast, and ptarmigan and golden eagle. There are some cliff heronries and coastal peregrine eyries, lochans with thirty pairs of arctic skuas, greenshank and many red-throated divers, two northern sites of great skuas, pintail, and a few black-throated divers on the larger, rocky lochs. One thousand nine hundred and sixty-five arctic, 130 sandwich and six little terns at Wester Burn (Wick) bred in 1974. Two pairs of slavonian grebes nest on one water. There are five coastal, and inland, peregrine eyries, slavonian grebes, scoter, inland nesting great black-backs, swifts as far north as Thurso and nesting redwings, grasshopper warblers (in the southeast), grey wagtails, redpolls, siskins, and occasional wood sandpipers and quail. Icelandic black-tailed godwits bred in the north in 1946, where four to five pairs of whimbrel nest, with red-throated divers. Kittiwakes nest by Scrabster jetty, and capercaillie, woodcock, teal, redpoll, etc., in Rumster Forest. Reay Forest, by the A836 on the northwest coast, has nesting sparrowhawks. Arctic tern have been recorded nesting inland with common terns on Loch Caluim.

An impressive array of visitors include king eider, yellow-billed cuckoo (Thurso, November 1970), roller (Reay, September), golden oriole (June), the first Scottish marsh sandpiper in September 1966, harlequin duck, hoopoe, bluethroat, white-winged and common black terns, barred warbler, black-eared wheatear, pectoral sandpiper (June 1973), white stork (Dounreay, May 1971), crane (May 1972), white-throated sparrow (Thurso, 1970), gyr, little auks, great grey shrikes, phalaropes and a collared pratincole at Loch of Mey in August 1973. Greenland whitefronts visit Broubster (a water rail haunt), Loch Scarmclate and Loch of Wester from Autumn to April, sooty and Cory's shearwaters are in autumn sea watches at Sarclet Head (A9), etc., and many gannets follow the fish shoals. One hundred and fifty-five purple sandpipers were at Brim's Ness in November. A winter roost of twelve thousand rooks is at Barrock House, Lyth. Corn buntings and twite nest on the moors, and collared doves at Wick docks. Good waters include Loch Scye; Loch Hempriggs (A9), St John's Loch and Loch of Mey on the seaward side of the A836 behind Dunnet Head, Loch Heilen, via Greenland east of Castletown in the north, Scarmclate and Watten on the northeast side of the A882. Lochar Moss has a black-headed gullery. The shore at Reay in the northwest (969649), and the Berriedale and Langwell Valley woods in the southeast (ND1122) are also interesting, as are Sinclairs Bay, Wick Bay, and Ackergill and Keiss dunes there. Gadwall nest.

Duncansby Head and Stacks: Protruding into the Pentland Firth, beyond John O' Groats, off the A9, this is the northeastern-most point of Scotland. Sandstone precipices over 200 feet (61 m), steep chasms, especially Long Coe or Gloup, penetrate the rocky 100 yards (90m) of headland, with 200 feet (60 m) stacks in the sea. There are nesting puffins, among vegetated slopes and guillemots (12 per cent bridled), kittiwakes, many razorbills, cormorants, rock-doves, jackdaws, hoodies and starlings are here. Sea watch is for sooty shearwaters in early autumn, gannets with fish shoals, and 200 twite in February. Freswick and Keiss attract shorebirds south of the Head. Skirza Head has kittiwakes.

Dunnet Head, Bay and Sands (203768): North Sea and Atlantic currents meet here in the Pentland Firth, beyond the B855 from Dunnet on the A836, in great waves in gales.

Coves and gulleys (car park by lighthouse, 350 feet—105 m) have a large colony of kittiwakes (Easter Head), many guillemots (10 per cent bridled), razorbills, puffins, a few black guillemots, fulmars, raven, herring gulls, peregrines, kestrel, hoodie, rockdove, rock pipit, wren. A cliff heronry on the east of the headland was deserted in 1971. On the moor by the head nest arctic and great skua, great black-backed gulls, twite, siskin and (in the Bay) arctic tern, ringed plover, oystercatcher, stockdove (in the sand dunes), a marsh sandpiper (Mid Sands, September 1966), ivory gull (December 1973). Seabird watch for sooty shearwaters early autumn, gannets with fish shoals, auks and up to five great northern divers in winter. Scrabster (Thurso) tides are 6 hours 7 minutes later than at Leith with 5 m springs.

Holborn Head: This is situated beyond the A882 from Thurso on the A836. There are nesting kittiwakes (including Clett Rock offshore, with razorbills). A seabird watch included king eider in the autumn and winter of 1973–4.

Noss Head (ND3855): Three miles (5 km) north of Wick, this headland is reached by the A9 and a by-road from Louisburgh. Its 100 feet (30 m) have nesting black guillemots, common guillemots, razorbills, puffins, kittiwakes, fulmars. Sea watch for gannets, etc. Ackergill (Wester Burn) beach attracts nesting little terns in nearby Sinclairs Bay and Loch of Wester by the A9. Wick Bay and, by the A9, lochs Hempriggs and Sarclet are bird haunts south of the head. Kittiwakes nest at Ires Goe, 3 miles (5 km) south of Wick, fulmars and kittiwakes at the Brough, a mile (1·6 km) south. Kittiwakes also nest at Clyth Stacks, Tod's Gote, Red Point and Sandside Head on the north coast. Ten thousand kittiwakes nest on Boch-ailean, $1\frac{1}{2}$

miles south of Berriedale by the A9 in the southeast. Forty pairs of Sandwich terns, and kittiwakes, nest at Bruan, fulmars at Dwarwick Head, and cormorants at Mid Clyth Stacks, north of Lybster, by the A9. Tides at Wick are 3 hours 23 minutes earlier than at Leith with 3·4 m springs. Migratory sooty shearwaters have been seen in June.

Ord of Caithness: This colony of 400–500 cormorants is Scotland's largest, and is near the A9, 3 miles (5 km) north of Helmsdale in the southeast.

Stroma: This is a low, round, green island with a lighthouse in Pentland Firth (from Ness of Huna, by the A9 from Duncansby). Possible storm petrels and Sandwich terns.

Information
Recorder: Mrs P. M. Collett, Sandyquoy, East Gills, Scrabster, KW14 7UH.
Society: Thurso Group, Scottish Ornithologists' Club, Hon. Sec., S. Laybourne, Old School House, Harpsdale, Halkirk, Caithness, KW12 6UN.

Inverness-shire
Although this is the largest county, some 1,102,420 ha (2,723,000 acres) in extent, only about one twenty-fourth of it is cultivated. A major British bird haunt, divided by the great northeast–southwest glen, Glen More, it is mostly mountains, or heath and moor with much sheep, cattle and deer grazing. Cultivation is mostly coastal and in the birch-sided valleys. It includes part of the Cairngorms and Ben Nevis's 4406 feet (1322 m) with their eagles and snow buntings, the Spey, Scotland's second longest river with its osprey eyries, and one of the largest state forests, the

Cairngorm–Glen More Forest Park. Mountainous south-western shores have many sea lochs and summer on the west coast is shorter than in Easterness. Their deep, steep-sided, Scandinavian-type fjords, unlike the eastern firths, have shallower bars at the entrance. Western Inverness (Wester-ness) is more cut up with glens, but its mountains slope northwest–southeast. There are very large lochs, especially Loch Ness. Good centres are Drumguish at the foot of Glen Tromie, Aviemore, Kincraig (835058), Kingussie (A9) and Nethybridge (002208) on the B970 from Spey Bridge to Grantown.

Forty-three pairs of slavonian grebes nest on eighteen lochs, one with twenty-seven or twenty-eight pairs with black-throated divers on waters along the Loch Ness system. There are also black-necked grebes on low lochs, and breeding pintail and spotted crakes, herons at Lynchan and a blackcock lek at Tulloch. Black-throated divers breed and ospreys fish on Loch Morlich. Snow buntings breed on the western and central Cairngorms and wrynecks on Speyside. Four to six pairs of snow buntings breed at 3000 feet (900 m) at six sites, mostly the Cairngorms. Bluethroats were claimed in 1968 and Temminck's stints nest occasionally in Easterness. Thirteen pairs of golden eagle nest in Monadh Liath and thirty-eight on Speyside. Five eyries are in range of Fort William. Peregrines nest in the Great Glen, on Speyside and the Cairngorms. Also there are hen harriers, redwings and, occasionally, whimbrel in the north and wrynecks, probably of Scandinavian stock, at Avie-more. Wood and green sandpipers nest in the west, crested tits in the northwest and east, Scottish crossbills and fieldfares in the east. Bramblings sometimes nest, and red-throated divers have several mainland haunts. It is the major breeding area of dotterel. Scoter, three pairs of goldeneye in nest boxes on one eastern water, gadwall, hen harriers, Reeve's pheasants introduced in Kinveachy Forest, peregrines (east and central), five colonies of little tern, and 150 Sandwich terns on the east coast in 1970 where none nested in 1973, are among its breeding interests. Its increasing ospreys are well known at several sites in Strathspey, etc. There are four pairs of black-throated divers, also capercaillie, even herring gulls nesting on buildings in Inverness. Snow buntings have been seen with dotterel above Rothiemurchus.

As many or more ospreys are seen on passage as nesting; snowy owls visit the Cairngorms and a red kite appeared in 1972. Britain's biggest goosander flock marks winter at the Beauly Firth (584458), with longtails, flocks of 414 goldeneye and other duck, and 3800 autumn waders. One thousand seven hundred and thirty-eight wigeon have been counted in November in Longman Bay. Canada geese flock from as far as Yorkshire to moult in Beauly Firth. Whoopers, greylags and a few brent come in winter, when odd greenshank remain. A citrine wagtail was recorded in September 1972. Fort William tide is 1 hour 52 minutes earlier than at Glasgow.

The spring aerial display of the light grey cock hen harrier conspicuously draws attention to its future territory.

Slavonian grebes returned by 21 February. Black-throated divers and common gulls breed too. The nearby Nairn valley is interesting. Ptarmigan range from 3000 feet (900 m) on Stob Ban, south of Ben Nevis, to Strathclyde and all the main mountains, including especially Glen Moriston and Glen Affric on the west and Creag Meagaidh–Carn Liath, Loch Treig, Cairngorm, Drumochter-gaick and Monadh Liath west of Spey. Fewer are at Loch Quoich, Ben Nevis, Mamores, Aonach Beag

and Stob Coire Easain, south of Spean Bridge, the
mountains around Corrieyairack and west of Loch Lochy,
Glen Roy, Ladhar Bheinn Sgritherall, the Saddle of Loch
Hourn, Sgurr na Ciche (Knoydart), Loch Eilloch,
Arkaig–Loch Morar, etc. The A9 affords good bird-
watching for motorists, with up to ten early morning
blackcock in fields between Aviemore and Kingussie, and
the soaring eagle between Crieff and Dunkeld. The three
great forests of Glenmore, Rothiemurchus and Abernethy
are unrivalled for capercaillie, crested tits, crossbills, eagles,
ospreys and occasionally goshawks, gyrs, etc. Crested tits
breed in many places like Strathnairn, Dulnan Forest,
Rothiemurchus and Glen Feshie, slavonian grebes on hill
lochs. In 1972 I found green sandpipers in June in Corour
Forest at 1300 feet (390 m), and oystercatchers nesting at
nearby Tulloch. Oystercatchers breed widely inland
because few parts are far from the intruding sea lochs.
Greenshank and common gulleries are widespread. Honey-
buzzard, hobby and wryneck possibly breed on Speyside.

Speyside: This is part of the Glen More, Aviemore,
Rothiemurchus, Nethybridge, Abernethy, Glen Feshie,
etc., complex, chiefly around A9–A95, between Kingussie
(755008) and Grantown-on-Spey (031278). Breeding birds
include several pairs of osprey, slavonian grebes on the lochs,
greenshank, capercaillie, Scottish crested tits and crossbills,
occasionally goldeneye and gadwall, many little grebes,
mergansers, goosanders, sparrowhawk, buzzard, eagle,
raven, redstart, dipper, coal tit, wood warbler, common
gull, dipper, oystercatcher, hoodie crow, siskin, occasionally
brambling, wryneck, bluethroat, pied flycatcher, long-
eared owl, redwing, fieldfare, wood and green sandpipers,
goshawk and the hen harrier. Morar Forest near Mallaig has

nesting dotterel, greenshank and summering wood-sandpipers occasionally. Bogs and forest north of Carrbridge on the A9/A938 junction have birds like crested tits, Scottish crossbills, greenshank and peregrines. 'Landmark' visitors' centre has a nature-trail. *Warden:* Kinakyle, Aviemore. The SWT has a 121·4 ha (300 acre) reserve, a pinewood, in Glen of Ryvoan beyond Abernethy Forest Lodge, with crossbills and crested tits.

Aviemore (A9) (896124): A peregrine eyrie marks a wooded cliff; slavonian grebes are on lochs. Craigellachie birch-woods, NNR (west of Aviemore) are rich in small birds, with Loch Puladdern.

Rothiemurchus: B970 east from Aviemore. Old Caledonian pine-forest with most of the crested tits, black grouse, crossbills, occasional buzzards (Pityoulish). Loch an Eilein pinewoods at Inverdruie (902111) have capercaillie, crested tits, crossbills, siskins, etc. Sandy-shored Loch Morlich to the east has fishing ospreys and red-throated divers but, like Glen More, it is spoiled by tourists. Short-eared owls are on the nearby hills to 1000 feet, crested tits and capercaillie in its pinewoods.
Warden: Achnagoichan Cottage, Rothiemurchus, (telephone Aviemore 287).

Glen More Forest (978098): Not the Caledonian Canal glen of this name. From Rothiemurchus to northwest Cairngorms, 7 miles east and signposted from Aviemore, it includes Loch Morlich and Queen's Forest from Glen More Lodge, NH974095, with YHA, camping and forestry 'hides' for blackcock and capercaillie. 1450 ha (3850 acres) of pine and spruce have three forest-walks and 92,000

acres of open mountains to the border Cairngorms.
Via Glen Einich from Rothiemurchus to Loch Einich,
for up to five eagles in the air, winter whoopers and visiting
greylags; the plateau with dotterel. It has golden eagles,
crossbills, crested tits, greenshank, redshank, woodcock,
hoodies, black grouse (Upper Tullochgrue), ptarmigan, etc.
Warden: Lilybank, Braemar (telephone 284), Deeside.

Much of the richness of Inverness-shire birdlife is in its
woods of ancient pines like Barrisdale, Glengarry, Glen Loy
and Loyne, Moriston, Loch Arkaig and Glen Mallie west of
the Great Glen, Strath Glass, Glen Affric, the pines of
Cannich and Strathfarrar, Guisachan and Cougie, Glen

Crested Tit, Speyside

Nevis, etc., many like Strathnairn with crested tits. Open areas in forests are often rewarding, like Gaick Forest moors.

Cairngorms: With an area of 23,839 ha (58,882 acres), this is the largest National Nature Reserve in Britain with 863 ha (2132 acres) of woods, a vast area from NH7208 to NN9187, at Strathspey over the southeast border. Parts in Mar and Glen Feshie are restricted in August–October shootings. A 3000 feet (900 m) massif is traversed by the passes of Glen Feshie, Lairig Ghru and Lairig an Laoigh with conifers to 2050 feet (615 m) on Creag Fhiaclach, Rothiemurchus. White Lady Shieling, 7 miles (11 km) from Aviemore, for 4084 feet (1226 m) Cairngorm (or via Glenmore Lodge) with ptarmigan ranging to the 2000–3000 feet (600–900 m) arctic-alpine zone, and on upper Lairig Ghru, dotterel on most hills of 3000–4000 feet (900–1200 m) also greenshank, short-eared owls, ptarmigan and snow bunting. Nesting birds of the Cairngorms include hen harrier, Scottish crossbill, crested tit, siskin, capercaillie and possibly red-throated diver, slavonian grebe, whooper swan, whimbrel and osprey. Continental birds like waxwing, fieldfare, redwing and brambling either stay in spring or nest. The northern side has golden plover and ptarmigan at Achlean, etc. Three or more nesting pairs of snow bunting, have both Iceland (dark rump) and Norwegian-Greenland (white rump) stocks. Several pairs of golden eagle, from 1500 to 2500 feet (450–750 m) in the Cairngorm and Braemar area are fewer than in the western Highlands, most nests being in pines or on cliffs off roads. Peregrines nest to 3200 feet (960 m), four pairs in the Spey and Dee forest hills. Greenshank are in moors and glens to 2000 feet (600 m), capercaillie in pines, oystercatchers to

1200 feet (360 m), goosanders on Loch Einich, etc., also black grouse, woodcock, golden plover, whinchat, wheatear, ring ouzel, twite, and occasionally dunlin and Temminck's stint (1956). Bluethroats were claimed near Loch Avon ('Arn'). Eagles nest and the snowy owl visited Loch Etchachan. Some northern parts are restricted for autumn shooting. There is a car park at 2500 feet (750 m) above Loch Morlich, and the information office is at Aviemore. *Warden:* Kinakyle, Aviemore (tel. 250).

Glen Feshie, Feshie Forest and Loch Insh (810025): This area is reached via Kincraig on the A9 8 miles (13 km) north of Kingussie (755008). Shoveler, teal, water rail, sedge and grasshopper warblers and other waterfowl nest at the

Young Crested Tits, Speyside

162 ha (400 acres) Loch Insh, where I saw the osprey
returning with pike when McNaughton the farmer took me
to its nest in a pine on the west end of Feshie Forest above
the loch. Capercaillie, black grouse, siskin, crested tit, etc.,
breed in the forest and the lake is visited in winter by
wildfowl and passage greylags and whoopers, hen harriers,
etc. Insh Marshes, towards Kingussie, is a 374 ha (917
acres) RSPB reserve with nesting duck, curlew, redshank,
oystercatcher, the occasional spotted crake and a black-
headed gullery. Visited by wood and green sandpipers,
quail, mallard, wigeon and other duck, hen and marsh
harriers, once the great reed warbler. *Warden:* Ivy Cottage,
Insh.

Greylags and pinkfeet visit Dell of Killiehuntly. Glen
Feshie's 7253 ha (19,133 acres), include the deep gorge of
Allt Ruadh (Red Burn) on the east side of the glen to the
craggy eagle heights of Creag Mhigeachaidh. Parts are
restricted in autumn shooting. Inshriach Forest walk
(NH841021) is 2 miles (3 km) along the by-road off the
B970, 3 miles (5 km) south of Kincraig. Near Insh lies Glen
Tromie with merlin, goosander (Loch an Seilich), and
other birds, with birchwoods above Killiehuntly Bridge,
pinewoods by Drumguish, and capercaillie, black grouse
and dipper. Glen Chomrhaig, between Feshie and Tromie,
is a winter haunt of their capers and blackcock. Badan
Dubh Forest (Feshie to Einich glens) has crested tits.
Winter parties of crested and coal tits visit the Craigeann
pines. Dotterel, peregrines and golden eagles nest in several
sites. Forest of Gaick is on the south side of Loch an
Seilich.

Abernethy Old Caledonian Forest (319716): Access is via
Nethybridge on the B970 between Grantown-on-Spey and

Aviemore, with nesting capercaillie, crossbills, crested tits, pied flycatcher, occasional goshawk, summering brambling, raven, oystercatcher, greenshank, woodcock, long-eared owl, redwing, fieldfare and sandpipers etc.; heronries (Lynchat and Broomhill), visiting hobby, occasional honey buzzard, marsh harrier and gyr (May 1972), and a winter roost of over 260 hoodies.

Loch Garten (NH977185): This is in the forest, signposted from Boat of Garten (944189) on the B970 north of Aviemore. This RSPB reserve of 614 ha (1517 acres) has a public hide; part is restricted. There are nesting ospreys late March to mid August, crested tits, tree creepers, wigeon, buzzards, sparrowhawks, redstarts, a blackcock 'lek', also sandpipers, capercaillie, visiting water rail, hen harriers, and a little bittern on the River Spey, Boat of Garten in July 1973. A winter gull roost here includes great black-backed gulls. The reserve includes Loch Mallachie and old pine forest.

Monadhliath Mountains and Laggan Hills (628968): North of Kingussie and Newtonmore on the A9, these uplands have nesting dotterel, snow bunting, four pairs of golden eagle (above Laggan Bridge, etc.), peregrine, raven, dunlin, golden plover, ring ouzel, ptarmigan (above Loch Laggan, etc.). Feral greylags and divers are on Loch Laggan by the A86, with peregrines nearby and to the south black-throated and red-throated divers. Ben Alder (3757 feet, 1127 m) on the north side of Ericht is another good bird haunt.

Loch Ness (250822): Twenty-seven miles (43 km) long and 1 mile (1·6 km) wide, this great chasm is 751 feet (225 m) at its deepest, between Inverness (266845) and Fort Augustus,

linked on the north bank by the A82 and on the southeast by
the A862 and the B852. Surrounding lochans have nesting
slavonian grebes, black- and red-throated divers, golden
eagles, etc., buzzards, dipper (River Ness), redpolls, etc.
Inchnacardoch (NH370090) has two forest walks from the
by-road to Auchterawe off the A82 north of Fort Augustus
(380094). Near the latter, are back-throated divers.
Glengarry Forest walk (NH307012) is off the A82 and A87
junction at Loch Oich, southwest of Fort Augustus.

Fort William (105740): Five eagle eyries are within bird-
watching range. There is a signposted road to Glen Nevis
car park (145684) and its confiding chaffinches, Achintee
and the easiest track to Ben Nevis (165713), 4406 feet (1322
m), in six to eight hours (the northeast face is for climbers).
Snow buntings and a few ptarmigan have nested here. We
found ptarmigan also at 3000 feet (900 m) on Stob Ban,
south of Nevis. Staying at North Ballachulish with its
collared doves, I saw black guillemot and red-throated
diver make daily visits flying past the ferry to Loch Leven.
Wood warblers, crossbills and buzzards breed in the forest.
Ardgour House (Corran) has woodland birds. The Lochaber Hills are the haunt of eagle, peregrine, crossbill,
redstart, dotterel, siskin, etc. Arctic and common terns,
common gulls, oystercatchers, ringed plovers, eiders and
mergansers nest scattered along the shores of Loch Linnhe,
while red- and black-throated divers and summering
whoopers occupy lochs from Shiel to Mallaig (675971).
Golden eagles had an eyrie in Glengarry Forest, and there
are greenshank and visiting tits, with occasional snow
bunting and brambling in summer above Glen Quoich.
There is a National Nature Reserve at Ariundle Oakwood
on Loch Sunart via the A861 road.

Glen and Loch Affric (228234): Via the A831 to Cannich Village, Strathglass, on the east–west route from Inverness to Loch Ness and Loch Beinn a'Mhead-hoin, then the Kintail road, for eagles, dotterel, ptarmigan, red- and black-throated divers.

Inverness and Beauly Firths (655472): Tidal entrance to Beauly Firth, where a summer moulting flock of 630 Canada geese from Yorkshire, Derbyshire and Nottinghamshire includes an occasional leucistic bird. One hundred and fifty pairs of common tern nest at restricted Fort George spit (762568), on the B9006 via the A96 near Whiteness Head (see under Nairnshire) at entrance. There is a ternery at Whiteness. Bunchrew Wood and Ness Bank (in Inverness town) are interesting in June, the latter in winter visited by whitefronted geese. Britain's largest goosander flock reached 1200 in January; there are also 450 greylags, 400 mergansers off Redcastle, flocks of tufted, pintail, scaup, whoopers and pinkfeet, over 400 goldeneye and autumn wader flocks of about 4000. Longman Point to Smithton below Inverness has flocks of wigeon, teal, mallard, pintail, shelduck, and wader flocks and gulls during the winter fishing season. Herring gulls nest on some buildings in Inverness. A heronry is in Munlochy Bay. Capercaillie and chiffchaff nest at the Black Isle peninsula between the two firths. (These are in Ross and Cromarty.)

Information
Recorders: R. H. Dennis, Landberg, Kessock, IV1 1XD (Black Isle Area). M. I. Harvey, Clach Bhan, Loaneckheim, Kiltarlity, Highland.
Society: Inverness Branch, Scottish Ornithologists' Club, Hon. Sec. W. G. Prest, 70 Culloden Road, Balloch,

Highland Region, IV1 2HH.

Literature: Brown and Waterston, *Return of the Osprey* (London, 1962).

Forestry Commission, *Forests of Northeast Scotland* (Edinburgh).

Glen More National Park Guide (HMSO, 1976).

Goodfellow, S. F., Birds of Corrour Forest, *Scottish Naturalist*, 70 (1961).

Nethersole-Thompson, D. and Watson, A., *The Cairngorms* (London, 1974).

Weir, D., Birds of Abernethy Forest, *Bird Notes* (magazine), 31 (1965).

Nairnshire

A small northeastern county of 52,267 ha (114,400 acres) on the Moray Firth, Nairnshire has a hilly south, and fertile lower valleys of the Findhorn and Nairn rivers, with the bordering Culbin Sands terns of Moray and nearby Loch Loy's occasional winter duck.

Whiteness Head: In Inverness-shire four miles (6 km) west of Nairn, off the B9092 from the A96 on the Moray Firth, this headland has 250 pairs of common tern, three to fifty pairs of little tern varying annually, occasionally arctic and Sandwich. It is similar to Culbin coast, with a sandspit and a public footpath to salt marshes. Great black-backed gulls began nesting in 1970; in 1970 a white-winged black tern was a July visitor. Flocks of up to 2000 bar-tailed godwits, 500 ringed plover and 1000 knot in autumn, occasional Richard's pipit, also shelduck, mergansers and scoter. Crested tits nest in the northeast. An oil-rig yard restricts some areas of the ternery.

Strathnairn: Access is via the B9091 from Nairn. There are pines with nesting crested tit, buzzard, also goosander, sandpiper, dipper, grey wagtail, oystercatcher, occasional bean goose (December 1973). Loch Flemington (from the B9090 off the A96 Nairn–Inverness road) attracts winter wigeon and other duck like goldeneye, scaup, etc., also greylags and whoopers. Other birds have nested in an area kept secret.

Information
Recorder: J. Edelsten, 14 South High Street, Portsoy, Banffshire, AB4 2NT.

Ross and Cromarty
Apart from its offshore Western Isles (see Chapter 16) these 809,732 mountainous hectares (2,003,065 acres) rise to 3860 feet (1158 m), with thirteen pairs of dotterel, forty-eight pairs of golden eagle, and ring ouzels so low as 400 feet (120 m), but they have few great rivers. Ecologically this is divided between the Atlantic Wester Ross with its rugged coast, deep bays, lochs and narrow-entranced, shallow firths with alluvial flats at their head, and the North Sea Easter Ross with wide Cromarty, Dornoch and Beauly firths. Ptarmigan nest on all the mountain ranges, down to 1085 feet (436 m), but there are not so many as in the Cairngorm area owing to fewer ridges and more peaty summits. There are two colonies of little terns and twelve pairs of red-throated divers. Great northern divers have bred and hybridised with black-throats there, while peregrines are above the loch, etc. Ospreys also nest. Golden eagles breed in Monar Forest, while seventeen pairs had young within 30 miles (48 km) of Applecross (710444) in 1971 (one in a cave). Winter brings the fifth largest flocks

of greylags and waders, 4000 wigeon to Nigg Bay and Tain-Ardjachie in October, also large flocks to Alness and Udale Bay; but Greenland whitefronts have declined at Loch Eye and Red Point. One hundred and seventy-five whoopers have been on Loch Evanton in March. The sea lochs are less wooded here than those of Argyll and Inverness-shire. Snow buntings, golden eagle and ptarmigan nest in Dundonnel Forest by the A832 south of Little Loch Broom, and black-throated divers and greenshank nest nearby in upper Gruinard valley. Snow buntings nest also on Beinn Eighe, etc. in Wester Ross, Torridon and Fannichs.

Wester Ross has a few pairs of dotterel, also ptarmigan and eagles. Fourteen pairs of black- and nine pairs of red-throated divers breed on lochs. There are occasional nesting slavonian grebes, scaup, redwings, stockdoves, great spotted woodpeckers (Inverewe gardens) and I found greenshank above Strath of Gairloch. A heronry is at Plockton. Corn buntings (northwest), grasshopper warbler (Gairloch), wood warbler, stonechat (northwest) and cormorant (Rhu Reidh, Eilean Mor) also nest. Storm petrels probably nest on Isle Ristol in the Summer Isles, and wrynecks have two inland sites, and fieldfares one.

Ben More, in the Coigach hills of Wester Ross is a reserve of the Society for the Promotion of Nature Reserves and includes four small groups of the Summer Isles. It is close to their other reserve Carn Iar and the National Reserve of Inverpolly. Among its predators are golden eagle, peregrine and raven and among its nesters eider, ptarmigan, greenshank, black grouse and both divers. Barnacles are winter visitors. It is managed in conjunction with the SWT.

Easter Ross has one of its best mountains in Ben Wyvis, with dotterel, crested tits (glens) and summer snow-buntings, with Strathpeffer at its foot and sandpipers nearby. Seventy-two pairs of Sandwich tern and 1000 arctic nest with twite and 400 great black-backed gulls at Morich Mor on south Dornoch Firth. There are thirteen pairs of dotterel, ptarmigan at Inchbae Forest, nesting crested tits (Heathmount), occasional whimbrel (1970), barn owls, great spotted woodpeckers, stonechats, grasshopper warblers, dippers and corn buntings, chiefly in the southeast. Kittiwakes nest on Castle Crag. Two hundred sooty shearwaters have been recorded in a two hour September sea watch at Tarbat Ness, Moray Firth, where fulmars and auks nest (NH9487). Fifteen hundred pinkfeet visit Evanton and 900 at Munlochy early in April, but there are very few bean geese. Occasionally a rough-legged buzzard may overwinter, and white-billed divers have been authenticated off Wester and Easter Ross.

Ptarmigan nest on all the ranges from Ben Wyvis in the east to Ben More in the west, including Coigach, Cul Mor, Torridon and Applecross forests (west), Spurr a' Charorachain, and Meall, Slioch, Strath Vaich hills, Beinn Dearg, the hills north of Strathcarron and Diebidale, Glencalvie-Inchbie (east), Sgurra 'Mhuillin (Strathconon) and near Killilan (Strome Ferry). In the south they breed on Attadale, Strathcarron, Sgurr nan Ceathramhnan, An Riathachan (Strathcarran-Affric), Glen Shiel, and Cluanie, Beinn Fhada and Five Sisters of Kintail, but fewer are on peaty Torridon An Teallach.

Inverpolly Forest (150126): This National Nature Reserve of 10,861 ha (45 square miles) is on the A835 from Ullapool to Drumrunie Lodge (permits are required here in the late summer and autumn from Nature Conservancy). The country varies from low moor to three eagle summits over

3000 feet (900 m), lakes, bogs, cliffs and screes, and includes diver-haunted Loch Skinaskirk and the tourist-tramped sandstone peaks of Stac Polly and Coul More. Also from the Lochinver coastal terminus of the A837 beyond Loch Assynt, Sutherland, where I have seen red-throated divers nesting by the road to Inverkirkaig, and the River Kirkaig. There are 330 ha (816 acres) of woodland at Doire-na-h-Airbhe with some of the few primitive birch-hazel in the northwest Highlands. Nesters include occasional redwings, occasionally snow bunting, eagle, black-throated diver, red-throated diver, red grouse, ptarmigan, raven, buzzard, peregrine, greenshank, merlin, ring ouzel at 400 feet (120 m), stonechat, twite, woodcock, fulmar, shag, greater and lesser black-backs (offshore islands), black guillemot, merganser, eider, a few greylags; in the glens (River Kirkaig) can be seen black grouse, wood warbler, (willow tit), woodcock, wood warbler, Scots crossbill, summering redwing, redpoll, etc. *Warden:* Strathpolly, Inverpolly, and Assynt Estate Office, Lochinver.

Ptarmigan nest outside the reserve on Seana Bhraigh southeast of Ullapool (124940), and redwings have bred. Pied flycatchers visit the birches near Dundonnell Lodge site (095878), off the A832, Little Loch Broom. Puffins formerly bred at NB9712-9101, the private Summer Isles off Loch Broom, and herons occasionally on Horse Island there. Cormorants, etc., nest on Eilean Mor (Gruinard Bay). These have July–August moulting flocks of greylags, and on Tanera more nesting greylags, red-throated diver, arctic tern, buzzard, black guillemot and eider on Carn nan Sgeir and gulleries on Glas Leac Beag, visited by 300 winter barnacles. Kittiwakes nest at Point of Stoer, north of Lochinver.

Beinn Eighe (995633): Britain's first National Nature Reserve, of 4759 ha (11,757 acres), includes 133 ha (330 acres) of woodland in Kinlochewe Forest bordering Loch Maree, by the A832, 45 miles (72 km) west of Inverness, or 24 miles (38 km) north of Kyle of Lochalsh via the A890 and Strome Ferry. Ranging from 30 to 3100 feet (9–930 m), the area includes old Caledonian pinewood with siskin, redstart, occasional crossbill, and Coille na Glas-leitire birchwoods at Loch Maree, where there are two nature trails and a forest walk (NG887719) on the south bank, 3 miles (5 km) northwest of Talladale on the A832. Loch Maree is 12 miles (19 km) long and 2 miles (3 km) wide and up to 350 feet (105 m) deep, with divers and feral greylag. Nesters also include two to three pairs of golden eagle, peregrine, buzzard, raven, dotterel, ptarmigan, occasional snow bunting, and redwing, black grouse, wrens at 2000 feet, dunlin, greenshank under Coire Domhain (I found a pair nesting within a few minutes of leaving the B858 on the southern border at Loch Clair). *Warden and Field Station:* Anancaun, Kinlochewe (tel. 204). Ptarmigan are also on Slioch, north of Maree.

Strathpeffer (248858): Five miles (8 km) west of Dingwall on the A834 and A832, or the A9 from Inverness, it is a convenient centre for Ben Wyvis (3428 feet — 1028 m) with occasional dotterel and snow bunting, also ptarmigan, dunlin, ring ouzel, wheatear and eagle; it can also be approached from Garbat on the A835 beyond Loch Garve. A strath on the west has nesting sandpipers; Strath Farrar (232838) on the Inverness border from the A831 west of Beauly has wood warbler and divers. Holiday Fellowship Centre, Balmoral Lodge, May–September.

Dornoch Firth (806876): Morrich More dunes and marsh below the military range between Tain (A9) and Whiteness Sands, Inver Bay, has a Sandwich ternery ranging from thirty to 1000 pairs, with other terns, varying with disturbance from visitors. A pair of long-tailed skuas was there in the summer of 1975. Tarbat Ness, the seamost ridge of rock where long-tailed duck flock in spring, has purple sandpipers, passing auks, skuas and shearwaters in autumn and seabird watches with 200 sooty shearwaters recorded in 2 hours in September. A drake king eider and two surf-scoters were off Golspie in autumn 1974, etc. Rockfield Cliff on the east has nesting fulmars and kittiwakes. Big flocks of autumn waders roost at Morrich More, where whitefronts are March visitors. Loch Eye, $1\frac{1}{2}$ miles (2·41 km) long, below Fearn (B9165, east of Tain) is visited by duck and waders. Waders and whoopers visit even Fearn railway pool beside the A9. Skibo Inlet and Loch Evelix also bring duck and whoopers close to the A9. Dornoch Firth is shallow and January wader flocks include 2500 bar-tailed godwits. Edderton Bay Sands, by the A9 west of Tain, are visited by scaup, goldeneye and autumn geese. Pintail visit the inner bay with the second best wigeon flocks (7500 in October in Edderton Tay Bay). Meikle (732858) has thirty to forty pairs of cormorants.

Cromarty Firth (788678): Nigg Bay on the north side is the major eastern haunt of wigeon (2500 in January), with pintail and a roost of 2000 pinkfeet. Its Zostera beds attract wildfowl, including 1200 winter goldeneye, 173 whoopers, and there are flocks of mergansers and goosanders. The Nigg Bay–Udale Bay (south side) tideline has the fifth largest wader flocks including 1000 bar-tailed godwits in autumn, and knot. Alness also attracts waders. These

shallow tidal flats are also visited by 1500 greylags. Corn
buntings nest alongshore. Southeast of Castlecraig Farm,
via the B9163 from the A9 from Tain, the grassy 450 feet
(135 m) cliff of the North Sutor, at the entrance to the firth,
has nesting cormorants, fulmars, kittiwakes, razorbills and
great black-backed gulls. South Sutor on the Cromarty side,
via the A832 north of Fortrose, has shags nesting towards
Ethie. The tide at Cromarty is 2 hours 51 minutes earlier
than Leith, with 4·2 m springs. Invergordon distillery
discharge attracts duck. The tide here is 10 minutes later
than Cromarty, with 4·3 m springs.

Moray–Beauly Firth (See Inverness-shire and Moray): Sabine's
gull visited Craighton Point opposite Inverness on the
Cromarty side in August 1969. Three hundred and forty
pinkfoot geese use the Black Isle (265860) by Beauly Firth.
Munlochy Bay (A832) has tidal wader flocks in autumn, as
well as whoopers, a nesting colony of fulmars, a heronry
with thirty-four nests, and a February–March field roost of
500 greylags. Another fulmar colony is in Rosemarkie Bay,
Fortrose (A832). Black-headed gulls, shelduck and mergansers nest in Beauly Firth, with autumn flocks of mergansers
and goosanders at Redcastle and North Kessock, opposite
Inverness, waders and field flocks of pinkfeet and greylags.
Common gulls nest at Avoch. Cory's shearwater appears in
the sea watch off Tarbat Ness. Munlochy Bay on the southeastern coast of the Black Isle is a sheltered estuary, a
Regional Reserve for wildfowl and waders (Highland
Regional Council).

Other waters: Loch Torridon (190856) has a National Trust
for Scotland reserve with ptarmigan at 1085 feet, cormorants nesting on Eilean Mor, heronry trees on Shieldaig

island, and sometimes wintering greenshank. Glen Shiel-daig Forest (819528) is here. They have a 3232 ha (8000 acres) reserve at NG8034-8126 at Balmacara, the Kyle–Plockton peninsula in Wester Ross, and Loch Kernsay with divers and mergansers below A832 at Poolewe 7 miles (11 km) from Gairloch (802779); also Loch Ewe (850840). I have seen black-throated divers nesting beside the A832, and in an evening stroll found greenshank nesting above Strath of Gairloch. Black-throated divers also nested by the A835. The Scottish Wildlife Trust has an 888 ha (2200 acres) reserve at NH0126-NG9913, at the head of Loch Duich by the A87 on the west coast, with nesting buzzard, raven, ptarmigan, siskin and twite, etc. on mountains including the Five Sisters of Kintail and Beinn Fhada (3283 feet—985 m); water-birds are also found on the loch. Lochs Carron and Eye (Tain) attract birds. Cormorants breed at Rudh'Ro where divers flock in autumn passage at peninsula tip beyond Melvaig on the A832 and B8021 north of Gairloch. Storm petrels nest on Longa Island in Loch Gairloch, while Red Point is a good sea watching site on the south side.

Woods: Corrieshalloch is a 5 ha (13 acres) National Nature Reserve, wooded (deciduous) gorge southwest of the A832 to Dundonnell from Braemore. Allt Nan Carnan is a thickly wooded gorge National Nature Reserve in moors northwest of Lochcarron, by the A890 north of Strome Ferry (863348). Rassal Ashwood (northernmost in Britain) and part of Allt Mor Gorge form another National Nature Reserve at the head of Loch Kishorn, by the B857 west of Strome Ferry. These state reserves are accessible. Inverewe National Trust gardens (859818) by the A832 at Poolewe, beyond Gairloch, have nesting chaffinches, willow warbler, robin, blackbird, etc. Golden eagles nest at 2500 feet in

Applecross Forest (west). Torrachilty forest walks are at NH195807 on the A835, 9 miles (13 km) southeast of Ullapool (Forest Garden), and NH455568 on the A834, 6 miles (9 km) west of Dingwall. Balblain trail (NH574955) is at Carbisdale Castle on the Arday–Invercroyle road; Lael forest walk (NC1977-96) is on the Inverness to Ullapool road, 6 miles (9 km) southeast of Ullapool; Morangel trail (NH753813) is 1 mile (1·6 km) south of Tain on the A9 Inverness to Wick road; Slatterdale trail (NG887719) is on the Dingwall to Gairloch road, 6 miles (9 km) southeast of Gairloch by Loch Maree. Old pines attract birds at Achnashelach, Coulin, West Loch Maree (Coille na, Glas Leitire), Shieldaig, Achnashellach Forest (River Carron), Strath Vaich (A853), Glens Einig and Rhidorroch (east of Ullapool), etc.

Eilean Na Creige Daibhe, the 1·13 ha (2·8 acre) Island of the Black Crags, is a rocky peat and pine covered heronry reserve of the SWT, 200 yards offshore near Plockton in Wester Ross, between Kyle of Lochalsh and Strome Ferry. Access is by boat from Plockton.

Information
Recorders: D. Macdonald, Elmbank, Dornoch, Sutherland. (Black Isle) M. I. Harvey, Clach Bhan, Loaneckheim, Kiltarlity, Highland.

Sutherland
Only a thirtieth of Sutherland's 525,443 ha (1,297,846 acres) is cultivated. The rest is mountainous with individual mountains separated by moorland plateaux with vast, undulating blanket bog and peat moors, wild valleys and extensive lochs between. Large areas are sheep grazing and there is much birch scrub with redpolls, chaffinches

and willow warblers. The coast varies from sandhills at Bettyhill in the north to high hills and grey rocks which echo the raven's croak. Ornithologically, the district is divided into the Atlantic northwest, with a precipitous coast with seabird colonies like Handa and deep sea lochs, and a flatter North Sea east, with sandy shores with the little tern (now reduced to eight pairs). A hundred to 208 pairs of arctic terns breed in the district, occasional whimbrel, scoter and redwings (two sites) in the north and eighteen pairs of golden eagle in the northwest. Wild greylags breed on one or two lochs with low islands and rushes, like Badenloch (also moulting flocks) and Loch Loyal, hen harriers at young fir plantations (Strathnaver), inland and coastal peregrines, nesting ospreys, snow buntings sometimes, eiders (Corpach, etc.), and ptarmigan down to 600 ft (180 m). Ten pairs of buzzard breed within 10 miles (16 km) of Bettyhill. Ten to twenty-three pairs of black-throated diver breed on lochs. Red-throated divers use lochs while great northern divers visit Loch Eriboll. Eighteen pairs of golden eagle hunt 358 square miles of northwest Sutherland. Eagles, black guillemots, occasional slavonian grebes, rare dotterel, capercaillie (Skibo and Balblair, Golspie) woods, buzzard (east), island petrels and shearwaters on the northeast, skuas, black grouse (Altnaharra, Syre, Rogart, Birrchen and Spinningdale in the southeast), golden plover in the moraines, Scottish crossbill (Loch Naver), merlins and many greenshanks, with dunlin, near rocks or dead fir twigs in the bogs and deafforested areas will be found nesting. Northern and southern types of golden plover have been found mated occasionally. Sanderlings are sometimes seen in display on the mountains in summer, when there are occasionally Temminck's stints, bramblings, wood sand-pipers, etc., on territories. Black-tailed godwits bred in the southeast in 1965. Spotted crakes bred in 1966. Red-legged partridge have been introduced to Rosehall, common partridge breed in the southeast, as do swifts, great spotted woodpeckers, crested tits, barn owls, occasional redwings, etc. Slavonian grebes are at certain waters. As in Wester Ross and Inverness-shire, the modern influx of breeding redwings may have levelled off or declined. Scottish and common crossbills nest in a few conifer woods.

Ptarmigan breed lower than in the south, on Ben Klibreck, Griam More and Beinn Stumanadh (east), Reay Forest (Ben Hee-Arkle, Foinaven), Ben Stack, Quinag and Canisp (west), Ben More, Assynt, Breabag (Inchnadamph), Cranstackie, Ben Hope, Loyal (south of Conamheall), on the low hills between the foothills of Conamheall (south of Cranstackie) and Ben Hiel (east of Ben Loyal), Meallam Liath (east of Ben Hope), Kyle of Durness-Kinnlochbervie, Farrmheall, Creig Riabach, Fashven and Sgribhis-bheinn, 600 feet (180 m) above Clo Mor, 900–110 feet (270–330 m) below Whiterhead, east of Loch Eriboll. They form the food of eagles. Snow buntings also breed.

In winter 2000 longtailed duck flock in Loch Fleet (808958) in the east, with flocks of 1000 velvet scoter; there are 1300 wigeon in Ardnacailce Bay and at Skibo in October. There are occasionally hoopoe, white-billed diver and snowy owl; rose-coloured starlings were at Scourie and Faraid Head in the autumn of 1972, a stilt sandpiper at Dornoch Firth in April 1970 and Bonaparte's gull in autumn 1967. Glaucous gulls come in winter and 650 barnacles in spring.

Handa Island (130480): This 310 ha (766 acres) unin-habited RSPB reserve off Tarbet village is 2 miles (3 km)

northwest of Scourie on the A894, off the northwest coast.
Access is by boat from the warden: Tarbet, Foindle, via
Lairg (582068). It has a bothy (permit from RSPB,
Edinburgh), a sandy beach on the southeast, 400 feet
(120 m) cliffs on the northwest and 500 feet (150 m)
guillemot stacks on the southwest. Breeding birds comprise
five pairs of great skua, one pair of arctic skua, 7000
kittiwakes, 2400 pairs of fulmar, 410 pairs of shag, 450–500
pairs of puffin, 8000 pairs of razorbills, 30,000 guillemots
(arriving mid December to January), one pair of red-
throated divers, fourteen pairs of eider, shelduck, raven,
ringed plover, lapwing, arctic tern, rockdove, red grouse,
snipe, pied wagtail, stonechat, wren, starling, willow
warbler, twite and corn bunting. Two hundred and fifty
Manx shearwaters an hour have been counted in May
seabird movements, and Manx and sooty shearwaters,
black-throated divers, Iceland gull and pomarine skua are
autumn and winter visitors. Corncrakes, grasshopper
warbler and sparrowhawk nest on the mainland, and a
heronry is on Eilean Ard, Loch Laxford. Handa's 'first'
accepted British trumpeter bullfinch (June 1971) possibly
escaped. Scourie Marsh is visited by rails, etc.

Badcall Bay Islands: This group is off the A894, 3 miles (5
km) south of Scourie (158446). There are 200 pairs of
cormorant nesting on Meall Mor and Beag, according to
persecution, and black guillemots breed on one island.

Bulgach Island (Eilean Bulgach, Am Balgh) (182588): Two
miles (3 km) off the northwest coast, southwest of Cape
Wrath, landing on this tiny island is difficult. There are
about 1000 puffins and lesser numbers of kittiwakes,
guillemots and cormorants which displaced the shags.

There are other species. Access is from the road north from the A838 at Rhiconich to Sheigra, then by a rough track to the coast.

Cape Wrath, Clo Mor and Kyle of Durness: These points are reached off the A838 to Durness on the northwest coast, then Keodale for the Kyle ferry and by bus to Cape Wrath (256750) for the highest British mainland cliffs with their nesting puffins. Four miles (6 km) east, Clo Mor cliffs (NC2973-3272) have thousands of breeding puffins, 25,000 pairs of guillemots, also razorbills, black guillemots, fulmars, peregrines, kestrels, ravens, shags, curlew and ptarmigan at 600 feet (180 m) inland on nearby Meall Sgribbish Bheinn, and golden eagles. Near Durness puffins may be observed. Cape Wrath has big passage movements of gannets. Far-Out, or Faraid Head, reached by a footpath from Durness (403680), is another good sea watch for storm petrels, etc., and has nesting fulmars, kittiwakes, puffins, guillemots, razorbills. It had a grey-headed wagtail in July 1970, and eleven great northern divers have been in the kyle in May. Sandwood Bay, southwest of Cape Wrath, has shorebirds, and kittiwakes nesting on the stack.

Loch Eriboll, Eillean nan Ron and Whiten Head: On the north coast, west of Tongue, these are also reached from the A838. Whiten Head (500690) at 1935 feet (580 m) on the eastern entrance to Loch Eriboll has nesting cormorants, shags, fulmars and puffins, and is a good summer-autumn sea watch for sooty and Manx shearwaters, skuas, gannets, auks, etc. Golden eagles nest. The A838 is convenient for Loch Hope, Ben Hope and the birch woods of Strathbeag (south). Snow buntings held territory on a mountain in 1975. Eilean nan Ron (Skerray) is a group of islands with

boatman access, off the mouth of the Kyle of Tongue, east of
Eriboll, separated from the mainland by a turbulent
current. The nearest, Eilean Coomb (Neave Island), is 200
yards (180 m) from land with the difficult Caol Beag
current, 28 ha (70 acres) in extent with cliffs to 213 feet
(63 m) and a landing on the south side. It has nesting
fulmars, eiders, goosander, shags, cliff buzzards and
sometimes puffins. The largest island, Roan, 1720 yards
(1·5 km) further out, is 1 mile (1·6 km) long with cliffs to
247 feet (79 m) on the north and 50 feet (20 m) on the
south, with nesting storm petrels, fulmars, black guillemots,
two pairs of great skuas, cormorants (Meall Halm), shags,
common terns, rock doves, eider, oystercatchers, greater
and lesser black-backed gulls and occasional peregrines and
puffins. Sooty and great shearwaters pass in autumn and
200–300 barnacles winter here. There is a rookery at
Tongue. Loch Loyal, on the A836 south from Tongue, has
wild greylags and mountains up to 2504 feet (751 m) have
merlins and sometimes eagles. A snowy owl visited Ben
Hope, Tongue.

Invernaver National Nature Reserve (NC6762-7059): Situated
on the A836 at the mouth of the River Naver, near Bettyhill
east of Tongue, this reserve's 550 ha (1363 acres) of scrub
and dune have nesting greenshank, red-throated diver, ring
ouzel and twite. Black-throated divers nest on lochs,
goosanders on the river. *Warden:* 89 Invernaver, Bettyhill.
From the A836 at Farr, a road and track north lead to Farr
Point sea watch, and there is a road from Invernaver to west
bank estuary shorebirds. Scottish crossbills, etc. nest and
Altnaharra on the west has nesting short-eared owls and
black grouse. Strathy Bog, another Nature Conservancy
reserve, is nine miles east, off the A836.

Dornoch Firth and Loch Fleet: Dornoch Point, reach by the
B9166 and B9168 south from the A9 in the southeast, and
the shallow Dornoch Firth, have wader flocks to 5000, the
second largest wigeon flocks, 7000 scoter in December, 2000
scoter in April, 2000 long-tailed duck in December and
1000 in May; there is one nesting site of little tern. Duck and
waders visit Dornoch ponds where dunlin bred in 1972;
sedge warbler, corn bunting, hen harrier (at the fir
plantation), crested tit and buzzard have all bred there.
Cuthill Sands attract the terns. Sooty and Manx shearwaters are on August and September passage, glaucous
gulls in winter and long-tailed skuas in spring. Rarer
visitors have included firecrest, lesser grey shrike (1972),
stilt sandpiper (April 1970) and a red-footed falcon at
Meikle Ferry (732858) in June 1973. Three miles (5 km)
long, tidal Loch Fleet (Skelbo level-crossing off the A9) has a
Scottish Wildlife trust reserve of 513 ha (1750 acres) with
winter flocks of wildfowl, autumn flocks of mergansers and
eiders (which nest), over 1000 waders in March, flocks of
wigeon, 800 long-tailed duck in April (Bar), a king eider in
1974–5, and a surf scoter in 1974–5. White-billed divers visit
it in March. Black-backed gull, eiders (Ferry Links),
Sandwich tern in 1971, fulmars at the Mound and Carrol
Rocks are among nesters. Strath Fleet (A839 inland) and
Mound Alderwood reserve, at Balblair Forest (on the north
side of the Fleet) have capercaillie and crested tits. Further
up the A9, Golspie and Brora on the north side of Dornoch
Firth attract 1000 eiders and as many velvet and common
scoter, 1300 long-tails in May (Golspie Bay and off Embo,
south of Loch Fleet), November wader flocks of 1700,
winter flocks of mergansers, up to ten pairs of nesting little
terns and rockdoves. Loch Brora, 4 miles (6 km) inland,
has nesting gadwall and feral greylags; but its duck

numbers vary with angling disturbance. Herons nest at Eilean Ard, Loch Laxford, in the west while fulmars nest on the ruined walls of Skelbo Castle and sit in old rooks' nests in nearby pine trees. Permits are required from Sutherland Estates office, Golspie, to visit Ferry Links Wood with its herring gullery on the north part of Loch Fleet Reserve, between Golspie and Littleferry, and a SWT permit for parts of the remainder. Terns, occasionally with Sandwich, occupy shingle spits below Balblair Wood. Many long-tailed duck and velvet scoter winter off Loch Fleet between Golspie and Embo, and waders feed on the loch sandbanks.

Other localities: Inchnadamph moor, a National Nature Reserve of 1292 ha (3200 acres) by the A837 at the head of Loch Assynt in the west (NC2521-2617), has nesting ptarmigan, sparrowhawks, etc. Divers breed on several lochs. Loch Shin (420200), the largest in the district, with nesting water-birds, is 17 miles (11 km) long and 1½ miles (2·4 km) wide, set in bleak moors, with a dam at Lairg at the junction of the A839, A836 and A838. Shin Forest (NC572016), 3 miles (5 km) south on the A836 Inveran road, has walks at Carbisdale Castle (NH574955) on the Ardgay-Inveroykel road, at NG604928 on the A836 1 mile (1·6 km) north of Bonar Bridge, at NH580950, 2 miles (3 km) further north, and at NH576994 opposite Shin Falls on the A836. Strathy Forest and Bog (284964) is a National Nature Reserve of 48 ha (120 acres) on the northeast coast at NC7953. Though mostly botanical, it has crossbills, etc. Loch Bottalie (58° 34′ N, 4° 48′ W) has common terns. Cross has greenshank and scoter. Black-throated divers nest on lochans. Gadwall nest on Loch Brora, and eagles elsewhere.

Information
Recorder: D. MacDonald, Elmbank, Dornoch.
Literature: Downhill, I. R., Notes from Island Roan, *Scottish Birds*, **2**, 6 (1963); **3**, 8 (1965).
Fisher, J. and Percy, K., Notes on Eilean Bulgach, *Scottish Naturalist*, **65** (1950).
Forestry Commission, *Kyle of Sutherland Forest Walks Guide* (London, HMSO).
Perry, Richard, *In the High Grampians* (London, 1948).
Pennie, I. D., A Century of Bird-Watching in Sutherland, *Scottish Birds*, **2**, 3 (1962).
Pennie, I. D., The Clo Mor Bird Cliffs, *Scottish Naturalist*, **65** (1951).

Check List
Nesters: Black-throated Diver, Great Northern Diver, Red-throated Diver, Slavonian Grebe, Little Grebe, Fulmar, Storm Petrel, Cormorant, Shag, Heron, Mallard, Teal, Gadwall, Wigeon, Pintail, Shoveler, Scaup, Tufted Duck, Pochard, Goldeneye, Scoter, Eider, Red-breasted Merganser, Goosander, Shelduck, Canada Goose, Greylag, Mute Swan, Golden Eagle, Buzzard, Sparrowhawk, Goshawk, (Marsh Harrier), Hen Harrier, Osprey, Peregrine, Merlin, Kestrel, Red Grouse, Ptarmigan, Black Grouse, Capercaillie, Red-legged Partridge, Common Partridge, Quail, Reeve's Pheasant, Common Pheasant, Water Rail, Spotted Crake, Corncrake, Moorhen, Coot, Oystercatcher, Lapwing, Ringed Plover, Golden Plover, Dotterel, Snipe, Woodcock, Curlew, Whimbrel, Black-tailed Godwit, Green Sandpiper, Wood Sandpiper, Common Sandpiper, Redshank, Greenshank, Temminck's Stint, Dunlin, Great Skua, Arctic Skua, Great Black-backed Gull, Lesser Black-backed Gull, Herring Gull,

Common Gull, Black-headed Gull, Kittiwake, Common Tern, Arctic Tern, Roseate, Little Tern, Sandwich Tern, Razorbill, Guillemot, Black Guillemot, Puffin, Rockdove, Woodpigeon, Collared Dove, Cuckoo, Barn Owl, Tawny Owl, Long-eared Owl, Short-eared Owl, (Nightjar), Swift, Kingfisher, Great Spotted Woodpecker, Wryneck, Skylark, (Shore Lark), Swallow, House Martin, Sand Martin, Raven, Carrion Crow, Hoodie Crow, Rook, Jackdaw, Magpie, Jay, Great Tit, Blue tit, Coal Tit, Crested Tit, Willow Tit, Long-tailed Tit, Nuthatch, Tree Creeper, Wren, Dipper, Mistle Thrush, Fieldfare, Song Thrush, Redwing, Ring Ouzel, Blackbird, Wheatear, Stonechat, Whinchat, Redstart, (Bluethroat), Robin, Grasshopper Warbler, Sedge Warbler, Blackcap, Garden Warbler, Whitethroat, Willow Warbler, Chiffchaff, Wood Warbler, Goldcrest, Spotted Flycatcher, Pied Flycatcher, Hedge Sparrow, Meadow Pipit, Tree Pipit, Rock Pipit, Pied Wagtail, Grey Wagtail, Starling, Greenfinch, Goldfinch, Siskin, Linnet, Twite, Redpoll, Bullfinch, Scottish Cross-bill, Chaffinch, (Brambling), Corn Bunting, Yellowhammer, Reed Bunting, Snow Bunting, House Sparrow, Tree Sparrow.

Migratory and rarer visitors: Large flocks of winter Long-tailed Duck, Eiders, Velvet Scoters and Wigeon, flocks of Greylag Geese and autumn tideline waders and groups of Great Northern Divers; there are good sea watching points for the autumn passage of Sooty, Cory's, Manx and Great Shearwaters, Long-tailed and Pomerine Skuas, Auks and Gannets are a feature of these northern bays, sea lochs and headlands. Marsh Tit, Green and Wood Sandpipers, the White-billed Northern Diver in summer plumage and Great Northern Divers are among summer 'visitors'.

Iceland and Glaucous Gulls, Waxwings, Grey Phalarope, Osprey, Harriers and Great Grey Shrike are regular visitors. A fair share of Scotland's rarer visitors include Surf Scoter, King Eider, Snowy Owl, Golden Oriole, Red-necked Grebe, Roller, Hoopoe, Pastor, Marsh Harrier, Hobby, Red-footed Falcon, Quail, White Stork, Lesser Grey Shrike, Gyr Falcon, Barred, Great, Reed and Icterine Warblers, Black-eared Wheatear, Harlequin Duck, Marsh Sandpiper, Crane, Citrine Wagtail, and American Bonaparte's Gull, Stilt and Pectoral Sandpipers, Yellow-billed Cuckoo and White-throated Sparrow.

Chapter 11

Lothian Region

East Lothian

Probably the most watched area, East Lothian's 42,510 ha (280 square miles) rise gently from the Firth of Forth, rich in nesting and migratory seabirds and shorebirds, to the 500–1000 feet (150–300 m) high East Lammermuir Hills on the Berwickshire border, a breeding ground of common gulls, red and black grouse, golden plover, dunlin, ring ouzel, merlin, woodcock and siskin, with a Scottish Wildlife Trust reserve at the East Deans. Marshy Danskine Loch is on their north side. Four-fifths is arable and the Lammermuirs are mostly sheep pasture. There are lowlands in the north and the west. The River Tyne divides the district and enters the mouth of the Forth in a sandy muddy bay at Dunbar, where the tide runs 8 minutes earlier than at Leith, with 5·2 m springs. It has a heronry at Tyninghame, and haunts of geese and waders. Offshore five island colonies include breeding gannets, puffins and terns, while Aberlady Bay, within easy reach of the coast road, is probably the most watched and most productive of all the bird haunts. Thirty-five little terns still breed in two colonies. There are fifty pairs of ringed plover, and many common tern. In January the Forth has Scotland's largest wader flocks and massive flocks of eiders, scaup and other duck. Eiders nest inland, and there are buzzards at Gifford and pied flycatchers at Humbie. In Dunbar (681791) 150 pairs of Kittiwakes nest on harbour warehouses and the castle wall. Rarer visitors include long-tailed skuas in spring and 'poms' in autumn, black-browed albatross, Caspian tern, waxwing, lesser grey shrike, red-necked grebe, little auk, spotted sandpiper and lesser yellowlegs. Lapland and snow buntings as well as shore larks visit the dunes, and divers visit the Forth in good numbers in winter when thousands of rooks roost at Stevenson Mains, Haddington. From the Forth to North Berwick in January one may see 2000 or 3000 scaup, long-tailed and other duck, godwits, purple sandpipers and Lapland buntings. For those not seeking rarities, there is Stenton forest walk (NT620725) on the B6370 at Press-meannon. East Lothian's woods are the hawfinch's most regular nesting haunts in Scotland. At least four white-billed divers have been authenticated on the Forth here.

Bass Rock (602874): This circular island of hard, terraced volcanic rock is 313 feet (94 m) high and 1 mile (1·6 km) in circumference, and is situated in the Forth 3 miles (5 km) northeast of North Berwick; accessible landing is on the east side according to wind and mists, by arrangement with the boatman (F. Marr, 24 Victoria Road, North Berwick), or the owner (Sir H. H. Dalrymple North Berwick). There is a gannetry of 6000–7000 pairs with the earliest arrivals in the second week of January, a peak in March–June, and the last in September. The east colony is more approachable than the west. Also nesting here are puffins (on the old prison walls), fulmars, shags, kittiwakes, lesser black-backed and herring gulls, razorbills, guillemots, eider, starling, pied wagtail, wren, rock pipit. Black guillemot, peregrine and, in 1967–8, black-browed albatross are rarer visitors. North Berwick pleasure launches make public non-landing trips around the island in summer. With a powerful telescope, I have had good views from the hill at the east end of the promenade and Tantallon Castle.

Craigleith: This small grassy island with cliff colonies is just

Gannets, Bass Rock, August (overleaf)

over 1 mile (1·6 km) off North Berwick, with boatman access. Breeding puffins (1400), fulmars, sixteen pairs of shag, cormorants, thirty-six pairs of razorbills, guillemots on the east cliffs, 5000 predatory herring gull nests, 350 pairs of lesser black-backed gulls, and great black-backed gulls and kittiwakes.

Fidra (NT514870): This is a rocky islet 2 miles (3 km) off North Berwick, RSPB-managed with boat. There are very fluctuating terneries, with up to 300 pairs of Sandwich some years, and none in recent years; roseates vary from eighty in 1970 to none in 1972–4; common terns vary from 300 to none, and there are twenty to 100 pairs of arctic. Also seven pairs of shag, fulmars, kittiwakes, eiders, ringed plovers, common gulls (1973) and razorbills (1972) can be seen. It is tidal to Castle Rocks with nesting fulmar, eider, oystercatcher and shag. The shore opposite Fidra provides good binocular watching.

The Lamb: Also managed by the RSPB, this is a grassy stack in the Forth between North Berwick and Fidra, with no official access. The Forth's main cormorant colony is here, with 245 pairs and there are also 244 pairs of shag, eight pairs of razorbill, guillemots, kittiwakes, lesser black-backed and herring gulls and eiders.

Eyebroughty: Four miles (6 km) west of North Berwick, via Gullane on the A198, this gull island has public access at the lowest tides. Nesting terns (occasional) and eider, but chiefly lesser black-backed and herring gulls. There are tidal merganser flocks and 2000 eiders flocking to mussel beds. Up to ninety-three purple sandpipers can be seen in April on shore at nearby Yellowcraig.

Roseate Terns, Fidra

Sandwich Terns, Fidra

Aberlady Bay (465799): This is a Reserve with public access at ebb tide. A line of gazing people, binoculars to their eyes, marked the shore as we stopped on the A198 some 16 miles (25·7 km) from Edinburgh and barely 9 miles (14·4 km) from North Berwick. This is the 'Cley' of Scotland, an unofficial meeting ground of bird-watchers (NT 4582-4580), 582 ha (1438 acres of sandy and rocky foreshore with 1¼ miles (2·5 km) of saltings, sand dunes, mudflats and sea buckthorn shrubs. Visitors walking out via Aberlady village (A6137 and A198 junction) and the wooden footbridge across the stream from the car park, on the ebb (tides only slightly earlier than Leith), should avoid disturbing vast carpets of wader flocks arranging and rearranging themselves on the mud, or the shingle-nesting birds whose eggs chill in cold winds. The ternery varies annually: Sandwich terns from 320 to none; 400 pairs of common tern in 1972; also arctic and occasionally roseate (1970). Eiders also include inland nests on the links, woods (with long-eared owls) and fields to the east. Coot and teal bred in 1971, and there are shelduck. The bay's major attraction are its flocks of waders feeding on the mudflats—twenty-four curlew sandpipers in September, godwits, knot, grey plover, greenshank, spotted redshank, ruffs (including winter), purple sandpipers, occasionally avocet (May), buff-breasted sandpiper (May 1974), and little ringed plover. Twenty-five arctic skuas have been seen in September; short-eared owls rest in the sea buckthorns, where there are shore larks, occasional water pipits, snow buntings and Lapland buntings on the dunes, together with the odd raven. Winter visitors include wigeon and red-necked grebes; there is a roost of pinkfooted geese. Two Caspian terns came in June and July 1971, and there have been white-winged black tern (July 1970), bearded tit (November 1971), lesser grey shrike (September 1971), white-billed diver (February 1972), and buff-breasted sandpiper.

Rocky Gullane Point, on the north of the Bay via the links road by the hotel, or Peffer Burn footbridge, with limited summer access, has had nesting little tern, shelduck and short-eared owl. It is a good sea watch in autumn-winter, with over 7000 eiders in September and waders like sanderling, long-tailed duck, velvet-scoters, divers, pomerine skuas (October winds), little auk (January storms) and a gull-billed tern in August 1967. Gosford Bay by the A198 west of Aberlady is good for long-tailed duck, divers and five grebes in winter, with thirty-five slavonians one March. Herons began nesting here in 1971. Many oystercatchers, ringed plover, turnstones, purple sand-pipers, curlew, redshanks, knot, dunlin and bar-tailed godwits winter on the rocky coast at Gullane Point–Tynemouth and Belhaven Bay–Blisdean Creek.

Tyninghame and the Tyne estuary (631808) : Access is by the A198 from the A1 west of Dunbar or the A1087 to West Burns. The area has 1000 pinkfeet in autumn–winter, with occasional greylags and brent. Sandy Hurst spit, on the north side, has waders including occasional avocet in July and April, and a spotted sandpiper in October 1971. Visiting duck include velvet scoter. There is a small heronry at Tyninghame, and many kittiwakes nesting on Dunbar harbour buildings. Fifteen pomerine skuas were noted in October 1971. Part of John Muir Country Park.

Information
Recorder :
K. S. Macgregor, 16 Merchiston Avenue, Edinburgh EH10 4NY.

Literature:

Hamilton, F. D. and Macgregor, K. S., Birds of Aberlady Bay, *Trans. East Lothian Antiq. & Field Naturalists' Soc.,* **8**, and *Scottish Orn. Club* (1961).

Midlothian

This county is the most watched and most recorded of all districts. Its 95,110 ha (244,900 acres) include 10 miles (16 km) of the Forth, which cuts across half the breadth of Scotland, bringing great winter roosts of eider, scaup and goldeneye, especially in frost, as well as August waders, including ruffs. A few brent visit the area, also red-necked grebe and short-toed lark. Four hundred and eighty-five tufted duck frequent the Edinburgh lochs in January, while Duddingston has Britain's record pochard flock. Great crested grebes summer in the Forth from here to Aberlady. The district is rich in reservoirs, with Gladhouse reservoir a major attraction to waterfowl and other birds, like Baird's sandpiper, a visitor in 1974. The Forth here has further island bird sanctuaries. The steep Pentland and Moorfoot hills, with most reservoirs, cut across the southwest and southeast, the latter reservoirs with nesting oystercatchers, golden plover, short-eared owls and, in 1973, herring gulls. Golden plover and other species nest in the Moorfoots. Wader roosts are at Morrison's Haven, Loretto, Newfield, etc. The North and especially the South Esk rivers are the breeding haunts of dippers and sandpipers. Pinkfeet visit the southeast border hills at Middleton 55° 49′ N, 3° W. A free-flying colony of night herons from Edinburgh Zoo (Corstorphine Hill) is a recorders' hazard. Lesser white-throats, rarely breeding in Scotland, nested at Cold-ingham and Cousland in 1974, and fieldfares elsewhere.

Edinburgh and Leith: Magpies, tawny owls and collared doves nest in Edinburgh suburbs, kestrels sometimes on St Mary's Cathedral and Princes Street GPO, and rooks at Gogar Mount and Hanley, Drum (Gilmerton), Mortonhall South Gate and a dozen lesser sites. In Roseburn Park a December kingfisher flew up the city's Water of Leith. I mentioned in *The Bird-Lover's (Watcher's) Week-End Book* how a flock of snow buntings spent 20 minutes on the rugby pitch at Murrayfield during an international match, feeding on grains of corn left from straw used overnight as frost protection. Robins, chaffinches, titmice, etc., have been tamed by hand feeding in the Royal Botanic Gardens in winter, where hawfinch, waxwing and crossbill are occasional visitors. Leith Docks and Seafield sea wall promenade, by the A198, A1 and B1348, form one of Britain's major winter wildfowl haunts 5 miles east to Portobello Bay, Esk mouth at Musselburgh lagoons and Cockenzie power station. Eighty-five per cent of British and Irish scaup reach up to 15,000–30,000 on December–February tides, when there are fleets of 20,000 eider, 8000 pochard, 4000 goldeneye, 1500 scoter, 300 longtails, mergansers, some shoveler, etc., as well as 400 great crested grebes. A new sewage scheme may lessen the future attraction of Seafield outfall. The sandy shore here has up to twenty curlew sandpipers in August, flocks of knot, plovers and godwits, and also forty purple sandpipers in winter and nesting common and arctic terns and ringed plovers. Waders flock to Musselburgh (335637) where the short-toed lark was a September visitor. I have seen migrating wheatears on Edinburgh's Calton Hill including the larger Greenland race.

Duddingston Loch (NF2872): This Royal Parks reserve of

the Ministry of Public Works, Edinburgh, is Holyrood Park's major attraction, with public access to the water from Queen's Drive, from the A6096 on the east of the city. Parts on the Duddingston Road side are restricted. One hundred and fifty-six species including thirty-one nesters have been recorded in its 12 ha (30 acres), of which 4·6 ha (11½ acres) are reeds, 1·4 marsh, 2·6 grass, scrub and trees. Nesters include great crested grebe, piping teal, diving duck, pochard, mallard, sedge warbler, whitethroat, redpoll, reed bunting, corn bunting, long-eared and tawny owls and green woodpecker. Also grasshopper and willow warblers, bullfinch, tufted duck, feral greylag and little grebe. The water rail has summered. Its dozen different duck include the winter roost of Forth (Seafield) pochard, attaining a record 8200 in January frosts; also tufted duck, gadwall, scaup and goosander as well as occasional turnstone and purple sandpiper, bittern, etc. Duck also visit Dunsappie and St Margaret lochs in Holyrood Park, while nesting stonechat and visiting snow bunting may be seen on 823 feet (247 m) high Arthur's Seat. Stonechats also nest in Midlothian at Cobbinshaw.

Bawsfinch, a 15 acre (6·07 ha) SWT reserve of thicket and grass adjoins Duddingston Loch.

Inchmickery Island (NT2080): This is an RSPB-managed reserve of just over 1 ha (2·4 acres) in the Forth, 2½ miles (4 km) from Edinburgh. There is no official access. Variable nestings depend on crows and herring gulls (recently culled). Thirteen hundred terns nest here, mostly about 450 Sandwich, 85–750 common, arctic, and up to 100 roseates. It has a bird-attracting small southern islet of Carcraig.

Inchkeith Island (295828): Four miles (6·5 km) north of

Leith, 450 puffins, five to six pairs of razorbills, herring gulls, shags and up to 750 pairs of common terns, as well as arctic, etc., nest here. It is also a migration watch point. This is officially Tayside.

Moorfoot Reservoirs: These attract waterfowl, especially the 160 ha (395 acres) of Gladhouse in the Upper Esk valley at Toxside, 13 miles (20 km) south of Edinburgh via the A701 and then B6372 from Penicuik and right turn at Upperside. Breeders include great crested and occasional other grebes, tufted duck, teal, shoveler, oystercatcher, 250 pairs of lesser black-backed gull and other species. One thousand greylags roost here October–December and in spring; up to 5000 pinkfeet roost in March. Pochard and snow bunting are winter visitors, and passage waders include wood and curlew sandpipers, ruff and occasionally white-rumped sandpiper. Spotted crakes are also visitors. Great crested grebes nest near Rosslyn Lee Station, south of Roslin (237664) off the A701, 6 miles (10 km) south of Edinburgh, which is also visited occasionally by Bewicks. Duck visit Rosebery Pool on the B6372 south of Gladhouse, Edgelaw by the B6372 west of the A7, and Portmore by the A703 before Eddleston across the southwest border. Pied flycatchers also nest at Roslin Glen.

Pentland Reservoirs: Cobbinshaw Station reservoir, by the railway south of West Calder on the A71, 12 miles (20 km) west of Edinburgh, has a black-headed gullery, nesting great crested grebes and mallard, and a winter pinkfoot roost. Greylags roost at Harperrig by the A70, 12 miles (20 km) south of Edinburgh, and great crested grebes nest at Threipmuir by the road from Balerno on the A70 6 miles (9 km) to the southwest of Edinburgh, and at Crosswoodhill by the A70 beyond Harperrig. These also attract winter duck, while Glencorse reservoir off the A702, Dunsappie, Lochend, Figate and St Margaret's reservoirs, and Bavelaw Moss at the west end of Threipmuir reservoir attract birds too. Common gulls nest at Auchencorth Moss.

Information
Recorder:
R. W. J. Smith, 33 Hunter Terrace, Loanhead.
Societies:
Edinburgh Branch, Scottish Ornithologists' Club, Hon. Sec. Mrs. D. R. Lansglow, 32 Campbell Road, Longniddry, East Lothian. Midlothian Ornithological Club (now informal).
Literature:
Connell, Anderson and Waterston, Birds of Duddingston Loch, *Scottish Birds* Supp., **1** (1961).

West Lothian (Linlithgowshire)

A small, inner Forth district of 31,095 ha (76,836 acres), West Lothian has summer haunts of sparrowhawk, peregrine, hawfinch (scarce), long-eared owl (Broxburn) and teal (Turnhouse), while the distribution of its autumn greylags and pinkfeet depends upon roosts available, e.g. near Grangemouth on the western border. Thirty puffins have been seen in summer off Horward Point below the Forth Bridge. Shags have nested in the inner Forth at Car Craig and fulmar, Sandwich tern and roseate have been noted at Inchgarvie. Linlithgow Park reservoir (300677), preserved by the Ministry of Works as a wildfowl refuge by the A9 (chiefly tufted duck and pochard), has nesting great crested grebes and has been visited by migrating ospreys. One hundred and fifty-four species have been listed at the

Almond estuary and Cramond Island, a passage haunt of waders and passerines, visited by duck and with nesting shelduck and rock pipit. Great crested grebes flock off Boness, and waders also visit the Esk mouth at Inveresk. The Scottish Wildlife Trust has a reserve at Pepper Wood. There is a winter rook roost at Lochcote House and a starling roost at Dundas Hill south of the Forth Road Bridge.

Information
Recorder:
R. W. J. Smith, 33 Hunter Terrace, Loanhead, Midlothian.

Check list
Nesters: Great Crested Grebe, (Black-necked Grebe), Little Grebe, Fulmar, Gannet, Cormorant, Shag, Heron, Mallard, Teal, Gadwall, Shoveler, Tufted Duck, Pochard, Eider, Red-breasted Merganser, Goosander, Shelduck, Greylag, Mute Swan, Buzzard, Sparrowhawk, Merlin, Kestrel, Red Grouse, Black Grouse, Common Partridge, Quail, Pheasant, Corncrake, Moorhen, Coot, Oystercatcher, Lapwing, Ringed Plover, Golden Plover, Snipe, Woodcock, Curlew, Sandpiper, Redshank, Dunlin, Great Black-backed Gull, Lesser Black-backed Gull, Herring Gull, Common Gull, Black-headed Gull, Kittiwake, Common Tern, Arctic Tern, Roseate Tern, Little Tern, Sandwich Tern, Razorbill, Guillemot, Puffin, Stockdove, Rockdove, Woodpigeon, Turtle Dove, Collared Dove, Cuckoo, Barn Owl, Tawny Owl, Long-eared Owl, Short-eared Owl, Little Owl, Swift, Kingfisher, Green Woodpecker, Great Spotted Woodpecker, Skylark, Swallow, House Martin, Sand Martin, Raven, Carrion Crow, Rook,

Jackdaw, Magpie, Jay, Great Tit, Blue Tit, Coal Tit, Willow Tit, Marsh Tit, Long-tailed Tit, Tree Creeper, Wren, Dipper, Mistle Thrush, Song Thrush, Ring Ouzel, Blackbird, Wheatear, Stonechat, Whinchat, Redstart, Robin, Grasshopper Warbler, Sedge Warbler, Blackcap, Garden Warbler, Whitethroat, Lesser Whitethroat, Willow Warbler, Chiffchaff, Wood Warbler, Goldcrest, Spotted Flycatcher, Pied Flycatcher, Hedge Sparrow, Meadow Pipit, Tree Pipit, Rock Pipit, Pied Wagtail, Grey Wagtail, Starling, Hawfinch, Greenfinch, Goldfinch, Siskin, Linnet, Twite, Redpoll, Bullfinch, Crossbill, Chaffinch, Corn Bunting, Yellowhammer, Reed Bunting, House Sparrow, Tree Sparrow.

Migratory and rare visitors: Ducks, Divers, Skuas including Longtails and Pomerines, Grebes including Red-necked from winter to spring, especially in East Lothian, waders including Spotted Redshanks, Curlew, Sandpipers, Purple Sandpipers, Knot, occasional Avocet and Caspian, White-winged Black Tern, Gull-billed Tern, Black-browed Albatross, Shore Lark, Short-toed Lark, Lapland Bunting and Water Pipit are among visitors to the Forth area, which includes the greatest winter flock of Scaup. Spotted Crake, Waxwing, Osprey, Rough-legged Buzzard, White Stork, Greater and Lesser Grey Shrikes, Pinkfoot and Greylag Geese, and American Lesser Yellowlegs are other visitors. The little ringed plover appeared at Gladhouse in 1974.

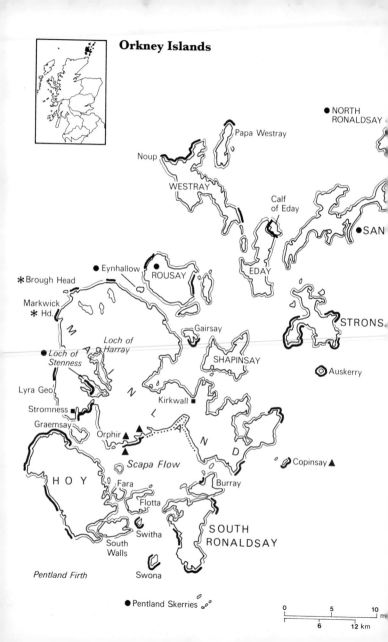

Chapter 12

Orkney Islands

Separated from the mainland by 10 miles (16 km) of fast
Pentland Firth tides, twenty-nine islands, thirty-eight
holms and many skerries, seventy-eight in all, with only
twenty-eight permanently inhabited, form these sandstone
outcrops with clay, peatmoss, ponds and farms. From over
300 listed species, seventy nesters include occasional scaup
(West Mainland), occasional goldeneye and gadwall,
shoveler and irregular pintail. Twenty-five thousand pairs
of arctic terns nest on eleven islands, most on Papa Westray
and Westray, and there are over 300 pairs of Sandwich
terns, but no little terns. There are twenty-seven peregrine
eyries. About forty pairs of hen harrier nest with short-
eared owls, 660 pairs of arctic skuas and 480 pairs of great
skuas and hoodies on the moors. There are seventeen to
twenty-five breeding pairs of red-throated divers, also
storm petrels (several holms and probably Hoy and
Copinsay), Manx shearwaters, 600 pairs of cormorants on
small northern isles, colonies of up to 2000 great black-
backed gulls, irregular nests of whimbrel but, unlike
Shetland, no red-necked phalaropes. It has Britain's second
largest seabird colonies on northwest Westray, the north
end of Papa Westray, Calf of Eday, north, southwest and
northwest Mainland, north and southwest Hoy, southwest
and southeast Stronsay, Auskerry, Copinsay, west and
southeast South Ronaldsay, Switha and Swona, with a
fifth of Britain's total arctic skuas, great black-backed gulls,
kittiwakes, arctic terns, guillemots and black guillemots,
and a tenth of its fulmars, cormorants, shags and puffins.
However, seventeen species breeding in Caithness and
Sutherland are not here for lack of trees, and twenty others

for ecological differences, whereas a larger number of voles give the region more breeding harriers, short-eared owls and kestrels. Many turnstones summer, coot are scarce, and willow warblers, yellowhammers, mistle thrushes and house martins are local. Eleven per cent of the guillemots are bridled. Black-tailed godwits bred in 1956, greenshanks in 1951 and black redstart in 1973. Cliff heronries are on the west of Mainland. Orkney is characterised by mild, moist winters and strong winds. Apart from Berriedale, Binscarth Woods and a few plantations, trees are rare, hence ground-nesting woodpigeons, song thrushes and kestrels. There are many lakes and springs, but no large rivers, though dippers probably bred at a burn. February flocks of over 2000 pochard and snow buntings, 1895 tufted duck on Loch Harray in October, Greenland whitefronts at Birsay and Loch of Tankerness, great grey shrike, snowy owl, Steller's eider, etc., characterise its winters. Cory's shearwater and up to forty-two sooties mark autumn sea watches. There are spring and autumn roosts of up to twenty hen harriers. Access is by sea daily from Scrabster (Caithness) or twice weekly Aberdeen, and by air from Wick, Aberdeen, Inverness or Glasgow to Kirkwall (except Sunday).

The Natural Environment of Orkney (164 pp., edited by R. Goodier, Nature Conservancy Council, Edinburgh, 1975), the proceedings of a symposium held in Edinburgh, describes population studies of hen harriers, seabirds, terns and auks, and of birds on Eynhallow. Among former nesters not breeding now it lists scoter, whooper, sparrowhawk, white-tailed sea eagle, ptarmigan, red-necked phalarope and sand martin. Golden eagle and dipper have returned to nest. Orkney was found to have more breeding seabirds than Shetland, and seventy to eighty breeding female hen

A Peregrine stripping prey

harriers, mostly on the mainland, with five to eight nests on
Rousay, four on Hoy and some on Eday. Great and arctic
skuas nest on Eynhallow, but not golden plover, storm
petrel, peregrine, puffin or black guillemot. The Westray
group has thirty-one colonies of arctic terns with 17,500
pairs (especially North Hill, Papa Westray, Noup Head
and Holm of Aikerness), shearwaters and puffins at
Rapness, puffins also at Swinedale, Noup Head and Neven
Craig; black guillemots at Swinedale, Aikerness, Rapness,
Neven Craig and Faray. North Hoy, Starling Hill and Dale
of Cortascarth, Marwick Head. The lochs of Harray and
Stenness and West Westray are noted as of outstanding
national importance. Important wader feeding sites are
Dingieshowe to St Peters Pool; Echna Loch and Loch of
Ayre are noted for visiting duck; Loch of Skaill and Loch of
Treadwall for nesting duck. Large rafts of shearwaters are
noted off Rackwick and Rousay and nine storm petrel
nesting sites are noted at Sule Skerry, Pentland Skerries,
Switha, Auskerry, Green Holms; and Faray, Rusk, Wart
and Skea Holms off Westray.

Mainland (Pomona): There are 200 miles (322 km) of good
roads on this 38,866 ha (96,000 acres) island, which is 23
miles long and 15 miles wide (37 by 24 km). The coastline is
deeply indented with bays and creeks, except in the west,
and inland is mostly flat moor and heath, except for
cultivated valleys. Two hundred and fifty-six Sandwich
terns, long-eared owls, cliff herons in the west, hen harriers,
red-throated divers, little grebes, red grouse, wigeon, arctic
skuas, great and lesser black-backed gulls, auks, eiders,
short-eared owls, merlins, fieldfares (1967), grey wagtails
(1974) and rooks in Kirkwall and Stromness are among its
breeding birds. The Kirkwall tide is 4 hours earlier than at

Leith, with 2·6 m springs. Birsay Moor (58° 8′ N, 3° 18′ W),
Burn of Rusht, is an RSPB reserve and botanical SSSI of
222 ha (550 acres) at the northwest tip. It has kittiwakes,
guillemots, short-eared owls, hen harriers, merlins, great
skuas, water-birds and gulls. One thousand sooty shearwaters have been counted in a day in autumn off the
Brough of Birsay. Costa Head at the northern tip has 400
feet (121·9 m) cliffs with guillemots, razorbills, puffins,
kittiwakes, fulmars, shags and ravens. It is reached by the
A966 to north of Loch Swannay, and a cliff path.
Cormorants nest at Brough Head. Marwick Hill and Head,
south of Brough, via the A967 and A986 for the B9056 to

Puffins have some of their biggest populations in Orkney

cliff path. Marwick Bay, has sheer rock faces with nesting fulmars, kittiwakes, shags, guillemots (15 per cent bridled), razorbills, puffins, peregrines and ravens and is a seabird watching point. The RSPB has this and moorlands, including Dale of Cortascarth, 135 ha (335 acres) with hen harriers, arctic skuas, black-backed gulls, short-eared owls, merlins, etc. Their Hobbister lease of 931 ha (2300 acres), partly restricted, at Waulkmill Bay off the Stromness to Kirkwall coast road near Orphir and Kirbisker Youth Hostel, has shore cliffs and small colonies of seabirds, fulmars, black guillemots, cormorants and shelduck. The adjacent moorland has great skuas, hen harriers, merlins, dunlin, golden plover, short-eared owls, snipe and curlew. It is opposite Scapa Flow (340000) with nesting great black-backed gulls, red-throated divers, wigeon (lochans), redshank, lapwings, teal, mallard and tufted duck. Winter seaduck come here and up to seventy-two great northern divers in April. *Warden:* Easter Sower, Orphir.

Other bird haunts include Loch of Skaill and Bay of Skaill, Loch of Swannay, Shunan, Tankerness and Lowrie; Stromness, Costa and Rerwick Heads, Sands of Evie, Sandside Bay (Deerness), Skara Brae, Dounby, Liod, Binscarth and Berstane woods. The latter has a winter rook roost. Fulmars nest on Stromness Hotel.

Stenness and Harray fork their joint way into the west as one great 1619 ha (4000 acre) sea loch via the A966 and B9055, the nesting haunt of teal, tufted duck, mergansers, shoveler, arctic and common terns, common gulls, hen harriers, eider and dunlin, and harbouring a herd of non-breeding mute swans. Duck wintering here include 2060 tufted and 3000 pochard on Harray in October, and 105 longtails and 300 scaup on Stenness. Stromness, at the mouth of Stenness with tides $5\frac{1}{2}$ hours earlier than at Leith, has nesting puffins, red-throated divers, guillemots, cormorants (Horse), and cliff herons (Lyra Geo). Cory's shearwater is a September passage migrant. Row Head has auks (guillemots). Kittiwakes nest at Tatcliff Bay, Rose Ness at the southern end. Costa Hill (Head) in the north has 1000 guillemots and kittiwakes, puffins (Standard Stac nearby), shags, red-throated diver and golden plover. Churchill Causeway connects the south with the nearby islands of Burray (474984), where the surf scoter occasionally visits Echinaloch Bay, and South Ronaldsay with its nesting kittiwakes and fulmars. Kittiwakes nest from Black Craig to Gaulton, black guillemots in Scapa Flow's Churchill Barrier. A diminishing heronry is with fulmars on Yesnaby Cliffs, and at Sandwick; cormorant colonies are on the twin islands of Boray and Taing Holms and on the 4 ha (10 acre) Muckle Green Holm. Two thousand one hundred and thirty-six pochard have flocked on Broadhouse Loch, and Binscarth Wood has nesting spotted flycatcher and goldcrest, with long-tailed tits, tree creepers, hawfinch and long-eared owl. A sea watch is at Graemsay at the southwest (272055, 58° 56′ N, 3° 17′ W). Puffins nest with kittiwakes, hen harrier and ravens at Evie. Storm petrels also nest on Rusk Holm and Faray Holm, and probably on Green Holm and Switha. Puffins breed also on Costa Head, Swona, St John's and Berry Heads.

Auskerry (HY6715): This little island east of Shapinsay has nesting storm petrels.

Copinsay: There is public access to this RSPB island of 151 ha (375 acres), 2 miles (3 km) east of Point of Ayre on the southeast of Mainland. Steep seabird cliffs at the lighthouse have 10,000 kittiwakes, 9000 guillemots, sixty-eight black

guillemots, 300 razorbills, 680 fulmars, fifty puffins (Black
Holm), sixteen pairs of cormorants, eighty-four shags,
ravens, arctic terns (Corn Holm), 230 great black-backed
gulls and herring gulls (The Holms), ringed plover,
shelduck and black redstart (1973). There is an autumn
passage of skuas. Rarer visitors are sooty shearwater, black-
browed albatross, goshawk, smew, dowitcher, white-
rumped sandpiper (October), greater yellowlegs, red-
footed falcon, pine, black-headed and rustic buntings,
icterine, barred, subalpine and yellow-browed warblers,
firecrest, red-breasted flycatcher, Richard's pipit, lesser
grey shrike, woodchat and scarlet grosbeak.

Eday and Calf of Eday (HY5640-5528) : Less than 2 miles (3
km) from Sanday, the island of Eday has towering
sandstone gull cliffs, $1\frac{1}{2}$ miles (2·4 km) long, sloping
gradually towards the south, where there is a landing strip
(subject to wind). Access is by Loganair from Kirkwall. The
Calf of Eday to the north is uninhabited. Many great black-
backed gulls nest here, also kittiwakes, puffins, guillemots,
cormorants, shags, arctic skua (Calf and Eday), occasional
hen harrier, whimbrel (probably 1968), and Orkney's only
regular tree sparrows (Carrick House). The snowy owl is
among occasional visitors. The Calf has the main seabird
colony.

Eynhallow : Between north Mainland and Rousay, with
strong tideways, this 80 ha (200 acre) rabbit-free verdant
island refuge has southeast beaches and northwest seabird
cliffs with a north–south ravine. There are nesting common
and arctic terns (Sheepsberry and Geory), arctic and great
skuas, fulmars (Ramnagoe, etc.), auks (black guillemots in
the northwest), puffins, common, herring and lesser black-

backed gulls, shags, cormorants, eiders, mergansers, golden plover, twite, rockdoves (ruins), oystercatchers, ringed plovers, occasional corncrake and storm petrel. Some fulmars lay on the grassy cliff summit.

Gairsay: This fulmar colony at 59° 6′ N, 2° 59′ W lies northeast of Mainland, with Taing Skerry and Holms (HY4322-4520). There are also nesting arctic skuas and cormorants.

Hoy (325998, HY1904-1700): Southwest of Mainland, Hoy's spectacular, second highest British cliffs, 1500 feet (450 m) are whitewashed with the excreta of 4000 nesting pairs of great black-backed gulls, fulmars, guillemots, razorbills, puffins, kittiwakes and ravens. One of Britain's welcome peregrine populations breeds here, and there are also buzzards, Orkney's only golden eagles, shags in the south, 100–150 pairs of arctic and great skuas on the hills, 800–1000 Manx shearwaters at Sneak Head in the north, merlin, ring ouzel, hen harrier, sedge warbler, goldcrest (plantations), stonechat, occasional greenshank (1951) and reed bunting. Hoy's eagles feed on fulmars. A black-browed albatross in August 1969 was one of its rarest visitors. Melsetter and Susiemer Burn are also good places.

Hoy is the largest and most westerly island, thirteen miles by six (25·9 by 9·6 km), mountainous and heathy. Access is by boat from Stromness to Longhope, three to six days a week according to season (and to Fara, Flotta and Graemsay islands), or by Loganair from Kirkwall. Arrangements for using hostel at Rackwick from Orkney Youth Leader, Education Office, Kirkwall.

North Ronaldsay (HY7856-7651): This is a low, grassy, fertile northern island with continental migrants similar to those of nearby Fair Isle, but with different breeders. There are a lighthouse and wader pools. It can be reached by Loganair from Kirkwall. Sandwich and arctic terns nest here and occasionally scaup, corncrake, twite, black guillemot and other rare species breed, but no longer red-necked phalaropes. One thousand sooty shearwaters have been seen in an August day, 111 in three hours, and on passage to October. Rarer visitors include woodchat; scarlet rosefinch, little bittern, pectoral sandpiper and melodious warbler (autumn 1971), dowitcher, black kite (1970), icterine warbler, arctic redpoll, Richard's pipit, gyr falcon (December), etc., while autumn whoopers visit the Loch of Anchum.

Papa Westray (HY5055-4849): In the far north beyond Westray, this island can be reached by Loganair from Kirkwall. It has many arctic and great skuas and occasional tree sparrows. Visited once by snowy owl, and once by a harlequin drake; it was a former nesting site of red-necked phalaropes and still has one of Britain's biggest arctic terneries. Puffins nest too.

Pentland Skerries (ND4678): These are the Orkneys' southernmost islands, situated between Duncansby Head (Caithness) and South Ronaldsay, with a ternery and nesting cormorants, storm petrels, etc., a lanceolate warbler among rarer migrants.

Rousay: Situated off the northeast coast of Mainland, this island of 9·6 × 6·4 km (6 × 4 miles) across Eynhallow Sound has a hostel (tel. 328). Seabird cliffs at Skaeburgh Head have nesting guillemots, razorbills, puffins, kittiwakes, fulmars and rockdoves. There are also arctic and great skuas, Sandwich terns, hen harriers, red-throated divers, red grouse and pheasants. Rafts of Manx shearwaters rest offshore. Apart from Hoy, it is the only island with extensive heather and peat moor. Via boat from Kirkwall.

Sanday: Shaped like a piece of jigsaw puzzle, east of Eday and reached by Loganair from Kirkwall, Sanday has nesting Sandwich, arctic, common and sometimes little terns, fulmars, great black-backed gulls, wigeon, teal, goldeneye, pintail, mergansers, dunlin, redshank, grebes (on the loch), golden plover, snipe, short-eared owls, corn buntings, arctic skuas and sedge warbler. In 1956 black-tailed godwits bred. The island is also a former nesting site of red-necked phalaropes.

Shapinsay: Lying east of Mainland, Shapinsay has nesting puffins and red-throated divers.

South Ronaldsay: The southerly island has seabird colonies on its northeast and southern cliffs. Nearby Lamb Holm, Glimps Holm and Burray are also interesting haunts.

Sule Skerry and Sule Stack: Lying 40 miles (64 km) northwest of Stromness and 35 miles (56 km) north of Sutherland, these twin, almost barren, rocks are ecologically part of the Western (Outer) isles, but have been recorded with Orkney. Stack Island (Stack Skerry) (59° 2′ N, 4° 30′ W; HX5617) is 2·5 barren hectares (6 acres) of island 5 miles (8 km) southwest of the Skerry lighthouse. Bereft of turf and puffins, it has 3500 gannets, 100 pairs of kittiwakes, 200 pairs of guillemots, and shags. The tide makes landing difficult. Skerry (59° 4′ N, 4° 24′ W) is a 40–50 feet (12–15 m) reef of 14 ha (35 acres), with a lighthouse and vegetation where 60,000 puffins breed. There are also storm petrels, kittiwakes, razorbills, black guillemots, cormorants, shags, eider, 500 pairs of arctic and common and, occasionally, Sandwich terns, skuas, great black-backed and herring gulls, rock pipits and rockdoves. Eggs of Leach's petrel have been taken. Access is by air from Kirkwall. This is the Sulisker area of deep sea fishermen.

Stronsay: Northeast of Mainland and Shapinsay, Stronsay can be reached by Loganair from Kirkwall. It has nesting puffins, shoveler, sedge warbler and the occasional hen harrier. Great black-backed gulls nest on the cliffs.

Switha: This is a small island between Hoy and South Ronaldsay, with nesting storm petrels and a seabird colony with puffins.

Swona: There is a seabird colony on this small island situated southeast of Hoy, where rarities have occurred among its migrants.

Westray: This northerly island (10 × 4 miles; 16 × 8 km) can be reached by Loganair from Kirkwall. Seabird cliffs at Noup Head have guillemots, razorbills, puffins, kittiwakes, fulmars, ravens and also occasional breeding scaup (1965), hen harrier, arctic and great skuas, sedge warbler, 15,000–27,000 arctic terns (North Hill, forming with Papa Westray Britain's biggest colony), and formerly red-necked phalarope. Steller's eider was here in October 1974. Storm petrels breed on the offshore islets of Faray, Rusk, Wart and Skea Holms. There is a daily steamer from Kirkwall.

Information
Recorder: D. Lea, Easter Sower, Orphir, KW17 2RE.
Societies: Orkney Field Centre, Links House, Birsay.
Orkney Field Club, Hon. Sec. Mrs C. Spence, Park
Cottage, Finstown.
Literature: Balfour, E., *Orkney Birds* (Stromness, 1972); 64
pp., 314 species.
Balfour, E., Breeding Birds of Orkney, *Scottish Birds*, **5**, p. 29
(1968).
Groundwater, W., *Birds and Mammals of Orkney.* 299 pp.
(Kirkwall, 1975).
Lack, D., Breeding Birds of Orkney, *Ibis*, **84**, 461; **85**, 1
(1942–3).
Lea, D. and Bourne, W. R. P., Birds of Orkney, *British
Birds*, **68**, 7 (1975).
Robertson, D. J., *Notes from a Bird Sanctuary* (Eynhallow), 65
pp. (Kirkwall, 1934).
Walker, K., *Island Saga—Story of North Ronaldsay* (Aberdeen,
M. A. Scott, 1967); 42 pp.
Orkney Bird Report, D. Lea, Easter Sower, Orphir KW17
2RE.

Check list
Nesters: Red-throated Diver, Little Grebe, (Slavonian
Grebe), Fulmar, Manx Shearwater, Storm Petrel, Gannet,
Cormorant, Shag, Heron, Mallard, Teal, Wigeon, Pintail,
Shoveler, Gadwall, Scaup, Tufted Duck, (Goldeneye),
Scoter, (Longtail), Eider, Red-breasted Merganser, Shel-
duck, Mute Swan, (Golden Eagle), Buzzard, Hen Harrier,
Peregrine, Merlin, Kestrel, Red Grouse, (Quail), Pheasant,
Corncrake, Moorhen, Coot, Oystercatcher, Lapwing,
Ringed Plover, Golden Plover, Snipe, Curlew, Whimbrel,
Black-tailed Godwit, Sandpiper, Redshank, Greenshank,

Dunlin, (Red-necked Phalarope), Great Skua, Arctic
Skua, Great Black-backed Gull, Lesser Black-backed Gull,
Herring Gull, Common Gull, Black-headed Gull, Kit-
tiwake, Common Tern, Arctic, Roseate, Sandwich, Razor-
bill, Guillemot, Black Guillemot, Puffin, Rockdove, Wood-
pigeon, Collared Dove, Cuckoo, Long-eared Owl, Short-
eared Owl, Skylark, Swallow, House Martin, (Sand Mar-
tin), Raven, Hoodie Crow, Rook, Jackdaw, (Great Tit),
(Tree Creeper), Wren, (Mistle Thrush), Fieldfare, Song
Thrush, (Redwing), Ring Ouzel, Blackbird, Wheatear,
Stonechat, Whinchat, (Redstart), (Black Redstart), Robin,
(Grasshopper Warbler), Sedge Warbler, (Whitethroat),
Willow Warbler, (Chiffchaff), Goldcrest, Spotted Flycat-
cher, Hedge Sparrow, Meadow Pipit, (Tree Pipit), Rock
Pipit, Pied Wagtail, (Grey Wagtail), Shetland Starling,
(Hawfinch), Greenfinch, (Siskin), Linnet, Twite, (Red-
poll), Chaffinch, Corn Bunting, Yellowhammer, Reed
Bunting, House Sparrow, Tree Sparrow.
   Water Rail, Little Tern, Dipper, Swift and Red-backed
Shrike may have nested.

Migratory and rare visitors: Flocks of Great Northern Divers,
Scaup and other sea duck characterise the bays. Autumnal
sea watches range from skuas and Sooty Shearwaters to a
Black-browed Albatross. Stray passage migrants have
included Icterine, Barred, Subalpine, Yellow-browed,
Lanceolated, Melodious and Arctic Warblers, Firecrest,
Red-breasted Flycatcher, Eastern Nightingale, White's
Thrush, Scops and Snowy Owls, Bluethroat, Scarlet
Grosbeak, Scarlet Rosefinch, White-rumped Swift, Little
Egret, Pine, Rustic and Black-headed Buntings, Goshawk,
Rough-legged Buzzard and Red-footed Falcon. Black and
White Storks, Great and Lesser Grey and Woodchat

Shrikes, Icelandic Black-tailed Godwits, Smews, Steller's Eider and Glaucous Gull are among visitors. American waders have included Dowitcher, Greater Yellowlegs, White-rumped and Western Sandpipers.

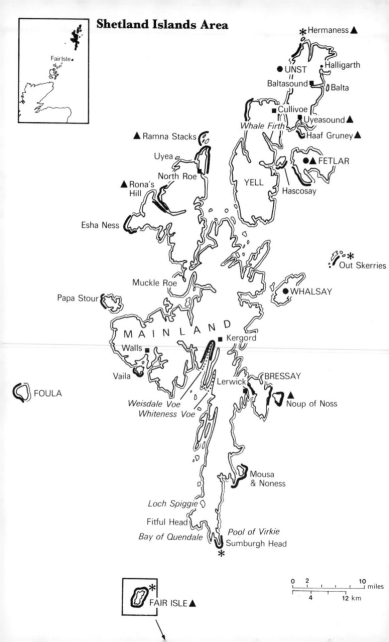

Chapter 13

Shetland Islands

Sixty miles (96 km) north of Orkney, the 117 Shetland islands (only twenty-nine of them inhabited), all with bays and bogs where duck and divers shelter in winter, bring an almost Scandinavian bird life into their 142,864 ha (352,876 acres). With coasts often rising sheer from the sea (Foula's cliffs tower precipitously to 1200 feet—360 m), only six degrees from the Arctic Circle, they harbour Britain's third largest seabird colonies, especially fulmars and great skuas. Calm weather is required to reach many islets without piers, but there are car ferries to Yell, Unst, Fetlar, Whalsay and Bressay, bridges connect Trandra and Barra to Mainland, and there is air transport from Aberdeen, Leith, Glasgow and Edinburgh. The highest hill, Rooness Hill on the north of Mainland, is only 1476 feet (443 m). Trees and hedgerows are absent (except woods at Hallgarth and Kergord); much of the ground is barren, or rugged, grassy peat except for some weather-bitten moutain ash or wild rose, some sheltered honey-suckle, and heather and crowberry moors and hills, with their wheatears, skylarks and meadow pipits. The midnight sun shows here on the longest day. With frequent lochs, voes and bays of eiders and mergansers, no part is more than 3 miles (5 km) from the sea. The lochs have bathing parties of skuas as well as the quavering blood-curdling calls of red-throated divers which ring like demoniac laughter through the summer night. Shags are commoner than cormorants along the coasts, which are shared by wrens and twites as well as rock pipits, snow buntings and purple sandpipers. Long-tailed duck summer on several waters, and curlew, mallard and common gull are more localised than in

Caithness and Sutherland; but there are five colonies of
red-necked phalaropes, nesting snowy owls, many whimbrel, arctic terns and arctic skuas (two-thirds dark) on the
moors of the northern isles. The darker, greyer Shetland
wren (misnamed 'robin') is typical near farms and villages,
except for the Skerries, and it migrates locally from Yell to
Unst. There are no little tern colonies, no nesting pochard
and the occasional cuckoo apparently has not been proved
to breed. Up to 22 per cent of the guillemots are bridled.
There are few kestrels because of few small mammals and
mostly only passing harriers and short-eared owls. The
scarce kingfisher is also only a migrant.

The general absence of chaffinch, robin, linnet, hedge
sparrow and yellowhammer is noticeable; but Shetland's
350,000 nesting seabirds have over 80 per cent of Britain's
great skua and whimbrel breeding populations, over 70 per
cent of the arctic skuas, 50 per cent of red-necked
phalaropes, 40 per cent of fulmars, 20–30 per cent of black
guillemots, arctic terns and shags, 10 per cent of puffins,
guillemots, red-throated divers, eiders, great black-backed
and common gulls and over 5 per cent of the gannets,
Leach's petrels, razorbills, kittiwakes and cormorants. It
has nearly half the northern hemisphere's great skuas.
Nesting fulmars include blue and white phases and the
large-billed *auduboni* race, comprising 117,000 of the
350,000 seabirds. They have occupied old raven nests.
White wagtails nest frequently. The Shetland wheatear has
a shorter wing than the slightly larger Faroe wheatear; the
Shetland starling is midway between the European and the
large Faroe race.

Two hundred and ten species recorded in 1974 included
a score of rarities. Winter flocks (or fleets) of up to 2000
long-tailed duck, 7800 eider, 300 whoopers (5–10 per cent

of the British winter population) and the main population of great northern divers are notable. Forty-six slavonian grebes have been counted in February and 23 glaucous gulls off Out Skerries in December. The rarer visitors are too extensive a list to mention more than a few: king and Steller's eiders, Hudsonian curlew (the American whimbrel), oven birds, Brunnich's guillemot, black-browed albatross, snowy owls (visiting seven islands at least), white-billed divers most winters, continental jackdaws, rare warblers, thrushes and October flocks of glaucous gulls, and occasional Ross's and ivory gulls. Shetland guillemots show more towards the dark underwing and flank-streaking of Faroese birds, which are winter visitors. By August the main exodus has left the massive seabird colonies and by November little auks become a common sight from the mailboats. Storm petrels nest on West Linga, Sandwick, Wetter and Hunder holms and on Fetlar. Glaucous and herring gulls hybridised in 1975–6 the first proof of a glaucous gull breeding in Britain.

It is peculiar that, apart from T. M. Fowler's 1926 claim in the Outer Hebrides (Frances Pitt, *Romance of Nature* (1937, p. 234), Shetland recently claimed Scotland's first nesting reed warblers. Its claim to the first British chestnut bunting, in 1974, like the ruddy duck at Unst, can best be relegated to the ever-growing list of escapees from captivity, probably miles away, and meaning less to the faunal history than even Mainland's introduced red grouse. There are four nesting sites of scoter, occasionally whoopers breed, also fieldfares (Mainland) and Faroe snipe, but cliff-nesting herons and house sparrows, and corncrakes, decline. The grey town of Lerwick is full of gulls when the fishing fleet returns, including Iceland and glaucous along the quaysides; but if you arrive hopeful of forgetting the collared dove's illiterate voice it will greet you in Lerwick, Scalloway and Unst. You can arrive by boat from Aberdeen or Kirkwall to Lerwick, or by air (except Sunday) to Sumburgh.

Mainland (Zetland): 33 miles (53 km) long, 99,040 ha (243,860 acres) in area, shaped like a jigsaw puzzle piece and with igneous and metamorphosed rocks rather than the sandstone of Orkney, this island has more rough grazing. Hotels are at Lerwick (whose harbour provides black guillemots, gannets and little auks, while glaucous and Iceland gulls visit the tip), Hillswick (by bus from Lerwick, with red-throated divers nesting on a loch, 1000 eiders with young in the bay, and gannets, shags, black guillemots, many fulmars, etc.), Scatsa and Scalloway (401391), the nesting haunt of red-throated divers, long-eared owls in heather, etc. Sumburgh Head (408077) at the southern tip, is reached by Loganair or Lerwick coach. 'The Roost' is the visitor's first sight of Mainland from an approaching boat, avoiding the roaring Fidal Current. Here nest 2920 pairs of fulmar, over 2000 guillemots (22 per cent bridled), 1400 kittiwakes, especially near the lighthouse, 1250 puffins, 360 razorbills, 500 shags, twenty-five black guillemot pairs, 200 pairs of lesser black-backed, also herring and common gulls, arctic and common terns, arctic and great skuas, red-necked phalaropes, red-throated divers, shelduck, mergansers and moorhen (lochs). On the east the Pool of Virkie attracts waders, like sanderling. Cory's and sooty shearwaters pass in August and September, 1500 moulting eiders may gather in September, icterine and Bonelli's warblers have been here on passage and winter brings barnacles and little auks. Castle Rock, an offshore stack, has auks, fulmars, etc. Waders visit nearby west of the Head, the Bay of

Quendale has summer great northern divers and long-tailed duck, with premigration flocks of up to twenty-eight of the former and 120 of the latter in April–May and over 600 moulting eider in August. Fitful Head, on the north side of the bay, has 8920 breeding fulmars, 1600 puffins, 840 kittiwakes, 600 guillemots, sixty razorbills, thirty-five pairs of black guillemots, fifty shags, and over 200 pairs of great black-backed gulls, as well as other birds. Loch of Spiggie, to the north at HU3717, is the freshwater black-headed gullery and breeding haunt of red-necked phalaropes, red-throated divers, black-headed gulls and great skuas, with

The Storm Petrel nests on the smaller northern isles

up to fifty long-tailed duck in May, winter duck, and up to
181 whoopers in November. Whiteness Voe (bay) in the
west is a haunt of great northern divers, skuas, swans,
waders and passerine migrants. Weisdale Valley and Voe,
just north, is the nesting haunt of duck, arctic and great
skuas, auks including black guillemots, kittiwakes, fulmars,
ravens, hoodies, divers, mergansers, eider, arctic and
common terns, sandpipers, wren, stonechat, white wagtails
and rarer birds. At the head of the valley, the 3·5 ha (9 acre)
Kergord Plantation has Britain's northernmost rookery and
winter roost, as well as long-eared owls, ravens, jackdaws,
occasional fieldfares, and chaffinches. In the northwest,
red-throated divers nest, and the headland lighthouse and
stacks of Esha Ness and Stennes are the breeding site of 4500
guillemots, 150 fulmars, great black-backed and herring
gulls, 3400 kittiwakes, 100 razorbills, and 400 puffins (at
Dore Holm). Ronas Hill and Voe, the 750 feet (225 m) cliff
National Nature Reserve via the A970 at the north
(HU3083), has great and arctic skuas, black guillemots,
razorbills and other seabirds along its 12 miles (20 km) of
coast, with an autumn passage of shearwaters and the
snowy owl among occasional visitors. The voe has red-
throated divers and is visited by great northern diver and
king eider. Two miles (3 km) north stand Ramna Stacks, an
RSPB reserve of eight small isles (thirteen rocks) with
fulmars, puffins, great black-backed and herring gulls,
cormorants, shags, kittiwakes, guillemots, etc., but no
normal access. Red-throated divers breed on North Roe
(Mainland) which also has skuas, seabirds, puffins and
rarer birds. The king eider is also a recent winter visitor to
Sullom Voe, which cuts deeply into the northeast. In the
southwest the Bridge of Walls at Sandness is a nesting haunt
of scoter, tufted duck and arctic tern. Arctic and great skuas

nest between Lerwick and Bigton. Puffins nest at the Nab, Corbie Geo, Sumburgh, Valley of Kame, Noups, Lyra Skerry and Vaila. Seabird colonies are also at Uyea (north), Braewick (northwest), Wats Ness and Westerwick (west), and No Ness (southeast).

Whimbrel, merlin and great skua nest on Mainland; fifty-six pairs of arctic skua nest between Lerwick and Bigton. Summer redwings and bramblings may be found, fieldfares have nested, lochs have scoters and red-throated divers, common gulls, arctic terns, tufted (Collaster and Ness Loch, Sandness), teal and shoveler (all three at Hillwell) near Spiggie. Around 1500–2000 long-tailed duck winter around Shetland. Girlsta (northeast) has special

Manx Shearwaters, breeders on lonely northern isles and passage-birds at sea-watch points

interests and arctic skuas, Gruitness has terns and Muckle Roe has cormorants. Flocks of up to 3000 moulting eider mark Salwick, and 124 long-tailed duck may be seen at Greengead. Thirty-one slavonian grebes have flocked at Tresta and Bixter Voes in February. Vaila in the southwest has large colonies of fulmar, guillemots, great blackbacks, with shags, kittiwakes, great and arctic skuas, razorbills, puffins, black guillemots and arctic terns. Dunrossness, Aithsting, Sandness, Melby, Jarlshof, Olna Firth, Mavis Grind, Sand Voe, and Lochs Hilwell and Girlsta are also bird haunts.

Bressay (495410): Boats approach Lerwick through Bressay Sound, marked by the sharp point of its Bard Head cormorant colony. One mile (1·6 km) east of Lerwick (440410) this rocky slate-quarried island, about 6 miles (9 km) long and 1½ (2·4 km) in breadth, has colonies with 3880 fulmars, 230 kittiwakes, 100 black guillemots, seventy puffins, ten pairs of razorbills, ninety-two pairs of great skua, eighteen of arctic, as well as 500 pairs of arctic tern, shags and peregrines. A woodchat visited it in June 1970.

Fair Isle and bird observatory (National Trust) (223725): Midway to Orkney, this is a National Trust property, 3 miles by 1½ (5 by 2·4 km); access is by air (Saturdays) May–September from Sumburgh, and by mail boat (Tuesdays and Fridays) via Grutness and Sumburgh (on Wednesdays, October–April). Its position makes it probably the greatest landfall and forward observation post of wind-drifted rarities, adding a score of new British bird records, with ninety-three species including White's thrush on one September day. An average of 214 species a year are ringed. Hostel bookings November–March (and prospectus) can be made through the Bird Observatory Trust, 21 Regent Terrace, Edinburgh EH7 5BT. April–October, to Fair Isle Bird Observatory, via Lerwick. Its cliffs and moors have 17,264 fulmars, 12,120 kittiwakes, 15,000 puffins, 180 arctic skuas, thirteen pairs of great skuas, 1530 shags, 1200 razorbills, 10,000 guillemots, 160 black guillemots, recently gannets, about fifty storm petrels (Fugli Stack, etc.), 450 pairs of Shetland wrens (mostly geos and beaches), peregrines (Sheep Craig and Keesta), eiders, corncrakes, rockdoves, common gulls, tree and house sparrows, oystercatchers, lapwings, ringed plovers, occasional cormorants, ravens (South Ramnigeo, Hoini, West Lotter), blackbirds, twites, pied wagtails, common terns and, in 1973, nesting whimbrel. Over thirty species nest. The main attraction is the great range of migratory visitors, varying from flocks of 2000 snow buntings in September and fifty glaucous gulls in January, to snowy owl, Icelandic water rail, Cory's and sooty shearwaters in autumn and a long list of rare waders (including North Americans), warblers, pipits, wagtails, buntings, thrushes, scarlet grosbeaks, etc., too numerous to give in full. Eastern nightingale and thrush nightingale, Cretzschmar's bunting, American hermit thrush, Steller's eider, gyr falcon, great bustard, collared pratincole, Hudsonian Whimbrel, gull-billed tern and little crake give some idea of the variety. Weather influences a bird week very much, e.g. the arrival of barred warblers and red-breasted flycatchers is associated with high temperature and light southwest or southeast winds in Germany. Scarlet grosbeaks are correlated with north or northeast winds in the North Sea and low temperature in Germany.

The first American myrtle warbler record was here in May 1977.

Fetlar (603917): Known as the 'Green Isle', Fetlar is reached via Yell and Lerwick by mail steamer. Its 4103 ha (10,135 acres) are the most fertile in the Shetlands. Its rugged high cliffs, seen on the east of Yell, and its fields with heather and grass moors have taken the fame from Unst since snowy owls returned to nest on Stakaberg Hill. The RSPB manages a 672 ha (1660 acres) wardened reserve with access restricted to an observation post. Here nest 13,000 fulmars, 700 pairs of kittiwakes, 750 of arctic tern, over 100 Manx shearwaters (East Neap and Lamb Hoga), fourteen storm petrels (East Neap, Sandwick, Watter, West Linga, and Hunda holms), 275 great skuas, 200 arctic skuas (Lamb Hoga Hill), 750 pairs of shag, 400 guillemots, 200 razorbills, 150 black guillemots, red-necked phalaropes at lochs and swampy, stony bogs, also red-throated diver, black-throated diver, whimbrel, many lapwings, two pairs of merlin, occasionally peregrines, corncrakes, wigeon, greater and lesser black-backs, common and a few black-headed gulls, curlew, dunlin, redshank, sandpiper, Faroe snipe, golden plover, Shetland wren and starling. Migratory visitors range from nightingale, red-flanked bluetail, lesser grey, woodchat and redbacked shrikes to bluethroat, American robin and icterine warbler, with up to twenty glaucous gulls in December, little auks in winter and sooty shearwaters in August and September. Between Fetlar, Yell and Unst in December, eiders total 5000 and long-tailed duck up to 230. Temminck's stint came in June 1975. Puffins also nest on Fetlar. In the absence of males, snowy owls did not breed in 1976–7 at Vord Hill reserve (615885).

Foula (395140): The sheer cliffs of this rock battleship face the Atlantic storms with the 1200 feet Kame in the north-west, Britain's second highest cliff, whitened by kittiwakes and guillemots. This most westerly Shetland isle is 16 miles (26 km) from Mainland and 35 miles (56 km) north of Orkney, with five peaks reaching 1373 feet (415 m) on Sneug and one valley. Often storm-bound, it is reached by boat from Scalloway or Walls, landing only at Ham Voe jetty. There is also an airstrip. Three and a half miles long (5.5 km), its 619 ha (4000 acres) reveal 176 species, including thirty-seven nesters. The latter include 1780 great skuas, which bathe in Mill Loch, 180 arctics, 1210 kittiwakes, 280 arctic terns, 530 razorbills (Muckleberry), sixty black guillemots, as well as Manx shearwaters, Leach's petrels and storm petrels (The Noup and South Biggins), many puffins (Gaada Stack, Swaa Head, Little Kame), guillemots (up to 30 per cent bridled), whimbrel, fulmars (light phase), ten pairs of red-throated divers, eider, teal, greater and lesser black-backed gulls, kittiwake and common gulls, 1700 arctic tern (Wurrno Bank), rockdove, corncrake, dunlin, snipe, oystercatcher, ringed plover, wren and skylark. Little auks are winter visitors, sooty shearwaters in autumn, and rarer migrants include barred warbler, American black-billed cuckoo and slate-coloured junco, as well as ruff and purple sandpiper.

Hascosay : Hardly over 260 ha (642 acres) between Yell and Fetlar, this little isle is the nesting haunt of black guillemots, great skuas, ten pairs of arctic skuas, occasional rarer birds also, arctic tern, ravens, eider, teal, occasional mergansers, fulmars, redshank, herring, lesser black-backed and common gulls and merlin.

Mousa (456245) : Stones of the prehistoric broch, marking the nesting haunts of fifteen pairs of great skua on this little island 11 miles (17 km) south of Lerwick, are seen on the left as boats approach Mainland. Over 1000 fulmars nest here and at No Ness, with three to four pairs of storm petrel, forty pairs of shags, six of arctic skua (village), 1000 kittiwakes, 600 guillemots, ninety-four black guillemots, seventy puffins, razorbills, 170 arctic terns, starlings, wrens, rockdoves, rock pipits and once fieldfares as well as rarer species. Parties of glaucous gulls come in November. *Warden*: Gunista, Bressay (tel: Bressay 217). Like Colsay island, Mousa is privately owned, with local permits from Bressay.

Muckle Flugga (608198) and Out Stacks: The rock lighthouse off the north was formerly stacked with puffins, kittiwakes, guillemots, black guillemots and rock pipits. Muckle Roe (west) and Muckle Holm by St Ninian's Isle (southwest) are cliff cormorant colonies.

Noss (NH5440): This small island of 313 ha (774 acres), 4 miles (6 km) east of Lerwick, is a Nature Conservancy reserve with spectacular 450 feet (135 m) seabird cliff scenery. Access is on Sundays and Mondays during May–August by boat from Bressay or Lerwick to Noss Sound, depending on calm weather. Four thousand three hundred gannets nest on The Noup, and there are also 2080 fulmars, 25,000 guillemots, 10,500 kittiwakes, 3100 razorbills, 1000 puffins, 140 shags, 220 pairs of great skua (moorland), forty pairs of arctic skua, fifty pairs of black guillemot, forty-five pairs of arctic and common terns, 240 great black-backed gulls, snipe, occasional white wagtails, lesser black-backed, herring and common gulls, Leach's and storm petrels (Noup), twelve to twenty pairs of rockdove, peregrines, teal, tufted duck, coot, ringed plover, rock pipit, twite, jackdaw (Noup), raven, corncrake, twelve pairs of wren, mallard, eiders (which flock under The Noup) and rarer species and there were formerly red-necked phalaropes. An American white-throated sparrow was among 1971 visitors.

Out Skerries : These are a group of three small, low-lying isles of 242 ha (600 acres), the highest rising to 170 feet with many stacks, holms and reefs with only thin soil and difficult to navigate. They lie northeast of Whalsay. There is a lighthouse on Bound Skerry on the east. Bruary is connected by a bridge to inhabited Housay, which has a good harbour. Gruney is the third island. Twenty-seven recorded nesting species include: storm petrel, 180 pairs of fulmar, fifteen of puffin, kittiwakes, 100 pairs of great skua, ninety pairs of black guillemot, twenty razorbill, common guillemots, 600 pairs of arctic and common terns, fifteen greater and lesser black-backs, ninety herring and twenty common gulls, fifteen rockdoves, oystercatchers and sixteen of starling. There are also eider, twite, wheatear, hoodie crow, rock pipit and occasionally swallow, blackbird, raven, lapwing and skylark. A cliff colony of house sparrows ceased recently. This easterly position brings the Skerries frequently into bird news with 160 species of chiefly Scandinavian migrants including recently: short-toed lark, red-throated pipit, bluethroat, ortolan, rustic and little buntings, tawny pipit, Scandinavian rock pipit, Siberian stonechat, red-flanked bluetail, scarlet rosefinch, arctic, greenish and other rare warblers, collared flycatcher, citrine wagtail, the first proven European ovenbird as well as American slate-coloured junco, bobolink, Hudsonian curlew and white-throated sparrow. Sooty shearwaters pass in autumn and little auk and king eider are winter visitors. Access is from Lerwick, on Thursdays.

Papa Stour : This seabird island off Sandness, to the west of the Shetland Mainland, has 1920 fulmars, 350 pairs of shag, twenty pairs of arctic and nine pairs of great skua, 2000 guillemots, 750 pairs of kittiwake, 100 puffins, fifty razorbills, and forty-five pairs of black guillemot, 1000 pairs of arctic tern and possibly storm petrels. The 393 pairs of great black-backed gull are less welcome predators.

Unst (594011): Reached by boat or Loganair from Lerwick, Unst is the northernmost island of Shetland, separated from Yell by narrow Bluemull Sound. Ten miles long by 3 miles wide (16 by 5 km), its 12,125 ha (29,950 acres) are mostly rocky moorland and bog, with freshwater lochans and their bathing parties of skuas and kittiwakes. There are cliffs, especially on the west. This island was once the most visited Shetland bird haunt. Crowning the Vallafield moor with 650 pairs of great skua (425 pairs nest elsewhere on Unst) and 130 pairs of arctic skua and merlin, the famous 960 ha (2383 acres) National Nature Reserve Hermaness head (601182) rises 657 feet (197 m) with its 500 feet (150 m) Neap, with public access to see 5900 gannets (HP6120-5912) and inaccessible Out Stacks, with the white stack of Muckle Flugga lighthouse beyond (613204). Here nest 16,000 fulmars (including the blue phase), kittiwakes, shags, razorbills, great and arctic skuas, guillemots (16 per cent bridled), 100 pairs of black guillemots, 21,000 puffins (The Moss), cormorants, kestrels, and possibly storm petrels. A black-browed albatross appeared off Hermaness about March from 1972 to 1975. Nearby, Saxa Head also has seabird colonies. Unst is the major haunt of arctic terns, with up to 1200 pairs, and with common terns, sixty-five pairs of whimbrel, forty-nine pairs of dunlin, fifty-eight pairs of golden plover, sixty-four pairs of ringed plover (including inland), and corncrakes, oystercatchers, common gulls, tufted duck, teal, eider, tree sparrows, house martins and reed buntings. Twenty-nine pairs of red-throated divers also fieldfares have nested, more welcome than its 354 pairs of predatory lesser black-backs. Occasional red-necked phalaropes, redwing (1974), black-tailed godwit and white wagtail nest. Hillsgarth plantation has nesting woodpigeons and summering redwings. In 1973, at Baltasound, it produced Scotland's first nesting reed warblers since the prewar Hebridean claim. One hundred and twenty pairs of black-headed gulls nest at Norwick. The freshwater Loch of Cliff has skuas, mergansers and sandpipers, etc and auks including occasional puffins occupy Burra Firth's cliffs. The little island of Uyea has 700 fulmars, 1000 guillemots, 450 kittiwakes, 2000 puffins, 100 pairs of razorbills and black guillemots, seventy shags, eighty arctic terns and a few great skuas. Peregrines nest. Its sheltered sound is a winter haven of whoopers (Eastern Loch) and their most northerly landing. Snow buntings sometimes summer on Moss, where January flocks reach 430. Long-tailed skuas may be seen in summer. The snowy owl is a visitor, a black-browed albatross was here in 1974, also a collared pratincole, occasionally a crane. Sooty shearwaters mark autumn sea watches and an American wigeon was recorded at Haroldswick in May 1973. Whoopers visit Uyea sound. Three miles southeast of Uyea sound, towards Fetlar, is the 18 ha (44 acre) uninhabited grassy isle of Haaf Gruney (HU6398), a National Nature Reserve with storm petrels nesting in mine workings, and fulmars and black guillemots elsewhere. A rough-legged buzzard visited Unst in March 1967. *Warden*: Sundraquoy, Uyeasound, Unst. Calm weather is necessary for landings.

Hermaness's single black-browed albatross since 1972 was nest-building in March 1977, and 1976, 'frustration' nests.

Whalsay: Accessible by boat or Loganair from Lerwick, Whalsay is situated off the east coast of Mainland. It has storm and Leach's petrels, fourteen pairs of red-throated divers, scoter, kittiwakes (Clett Head), whimbrel, occasional arctic skuas, arctic and Sandwich tern, razorbills, dunlin, merlin, golden plover, redshank, black-headed and common gulls, mallard and white wagtail among its nesters. Little stints are regular spring and autumn passage migrants, and a terek sandpiper was here in June 1975. Visitors include Bewick's swans, 120 little auks between here and the Out Skerries in January, Sabine's gull, flocks of up to fifty-eight longtails in March and rarities like red-footed falcon and red-rumped swallow, arctic, barred and thick-billed warblers, yellow-breasted bunting and American white-throated sparrow and pectoral sandpiper. Cormorants breed on the small Tain and Skaw Skerries towards Out Skerries.

Yell: The second largest island of the Shetlands, 17 miles by 6 (27 by 10 km), Yell is northeast of Mainland with hills, peat moor and seabird cliffs especially in the west; it is reached by boat from Lerwick and Mossbank, across the fast tides of Yell Sound. A guesthouse is at Couvafield, Mid Yell. Kittiwakes nest near the lighthouse, red-throated divers around the peaty lochs of Mid Yell and arctic and great skuas. There are also guillemots, black and common razorbills, puffins on Red Geo, storm petrels (Cuppaster), whimbrel with dunlin, mallard, hoodie, and eider, arctic and common tern (Loch of Lumbister, where arctic and great skuas nest on the nearby Alin Knowes ridge), scoter, occasional shoveler, golden plover and merlin. Faroe snipe, raven, curlew, eider and arctic skua nest at Mid Yell, there are black-headed and common gulls, arctic and great skuas on the northern ridge, eiders on inland rocks and peat, blackbirds, Shetland starlings in the pier, and in the past red-necked phalaropes. In April Colgrave Sound has had 1100 black guillemots and twenty-seven great northern divers; 100 little auks have been in Yell Sound in January. King eider, Ross's gull (October 1969), Bewick's swan, osprey and golden oriole are other visitors. Access via ferry, Mossland (Mainland from Lerwick). The main seabird colonies are at North Neaps, Birrier (east) and Burravoe (southeast).

Information
Recorders:
R. J. Tulloch, Lussetter House, Mid Yell. (Fair Isle) R. A. Broad, Bird Observatory, Fair Isle.
Society:
Shetland Bird Club, Hon. Sec. P. K. Kinnear, 2 Mounthooly Street, Lerwick, ZE1 0BJ.
Literature:
Tulloch, R. and Hunter, F., *Guide to Shetland Birds* (Lerwick, 1970); 64 pp.
Shetland Bird Club, *Shetland Bird Report*.
Venables, L. S. and U. M., *Birds and Mammals of Shetland* (Edinburgh, 1955).
Goodier, R. (ed.), The Natural Environment of Shetland, *Nature Conservancy Symposium* (Edinburgh, Nature Conservancy Council, 1974).
Jackson, E. E., Birds of Foula, *Scottish Birds*, Supp. (1966).
Fabritius, H. E., Notes on Birds of Foula, *Ardea*, **57,** 158 (1969).
Mitchell; D R., Birds of Unst, *Bird Notes*, **27** (1956).
Williamson, *Fair Isle and its Birds* (Edinburgh, 1965).
Yeates, G. K., *Bird Haunts in North Britain* (London, 1948).

Shetland Tourist Organisation, *Where to Stay in Shetland*.
Access: Central Shetland Tourist Organisation, Alexandra
Wharf, Lerwick (tel. 34). North of Scotland, Orkney and
Shetland Shipping Co., Matthews Quay, Aberdeen, run
boats twice weekly to Kirkwall and Lerwick, Grutness, etc.
Loganair (tel. Sumburgh 359, Kirkwall 3025, Aberdeen
Dyce 34441, Glasgow 041-889 3181) flights from Sum-
burgh to Lerwick, Whalsay, Fetlar and Unst.

Check list

Nesters: Red-throated Diver, Little Grebe, Fulmar, Manx
Shearwater, Storm Petrel, Leach's Petrel, Gannet, Cor-
morant, Shag, Heron, Mallard, Teal, Wigeon, (Pintail),
Shoveler, Tufted, Scoter, Velvet Scoter (1945), Eider,
Red-breasted Merganser, Shelduck, (Whooper), (Spar-
rowhawk), Peregrine, Merlin, Kestrel, Red Grouse,
(Pheasant), Corncrake, Moorhen, (Coot), Oystercatcher,
Lapwing, Ringed Plover, Golden Plover, Faroe Snipe,
(Woodcock), Curlew, Whimbrel, Icelandic Black-tailed
Godwit, Common Sandpiper, Redshank, (Greenshank),
Dunlin, Red-necked Phalarope, Great Skua, Arctic Skua,
Great Black-backed Gull, Lesser Black-backed Gull,
Herring Gull, Common Gull, Black-headed Gull, Kitti-
wake, Common Tern, Arctic Tern, (Sandwich Tern),
Razorbill, Guillemot, Black Guillemot, Puffin, (Stock-
dove), Rockdove, Woodpigeon, Collared Dove, Cuckoo,
Snowy Owl, Long-eared Owl, Skylark, Swallow, House
Martin, (Sand Martin), Raven, Hoodie Crow, Rook,
Jackdaw, (Tree Creeper), Shetland Wren, (Mistle
Thrush), Fieldfare, (Song Thrush), (Redwing), Black-
bird, Ring Ouzel, Wheatear, (Stonechat), (Whinchat),
(Redstart), (Robin), (Sedge Warbler), (Blackcap),
Whitethroat, (Willow Warbler), Goldcrest, (Spotted

Flycatcher), (Hedge Sparrow), Meadow Pipit, (Tree Pipit), Rock Pipit, Pied and White Wagtails, Shetland Starling, Twite, Redpoll, Chaffinch, Corn Bunting, Reed Bunting, House Sparrow, Tree Sparrow.

Quail, Spotted Crake, Swift, Wood-Warbler, Pied Flycatcher and Greenfinch may have bred.

Migratory and rarer visitors: Autumn passage of Great, Sooty and Cory's Shearwaters, and a rich range of Scandinavian and some North American passerines, European and North American waders. The continental birds, chiefly to the eastern islands, are a feature, with many additions to the British list. Summering Glaucous Gulls, Turnstones, Snow Buntings, Bramblings and Black-browed Albatross are noted and in winter Ivory, Sabine's and Ross's Gulls, King and Steller's Eiders and, before departure, spring concentrations of Little Auks, Great Northern and White-billed divers, Glaucous Gull, etc. Hen Harrier, Short-eared Owl, Swift and several Titmice and Warblers breeding elsewhere in Scotland are here known only as visitors. Waders have included Marsh Sandpiper, Avocet, Ruff with autumn flocks to eighty-four, Great Snipe, Hudsonian Curlew, Greater and Lesser Yellowlegs, Upland Sandpiper and Dowitcher. Flocks of sixteen Slavonian Grebes have been in estuaries in March. Northern Great Spotted Woodpecker, Great Grey, Lesser Grey and Woodchat Shrikes, Snowy Owl and Scandinavian Lesser Black-backed Gull are among winter visitors. Other visitors have included Quail, Gyr and Red-footed Falcons, Black Kite, Osprey, Pallid Harrier, Hoopoe, Bee Eater, Roller, Scarlet Grosbeak, Brünnich's Guillemot, Pied and Red-breasted Flycatchers, Red-flanked Bluetail, Icterine, Aquatic, Arctic, Dusky, Subalpine, Great Reed, Bonelli's, Barred and Greenish Warblers, Thrush Nightingale, Black-throated Thrush, Siberian Stonechat. Short-toed Lark, Parrot Crossbill, Scarlet Rosefinch, Yellow-breasted, Rustic, Little and Cretzschmar's Buntings, Rufous Turtle Dove, Tawny, Olive-backed and Pechora Pipits, Black-headed, Grey-headed and Citrine Wagtails, Woodchat and Lesser Grey Shrikes, Baltimore Oriole, Wilson's Phalarope, North American Laughing Gull and Black-billed Cuckoo. Occasional Rough-legged Buzzards may overwinter. A black-throated thrush, Scotland's third, visited Tolob in October 1974.

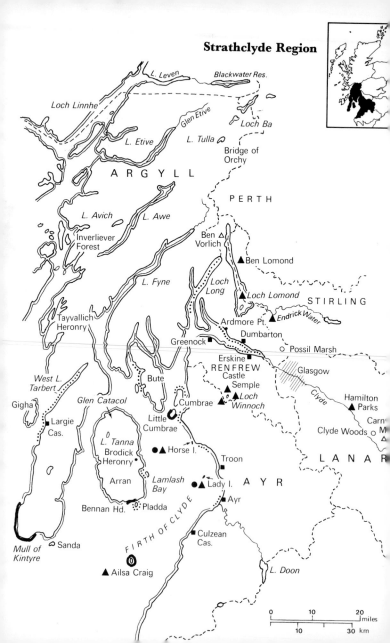

Strathclyde Region

Chapter 14

Strathclyde Region

Argyll (excluding Inner Hebrides)
This second largest district, with over 843,400 ha (2 million acres), includes four mountains over 3000 feet (900 m), with the southwest highlands, great arms of the sea like lochs Stuart, Linnhe, Leven, Etive, Fyne, Tarbert, Riddon, Storven and Long the haunt of divers, mergansers and eiders, several freshwater lakes with divers and goosanders, and boggy greenshank country, a stride from A82 car parks. Fifteen pairs of golden eagle in the south suffered recent failures due to sterile eggs or disturbance in their forests; twelve pairs hunt the north and the border area. Eight peregrine eyries are inland and coastal. Bastard Rock has kittiwakes. Forests harbour nesting siskins, capercaillie (Inchcailloch), black grouse (Garasdale, Dalmally, Inverliever), woodpeckers, buzzards and hen harriers, the latter including Tayvallich near Crinan, Lochgilphead, Kintyre, Connel forestry (northwest), Corrour and Knapdale. There are four colonies with fifty-two pairs of little tern, two sites of scoter, many hoodies, crossbills at Achnamara, Lochaber and Glanbranter, shovelers at Machrihanish, and the Irish dipper in Kintyre. I have watched house martins nesting on lonely Bridge of Orchy inn. Argyll's rocky lochs with low islets were once the western limit of mainland black-throated divers. Red-throated divers are fewer, though both nest in Corrour border forest. Black guillemots may be seen at Loch Linnhe, Lismore, Sanda (off Kintyre) and Pladda, ospreys summered recently, eagle and hen harrier, short-eared owl, crossbill, jay, magpie and the ubiquitous hoodie in Knapdale (north of Kintyre). Swifts breed in the north, kingfishers and

garden warblers in the mid south. Declining heronries mark
Coilessan, Ardentallan Park, Loch Feochan, Largie and
Torriedale castles (Kintyre), Rudh nan Daimh, lochs
Sween (Tayvallich) and Sunart, Rudh nan Eoin, Loch
Long and Tay Vallid. Loch Sunart (Rudha nan Eoin)
attracts waterfowl. Great crested grebes are only irregular
nesters on Loch Tulla, though recently visiting Goil.
Ptarmigan nest on Glencoe's Stob ban Ghabhar (3656
feet—1097 m) beside the A85, Ben Sturav, Ben Cruachan
(with golden plover), Clach Leathad (Black Mountain),
Beinn Trilleachan (Loch Etive), Beinn a' Bheithir (Bal-
lachullish), Arrochar Hills, Ben Arthur (Cobbler), Ben
Donich, Brack and an Lochair (Ardgoil), Ceann Gobh and
Beinn Bhuidhe (north of Loch Fyne), Garbh Bheinn
(Ardour), Ben Bhuiridh (2250 feet—675 m) Creagh Bheinn
and Fuar Bheinn, Ben Resipol (Ardnamurchan) and
Scarba. Ardnamurchan, the most westerly point, has
nesting eagles, peregrines and ravens. Japanese (green)
pheasants have been introduced by game preservers. Ben
Lui moor, Benmore Gardens (Dunoon) and Ariundle
oakwood interest us. Hebridean choughs sometimes visit
the Kintyre coast, and we have seen whoopers in June on
Loch Awe, Blackwater Reservoir and up Glen Etive. Wood
sandpipers are also seen sometimes in summer. In winter
come greylags, Greenland whitefronts (the mainland and
islands are a major haunt) and a few barnacles, with great
northern divers and duck in Oban Bay, 1150 moulting
mergansers at Tayinloan (July 1973) and the king eider a
modern visitor to Kintyre, Innellan, etc. Ivory gull,
laughing gull (Loch Skerrols 1974) and vagrant crested tits
have also been seen. Tides at Loch Long and east Loch
Tarbert are 5 minutes earlier than at Greenock, with spring
tides over 3 m; Oban is 5 hours 45 minutes later, with 4 m

springs. Campbeltown is 32 minutes earlier with 3 m springs. Oban is the main port for the outer isles. The whole Taynish peninsula with the largest native deciduous woodland in Scotland at Knapdale is a National Nature Reserve of 353 ha. Capercaillie nest at Inchcailloch and visit other forests. Crossbills nest in some conifer forests.

In a light snowstorm in mid May, I tramped from the A82 road across a well known greenshank moor and paused to watch a golden eagle overhead joined by a second in aerial display. A migrating pack of greylags dropped down towards the loch where I had been watching nesting black-throated divers, wigeon and mergansers. Suddenly the cock eagle came hurtling down through the geese like a thunderbolt.

Glencoe (180560, NN1358-1851): From Bridge of Orchy (298397) the A82 approaches Loch Tulla on the left, with a track beside its north bank, while the A8005 follows the southeast bank to Glen Orchy. At the far end I have seen goosanders, redshank, great crested grebe and reed bunting breeding and greenshank have been recorded nearby. The A82 continues north for 3 miles (5 km) to diver lochs, where I have seen nesting black-throated divers, great crested grebes, mergansers, wigeon, sandpipers and black-headed gulls, and, on the boggy moor at the head of a loch, greenshank, golden plover, dunlin and red grouse. It is a prodigious walk across the bog to Rannoch Moor on the Perthshire border, firmer for us in dry summers like that of 1975 than wet ones like that of 1973. Black-throated divers sometimes haunt huge Blackwater Reservoir. A National Trust area of 5180 ha (12,800 acres) includes the ptarmigan mountains of Buachaille and Etive Mor. Bird-watchers motoring non-stop through the glen on the A82, eager to reach Fort William and Ben Nevis eagles, overlook birds frequently overhead from Glen Etive. Etive's 3602 feet (1081 m) Clach Leathad also has these rock grouse. There are buzzards and ravens, peregrines and ptarmigan (on Meall a Bhuriridh). Ptarmigan chicks were also recorded on the north spur of Sgorr Dhearg in Glenduror Forest above South Ballachulish (062590) and peregrines above the Pass, but climbers often disturb them. An information centre is at the north end of the Pass. A dead end road leads up Glen Etive. Tidal west Loch Etive is approached from Loch Aweside.

Loch Awe: This freshwater loch is 22 miles (35 km) long and 1 mile (1·6 km) wide, with islands. It has mergansers, ringed plovers, oystercatchers, grey wagtails, regular divers, teal, wigeon, goosanders and, among the wooded northern banks, wood warblers, tree pipits, tree sparrows, and grey crows. I have seen siskins visiting conifers in the garden of Loch Awe House, the HF centre where woodcock rode at dusk. Lochans cupped in hills have red- and black-throated divers and other waterfowl. I found only golden plover on Ben Cruachan (207730), and I saw black grouse in Longworth Moor pines, between Tyndrum (338302) and Dalmally (161271), and occasionally buzzard and visiting caper. The National Nature Reserve of Glen Nant, a mixed deciduous woodcock, blackcock and buzzard wood of 42 ha (104 acres) lies alongside the B845 and its stream to the far Bailey Bridge car park (and forest road), reached via the A85 from Lochawe to Taynuilt (where I listened daily to a corncrake creaking, not in the corn, but in the usual hay). This is the roadside part of Inverliever Forest where pied flycatchers nest and twice I heard the green woodpecker's mirthful, lunatic laugh (as well as the great spotted), a newcomer to Argyll in its modern increase over western Scotland. Tree pipits and redstarts gladdened these woods, with bullfinches, jays, siskins, goldcrests, tree creepers, long-tailed tits and garden warblers. I found only goosanders at Loch Tromleg. Further south one leaves the B845 at Kilchrenan for the west loch-side road to Inverinan Forest (979127) with a misleading 'Osprey Point' at Dalavich, marking a historic nineteenth century eyrie. A mile before this, one turns right at the Lodge fork (Barmaline car park) to come out at the head of Loch Avich and its forest walk. Blackcock, hen harriers, buzzards, sparrowhawks and short-eared owls

The Ptarmigan, here on a clutch of seven in June snow, nests on mountain heights progressively lower further north

edge the forest. A golden eagle may sometimes be seen according to wind and season, but crossbills, depicted in the Forest Guide, are autumn visitors. Female capercaillie are seen occasionally. First morning light is always the best time for forest bird-watching, especially for blackcock. A forest walk begins at Inverinan House. Whinchats and golden plover mark hill walks to the diver and wader lochs. Glen (Strath) Orchy's riverside (B8074 from Dalmally to Bridge of Orchy) reveals nesting goosanders, dippers, teal, oystercatchers, redshank and sandpipers skimming the water, and its ancient Scots pines are worth looking over. Peregrines and eagles also nest. At one forestry village I visit a hen capercaillie comes each morning at 7 or 8 am to the village school to be fed.

Loch Etive: The A85 from Aweside leads north to Taynuilt and this long sea loch. At Bonawe ferry car park one is usually met by a reception committee of Roman-nosed eiders and sleek, diving mergansers, creaking cries of terns, and a few tatty black hags of cormorants. Here an arctic skua hunted above me in summer. Along the southwest stream's bank thickets I found sedge warblers, blackcaps, stonechats and sand martins nesting. Goosanders, tree creepers and long-tailed tits bred along the River Awe. I saw a great northern diver in summer plumage below Dunstaffnage Castle in May 1976. Though the eagle (larger than a raven) flies sometimes above the head of Loch Etive, a mistaken buzzard (less than a raven's length) often satisfies the ferry trippers. Regarding other sea lochs, arctic terns and common gulls nest along the stony shores of Loch Linnhe where one may also see shags, black guillemots (nesting Lismore island, Creag, Pladda) and even great northern divers in summer. Doire Donn, near Ardgour, is a

The Loch Ness monster? Shag calling when surfacing wet with crest depressed. Below, on nest

Scottish Wildlife Trust reserve. Cormorants nest on Loch
Fyne's Eilean Buidhe while the 10 miles (16 km) of West
Loch Tarbert, opposite Kintyre, produce flocks of mergansers and goldeneye in winter, flocks of whitefronts opposite
Ghiga and barnacles in spring. I soon began seeing black
guillemots on my way to Jura and Islay. Great northern
diver, slavonian grebe, velvet scoter, long-tailed duck and
eider also visit it. Further up the west coast lochs Sween
(with Tayvallich heronry and boat to Fairy Isles' duck
haunts, also breeding eiders in Sween, Linne Mhuirich and
na Cille) and Sunart are worth visiting, the latter area with
crossbills nesting in the forest sides. Loch Riddon (A886
from Loch Fyne, opposite Bute) has Sandwich terns and in
April 1973 an American dowitcher was recorded here.
Forty-nine species nest on Lunga Island, off Luing.

Kintyre: This 810 ha (2000 acres) peninsula pointing to
Ireland (and with Irish dippers) from the isthmus of
Tarbert (865686) to the Mull of Kintyre is 40 miles (64 km)
long and averages 7 miles (11 km) wide, mostly moor and
coast with nesting eagles, hen harriers (Knapdale), peregrines, black grouse, redpolls, redstarts, tree pipits,
blackcaps and goldcrests, and shags on its islets. Sanda
island, southeast of the Mull, is about $1\frac{1}{2}$ miles long and has
up to 100 pairs of black guillemots as well as puffins and
kittiwakes. Rockdoves nest on Ghiga Island, Greenland
whitefronts visit Campbeltown airfield and opposite Ghiga
(A83), where greylags and barnacles are also winter
visitors. Choughs sometimes visit the coast from either
Islay or Rathlin (Ireland) and the king eider has
been a recent December visitor to Clachan. Three forest
trails and a heronry are near Torriesdale Castle (with
Forest Walk at NR800382), Carridale (B842/879 junction)

in the southeast. Another heronry is at Largie Castle (A83, Tayinloan, opposite Ghiga). Ghiga is listed with the Inner Hebrides. Ten miles (16 km) of West Loch Tarbert are the winter haunt of great northern diver, slavonian grebe, longtail and velvet scoter duck, whitefronts and, in spring, barnacle geese at the loch mouth. The A83 gives access (and bus from Glasgow), or boat from Gourock to Tarbert. The coast by the A83 from Tayinloan north is a winter haunt of divers, grebes, scoters and whitefronted and greylag geese.

At Carradale Point off the B879 in Kintyre, the headland and a small island comprise a 70 ha (173 acre) public reserve of the SWT, with rocky cliffs overlooking Kilbrannan Sound. Its seabird watch includes passing gannets, mergansers and eiders. Access is by a southerly track from the road midway between Carradale Mains and Carradale village. Cars are left near Carradale beach.

Argyll National Forest Park (Loch Eck): 24,292 ha (60,000 acres) of rugged hills and sea lochs from Argarten to the east shore of Lomond, with eagles, ring ouzels, dippers, long-eared owls, golden plover, grey wagtails, etc. Forest walks include several from Benmore in the south (NS145845), 1½ miles (2·4 km) south of Loch Eck on the A815 Strachur to Dunoon road, Glenbranter village in the northwest (NS123976) 15 miles north of Dunoon on the A815, and at Ballemeanoch (NN106006) on the by-road 1 mile (1·6 km) southeast of Strachur. Other forest walks start at 2 miles (3 kms) northeast of South Ballachullish on the A82 Glencoe road, in Knapdale (NR790910) via the A816 from Lochgilphead for B841 at Cairnbaan then south on the B8025 at Bellanoch, and on the by-road continuing the A886 (NR000753) for 3 miles (5 km) north of the common gullery at Tighnabruaich up the Kyles of Bute. Tighnabruaich has a wildlife centre and hides. Black Mount, Ardgour, has ancient Scots pines of interest to birds. Cory's shearwater was off Machrihanish in August 1975. The coastal strip north of Tayinloan is visited by many white-fronted geese, finches and other winter birds.

Information
Recorder: M. J. P. Gregory, Duiletter, Kilmory Road, Lochgilphead, PA31 8NL.

Society: Mid-Argyll, Kintyre and Islay Tourist Association, Campbeltown.
Literature:
Forestry Commission, *Guide to Argyll Forest Park* (HMSO).
Scottish Centre for Ornithology, *Check List of Birds of Argyll*.
Williamson, K., Breeding Birds in a Deciduous Wood in Mid-Argyll (Glen Nant), *Bird Study* (magazine), **21**, 29 (1974).

Ayrshire
Eighty miles (50 km) of the Clyde and North Channel coast vary the hilly and, in parts, industrialised areas of Ayr's 25,595 ha (735,262 acres) with waders and seafowl. Ailsa Craig is a famous oasis of seabirds in the busy shipping routes of the Firth of Clyde, while lesser in-shore islands struggle to save their terneries. Red- and black-throated divers, dotterel, inland peregrines, Irish dipper, (Glendipp and Ballantrae), yellow wagtails, sand martins, magpies and bullfinches in the north, twenty pairs of buzzard, five pairs of great crested grebe, and six to nine pairs of little tern at one site, are among breeding birds. Hen harriers nest in the south, peregrines and sparrowhawks in the centre and south, pied flycatchers and long-eared owls at Dalmelling-

ton, and willow tits there and at Stinchar valley, Ballantrae, Barassie and Skelmorlie. Occasional corncrake and quail breed, but herons (at Bargany, Brownmuir Beith and Kelburn Castle, Largs) are declining, whereas thriving herring gulls nest occasionally on buildings in Kilmarnock. As well as August–September waders, like curlew sandpipers (Barassie) in the estuaries like Irvine Flats and even near Prestwick, up to 500 ringed plover, and later on rocky parts of the coast, purple sandpipers, glaucous, Iceland and Scandinavian lesser black-backed gulls are annual visitors; greylags visit Loch Goosey and occasionally a few brent come. King eider (River Irvine) and snowy owl have been recent visitors, also the lesser yellowlegs at the Carse of Ardersier and a little bittern was at Calgean in March. Tides at Ayr and Troon are 20 minutes earlier than at Greenock, with 3 m springs. Kittiwakes nest on the southwest cliffs.

Ailsa Craig (NS0200, 202600): 10½ miles (16 km) from Girvan. Permits can be obtained from the Information Office, Town Hall, Girvan, or from the Marquis of Ailsa. Landing is on the south side, or there are non-landing cruises from Brodick (Arran), etc. There are precipitous 1100 feet (440 m) seabird cliffs on the west with 1000 gannets, northern and southern guillemots, black guillemots, razorbills, few puffins now, fulmars, kittiwakes, cormorants, twite, occasionally peregrine, greater and lesser black-backed and herring gulls.

Horse Island (NS2141, 314311): This 2 ha (5 acre) RSPB-managed, low, rocky island 1½ miles (2·4 km) off Ardrossan, has no normal access. Breeding birds include 300 common, 87–300 arctic, up to 120 Sandwich, and occasional (up to 22) roseate terns, with great and lesser black-backed, black-headed, common and herring gulls, eider, shelduck, oystercatcher, ringed plover and rock pipit. The terns have declined and gulls increased in recent years.

Lady Isle (NS2729): This local reserve (owned by J. M. McKellar) lies off the coast at Troon (OS232631). It is a small, grassy island formerly managed by the Scottish Society for the Protection of Wild Birds, with a declining ternery; formerly there were 400 pairs of roseates, also common, arctic (none in 1973) and Sandwich. Also there are shelduck, eider, oystercatcher, ringed plover and rock pipit. A king eider visited Troon in March 1973, and flocks of 3000 waders are on the Barassie Sands (north) side, November–March, where eight curlew sandpipers at a time are there in the August–September passage. Further north, the River Irvine estuary flats (A78) have January flocks of over 6000 waders, with a king eider recently among winter eider flocks. Stevenston, on the coast towards Saltcoats, is another wader haunt. At Prestwick, south of Troon, purple sandpipers reach seventy in May, and sixty-five at Turnbury Bay, on the A719 south of Ayr.

Girvan and Coast: Glaucous and Iceland gulls are winter visitors to Girvan and Ayr harbours. The southwest coast by the A77 further south, has up to three pairs of nesting little tern, thirty-five pairs of common tern, twenty pairs of arctic, fifteen pairs of ringed plover, also oystercatchers and fulmars, while nightjars breed in a nearby glen, and cormorants at Corrarie Point. Fulmars nest at Portencrosi and Dunure in the south. Late summer tides bring apparently moulting flocks of eiders and mergansers near Hunterston Sands. Maidens Harbour and Turnberry Point attract tidal waders, as Wemyss Bay (A78, north of Largs), Fairlie Flats (Hunterston Power Works), Dipple Shore at Girvan, with 2600 in April, Seamill (West Kilbride), Hunterston Sands (south of Fairlie) with 2790 in January. Irvine Meadows have 5000 February dunlin, curlew sandpipers in autumn and twenty breeding pairs of shelduck. Flocks of 150 twite have been at Turnberry, and Sabine's gull was at Largs in September 1972 and a king eider 1971–4. Wigeon and other duck, godwits, etc., may be seen north of Ardrossan. Barassie sand flats north of Troon are good for waders. Dipple shore near Girvan is good for waders and seabirds.

Little Cumbrae (152514): This 243 ha (700 acre) island, $1\frac{3}{4}$ miles by 1 mile (3 by 1·6 km), lies southwest of Fairlie (A78) and is more accessible from here than from Bute. Owned by Little Cumbrae Estates Ltd and Highland Engineering Ltd, it has guillemots, razorbills, great black-backed gulls, black grouse, wheatears, whinchats, rockdoves and occasionally other birds.

Loch Doon: This area of 507 ha (1500 acres), reached via Dalmellington on the A713, has five pairs of ringed plover and was visited by a snowy owl in June 1973. Nearby private Ness Glen (owner A. B. Gavin) has redstarts, pied and spotted flycatchers and willow tit. Doonfoot (Scour of Doon) just south of Ayr on the A719 has flocks of up to 3300 waders including up to forty-eight sanderling, a roost of 6000 common gulls and visiting water pipit. Goosanders nest at Bogton Loch, great crested grebes on Creoch, Fergus, Martnahan (B742, southeast of Ayr; private) and Loch of Lowes (New Cumnock), while Loch McCaterish (Carsphairn) has a black-headed gullery. Greylags visit

Mochrum Loch (A77, southwest Maybole) in March; water rails breed at nearby Trabboch Loch. Up to sixty-two whoopers visit Bogside in February. Other bird waters include Glenbuck Loch (reservoir) by the A70 on the eastern border past Muirkirk, Craigendunton, Camphill Reservoir by the A760 southeast of Largs and Martnaham Loch, Shankston. Blackcock lek near Patna.

Culzean Castle Country Park: These 226 ha (560 acres) of National Trust land can be reached via Girvan on the A77 north to the A719. Rocky shored Culzean Bay waders include purple sandpipers, and there are woods with nesting woodcock and siskins, a pond, and a nature trail. A little bittern was here in May 1973. Gadwall nested in 1974. Enterkin Wood, near Ayr, is a Scottish Wildlife Trust nesting site of redstarts, redpolls and warblers. Other 'bird walks' include the Archincruive Estate of the West of Scotland Agricultural College, Drumlanrig Castle (Duke of Buccleuch), and thousands of winter rooks roosting at Ailsa Hospital, Auchenleck House and Eglinton Park. Short-eared owls nest at Barr (on the B734 east of Girvan). Declining heronries are at Melburn Castle, Largs, and Barganny (Girvan). Stairaird Estate, near Mauchline (Lord Glenarthur) is a haunt of jays, woodpeckers, etc., by the River Ayr.

Information
Recorder:
Ian Gibson, Arcadia, The Glen, Howwood, Renfrewshire.
Society:
Ayr Branch, Scottish Ornithologists' Club, Hon. Sec. R. M. Ramage, 57B St Quivox Road, Prestwick, KA9 1JF.

Literature:
Gibson, J. A., Breeding Birds of Ailsa Craig, *Scottish Naturalist*, **63** (1951).
Hardy, E., Birdlife in the Western Highlands, *Scottish Field* (November 1972).
Paton R. E. and Pike O. G., *Birds of Ayrshire* (London, 1929).

Bute
Only a small part of the 56,450 ha (139,432 acres) of these islands is cultivated. The largest, the Isle of Arran, is the most interesting for bird-watchers. The 12,120 ha (30,000 acre) Island of Bute is 15 miles by 3½ miles (24 by 6 km), rising to 875 feet (263 m) at Kamas Hill, with several lakes, the largest, Loch Fad, being 2½ miles (4 km) long. Smaller islands are Inchmarnock (with fulmars on its west side) and Great Cumbrae, 3½ miles by 1 mile (6 by 1·6 km), in the Firth of Clyde, which was visited by a white-billed diver in 1973 and a king eider in June 1974, and has a backbone ridge of hills, and five bays and Eileans (islands). The Mull of Kintyre separates Bute from the Hebrides. Irish dippers breed at Ettrick Burn and on Arran, a few corncrakes still nest, and there are many eiders and mergansers and a few eagles, peregrines and hen harriers.

Arran (950370): In the Firth of Clyde, this 25 miles (40 km) long island of 42,839 ha (105,814 acres) has tourist car ferries from Ardrossan, Gourock and Fairlie to Brodick (014365) with its heronry in Markland Wood and a coast road (A841) whose bus service, mainly in the southern part, has its timetable delayed when the ferries arrive late. Northern mountains and wilder glens include Glen Catacol (A841 in the northwest) below Glen Diomhan National

Nature reserve (botanical), with nesting golden eagle and peregrines. Goatfell is reached via Brodick's Castle Woods. Loch Tanna has nesting common gulls, sandpipers and other species. I reached it over the private deer forest from the A841 at Dougrie Lodge and Glen Scaftigill in the west (with permission from the owner, Lady Boscover), through the boggy saddle between Beinn Bharrain and Sail Chalmadale when the genial weather late in May favoured me with nesting curlew, red grouse, golden plover, common gulls and hen harriers. Harriers also nest by a black-headed gullery, and there are red-throated divers on northern lochs. Goosander and merganser nest at Glen Iorsa and Loch Ranza. The top of Glen Sannox and Glen Iorsa the National Trust's 2618 feet (785 m) Cir Mhor has merlins, ravens and other species. The rolling heather-clad southern uplands and pastures, in contrast, are the haunt of stonechats, whinchats, woodcock, grasshopper warblers, barn owls, sparrowhawks, tree creepers, siskins, redstarts, grey wagtails, green woodpeckers, black grouse, hoodies, water rails, six pairs of nightjars (including Brodick), three pairs of kestrel, goldfinches and a few corncrakes (Lamlash). Each evening after dinner when staying at Altachorvie, the HF lodge on the north shore of Lamlash Bay (040305) in the east, the base for our bird studies which listed seventy-two nesting species, I stood at the door to watch the woodcock roding overhead. Eiders nested along the coast, mergansers in the Bay, ravens and other species on steep Holy Island (053309) off shore. I found a small heronry in a plantation behind the quay, while buzzards nested up Glenashdale, above Whiting Bay (048262), and like harriers, by inland plantations. Lamlash tides are 26 minutes earlier than at Greenock, with 3·2 m springs. The old wartime observation post at Largybeg Point at the south end of the Bay, is useful for observing the habits of the procession of gannets fishing the Firth from the distant white rock of Ailsa Craig. Within reach of the A841 along the south coast, merlin, buzzard and stonechat nest at Levencorroch. Another heronry is above Kilmorry while at Bennan Head I had to go along to Levencorroch before I could reach the bouldery shore and make a low-tide return, almost an obstacle event, to the Black Cave below. Fulmar, house martin and rockdove also nest on the Head, and the Hebridean rock pipit is a feature of this coast. Teal, shelduck and shoveler nest on Arran and up to 1000 greylags and Greenland whitefronts visit Whiting and Lamlash bays in winter. In the quiet of evening after the speedboats have finished, I have watched arctic skuas pursue common, arctic and Sandwich terns in Lamlash Bay, late in May. Ptarmigan were rarities on Caisteal Abhail in 1974.

Isle of Bute: Two hundred and fifty moulting mergansers mark the Kyles in August. Waders flock on the tides and greylags are winter visitors. About fifteen miles long with 875 feet Kames Hill, Bute has very mild winters. Red-throated divers nest, also rockdoves, nightjars, one pair of peregrines and one pair of hen harriers. The king eider has been a recent visitor at Rhubodach, etc., staying three years between here and Ayr. Up to 500 ringed plover winter here. A large winter rook roost is at Kerrycrusack Wood, Loch Ascog.

Information
Recorder:
Ian Gibson, Arcadia, The Glen, Howwood, Renfrewshire.

Literature:
Gibson, J. A., *The Birds of Arran* (Rothesay).
MacWilliam, J. M., *Birds of the Island of Bute*.
Bagenal, T. B., and Millar, R. H., List of the Birds of Great
Cumbrae, *Glasgow & West of Scotland Bird Bulletin*, **3** (1954).
Hardy, E., Birdwatching on Arran, *Birds Illustrated* (1963).

Dunbartonshire
Despite its lower industrial areas towards Glasgow much of
this district is mountainous country, up to 3000 feet
(900 m), which is enriched with eagles and a few ptarmigan
where the Leven meets the Clyde, extending to Loch
Lomond and its islands, and the Gareloch peninsula. It has
five pairs of hen harrier, green woodpeckers at Overtoun,
and pied flycatchers at Invernarnan, while along Clydeside
gather Scotland's third largest wader flocks. Black-headed
gulls nest in the Kilpatrick Hills. Along its Stirlingshire
border the Endrick Marshes of southeast Lomond attract
many waders, winter duck and greylags (which also visit
Wards Dam). Even in the industrial southeast Milngavie
reservoirs attract duck beside the A81. A few ptarmigan still
nest on Ben Vorlich, Ben Vane, the Arrochar Hills of
Beinne Inne, Beinn Narnain A'Chrois and Ben Arthur (the
Cobbler). Great crested grebes and pintail seem no longer
to nest at Boturich Castle (Lomond). The rough-legged
buzzard has been a spring visitor, and scoter still nest.

Inner Clyde: Wader flocks usually peak in January,
especially at Helensburgh, Rhu (Gareloch) and Ardmore
points, the latter a Scottish Wildlife Trust reserve by the
A814 north of Cardross, with knot, golden plover, shelduck,
wigeon, divers, grebes, and a heronry at Ardmore House.
Shelduck flocks reach 2330 at Cardross Point in February

and grebes also flock on the river. Up to 150 scaup flock off Helensburgh.

Loch Lomond : Despite the weekend pressure of tourists on the southern and western shores and the wooded islands of Torrinch, Inchlonaig, Inchconnachan, Inchmoan and Inchmurrin, visited by boats from Luss, there are occasionally common tern, oystercatcher, redshank, sandpiper, common gull, merganser, goosander, buzzard, woodcock, dipper, grey wagtail, wood warbler, redstart, peregrine and capercaillie nesting. Winter duck are always worth noting. I find fewer tourists north of Tarbet (315046) using the A82 up the western shore, though one turns off at Balloch on the south end for the A811 to the richer Stirlingshire corner. A winter rook roost is at Rossdhu House. *Warden :* Dubhaneil, Gartocharn, Alexandria; and The Boatyard, Balmaha (tel. 214). Whoopers sometimes visit the south end. Luss islands are owned by Sir Iver Colquahoun.

Loch Long : This narrow arm of the sea lying northeast from the Clyde to Arrochar (298044) is 16 miles (24 km) long, with the A814 along the eastern shore. Here I have seen shags, cormorants, mergansers, etc., as well as shore birds away from its industrial wharfs. Flocks of wigeon whistling with surprise and mallard mark it in winter with tufted duck but few pochard and goldeneye. The Argyll border mountains beyond Arrochar have golden eagles and there are ptarmigan on Vorlich, Narnain and the Cobbler,

Information
Recorder : Ian Gibson, Arcadia, The Glen, Howwood, Renfrewshire.

Literature: Clyde Area Bird Report.

Lanarkshire (Clydesdale)
This much populated and industrialised 228,537 ha
(564,284 acres) includes Glasgow, the largest city of
Scotland, with great spotted woodpeckers and blackcaps in
Linn Park, an avian slum of starling roosts, and suburban
magpies. However, mountains to 2000–3000 feet (600–900
m) of moors and sheep grazing mark wilder curlew country
above the popular wooded Falls of Clyde to Corehouse,
whose thin central valley, a haunt of yellow wagtails
(Carstairs) of largely southwestern distribution in Scotland,
is in marked contrast to the scummy scurge where industry
and housing vomit their sewage and an Iceland gull once
favoured Glasgow's riverside. The modern motorway has
reduced the wildfowl visiting Hamilton Parks bird sanctuary, but Possil Marsh and the reservoirs north of Glasgow
continue to attract waders and duck, with the little ringed
plover beginning its colonisation at the Renfrew border.
Greylags roost at the Haughs near Quothquan, at White
Loch (Carnwath) which numbers the lesser whitefront
among its recent visitors, Lenzie Loch and the Clyde floods
south of Libberton. Pinkfeet roost at Upper Cowgill and
Culter reservoir in the Lanark Hills and feed near the B7016
between Carnwath Moss and Biggar. Whooper swans visit
Glenbuck by the A70 east of Muirkirk. Pied flycatchers nest
in the south, green woodpeckers at East Kilbride and
kingfishers along the White Cart River where lesser
whitethroats are visitors. Sharp-tailed and solitary sandpipers have visited Lanark, and a spoonbill visited Douglas
Water in July 1973. Bothwell Bridge in modern times had
Scotland's largest heronry, beside the Clyde. Marsh Tits first
nested in 1974, at Langholm.

Possil Marsh and Loch (NS5771–5869) : This Scottish Society for the Protection of Wild Birds reserve between the A81 and the A879 to the north of Glasgow has seen better days. Once short-eared owl, divers and whoopers visited the loch. Its great crested grebes ceased nesting in recent years. In less than a decade breeding sites have been reduced from twelve to three sites: Woodend Loch, Gadloch where curlew sandpiper have been recorded on the Stirling border, and Hamilton Parks. Several waterfowl reservoirs surround Glasgow, especially Lenzie Loch 4 miles (6 km) northeast on the Dunbartonshire border, with its flocks of wigeon, teal and greylags, some waders and whoopers; there are pochard on Hogganfield Loch by the B808 and A80 junction, and tufted duck on Johnston, Drumpeller and Bishop lochs northwest of Coatbridge to the east. Balgray, Carmunnock and Rogerton reservoirs (Motherwell), Brother Loch and Dunwan Dam, southwest of Glasgow, are further waters to visit, chiefly in winter. Carnwath (crane) Loch in the southwest has a black-headed gullery. Also in the southeast is Biggar Common. An American least sandpiper visited Wilderness Sand Quarry, near Buchley Farm, Cadder (591722), in September 1965, a haunt of ruff, sandpipers, little stint and other passage waders.

Hamilton Low Parks and Reservoir: Strathclyde County Park reserve on the Hamilton and Kinneil Estates (NS7355) by the racecourse. Lying between the A723 and the A74, it is divided by the M74 motorway. Part is flooded by the Upper Clyde. It has nesting tufted duck, mallard, teal, great crested grebe, yellow wagtail and heron (Bothwell Bridge), and it is visited by waders (including grey phalarope, pectoral and curlew sandpipers, greenshank, ruff, spotted redshank, wigeon, teal, pintail, shoveler, goldeneye, pochard, etc.) (authority District Clerk). A winter rook roost is at Hamilton Palace. At certain times access to the park is restricted. The SWT has a reserve at Corehouse.

Information
Recorder: Ian Gibson, Arcadia, The Glen, Howwood, Renfrewshire.

Society: Glasgow Branch, Scottish Ornithologists' Club, Hon. Sec. Mrs I. T. Draper, Otter's Holt, 37 Dumbrock Road, Strathblane, G63 9DG.
Literature: Clyde Area Bird Report (Scottish Naturalist, 1955, etc.*).*

Renfrewshire
This 63,478 ha (156,785 acres) district of industrialised Clydeside varies from a hilly ring ouzel and raven southwest, whose lochs have grebes and Canada geese, to the 1200 feet (360 m) of the southeast coalfield. A few buzzards breed; it has twelve pairs of great crested grebes, six pairs of inland nesting ringed plover at Queenside Muir 1200 feet in the west, a pair of hen harriers with varied success, two pairs of red-throated divers, redstarts in Brisbane Glen, Irish dipper and, in 1956, black-necked grebes. Clyde mudflats from Gourock upriver attract wader flocks, where greenshank sometimes overwinter and yellow wagtails nest by its tributaries. Lesser blackbacks nest at North Kessock. The Wildlife Trust has Corehouse Estate. Blackcock lek at Kelly Glen.

Lochwinnoch: This is 159 ha (375 acres) of RSPB leased reserve by the A737 and the A760 Barr Loch and Aird

Meadows southwest of Paisley (492641–5835). A substantial wintering population of duck is visible from the roads, which includes wigeon, teal, goldeneye, tufted duck and mallard, with a few greylags and whoopers. A rook roost is at Castle Semple. Nesting birds include great crested grebes, sedge warblers, yellow wagtail, duck and a small heronry. There are also marshes and Aird Meadows. There is no normal access (warden). Loch Barr and meadows on south had a black-headed gullery, nesting water rail (drained), tufted duck, great crested grebe, and visiting wigeon, smew and whoopers. Other bird waters include Rowbank Reservoir, Loch Thom, south of Greenock, with nesting Canada geese, dunlin, 250 pairs of common gulls, and great black-backed gull in recent years. Loch Libo, a Scottish Wildlife Trust reserve of 18 ha (44 acres) in the south has nesting duck, great crested grebes and winter wildfowl. Grebes nest also on Harlaw Dam, and waterfowl visit Balgray reservoir, at Barrhead Dams, Stanley Dam (southeast of Paisley), Barcraig Dam, High Dam (in the south), Eaglesham and Dunwan Dams (south of the B764), Lochgoin in the southeast, Linn, Lyoncross, Ryat and Waulkmill dams.

Inner Clyde: At Langbank (on the A8), where the 4 m spring tides are 20 minutes later than at Greenock, waders flock on the mudflats. At Erskine Bridge above it (A726) over 5000 redshank have been counted in December. Curlew sandpiper are autumn visitors, even an October Leach's petrel was blown inland. Garden warbler and green woodpecker nest nearby. Up to twenty pairs of shelduck nest at Longhaugh Point nearby, where flocks have been recorded up to 1331 in July, and scaup flock in winter.

Loch Libo: An SWT reserve and an SSSI of 17·8 ha (44 acres), near Uplawmoor, by the A735 four miles from Barrhead. It comprises wood and marsh, a winter wildfowl haunt with tufted duck, pochard, wigeon and goldeneye. It has nesting little grebe, water rail, tufted duck, redshank, snipe, and common sandpiper.

Paisley Moss: Attracts autumn waders like green and curlew sandpipers and in May 1968 the little ringed plover came to Scotland this way. The bittern has also been a modern visitor.

Europe's first known American Cape May warbler sang at Paisley in June 1977.

Information
Recorder: Ian Gibson, Arcadia, The Glen, Howwood, Renfrewshire.

Society: Paisley Naturalists' Society, Paisley Museum.
Literature: Gibson, J. A. (ed.), *The Natural History of Renfrewshire* (Renfrewshire Natural History Society, Foremount House, Kilbarchan).
Gibson, J. A. (ed.), The Breeding Birds of Renfrewshire, *Glasgow & West of Scotland Bulletin,* **4** (1955).

Check list
Nesters: Black-throated Diver, Red-throated Diver, Great Crested Grebe, (Black-necked Grebe) (Slavonian Grebe), Little Grebe, Fulmar, Gannet, Cormorant, Shag, Heron, Mallard, Teal, Gadwall, Wigeon, (Pintail), Shoveler, Tufted Duck, Pochard, Scoter, Eider, Red-breasted Merganser, Goosander, Shelduck, Greylag, Canada Goose (Whooper), Mute Swan, Golden Eagle, Buzzard, Spar-

rowhawk, Hen Harrier, (Osprey), Peregrine, Merlin, Kestrel, Red Grouse, Ptarmigan, Black Grouse, Capercaillie, Partridge, (Quail), Pheasant, Japanese Pheasant, Water Rail, Corncrake, Moorhen, Coot, Oystercatcher, Lapwing, Ringed Plover, Golden Plover, Snipe, Woodcock, Curlew, Sandpiper, Redshank, Greenshank, Dunlin, Great Black-backed Gull, Lesser Black-backed Gull, Herring Gull, Common Gull, Black-headed Gull, Kittiwake, Common Tern, Arctic Tern, Little Tern, Sandwich Tern, Roseate Tern, Razorbill, Guillemot, Black Guillemot, Puffin, Stockdove, Rockdove, Woodpigeon, Collared Dove, Cuckoo, Barn Owl, Tawny Owl, Long-eared Owl, Short-eared Owl, Nightjar, Swift, Kingfisher, Green Woodpecker, Great Spotted Woodpecker, Skylark, Swallow, House Martin, Sand Martin, Raven, Carrion Crow, Hoodie Crow, Rook, Jackdaw, Magpie, Jay, Great Tit, Blue Tit, Coal Tit, (Crested Tit), Willow Tit, Long-tailed Tit, Tree Creeper, Wren, Dipper, Mistle Thrush, Song Thrush, Ring Ouzel, Blackbird. Wheatear, Stonechat, Whinchat, Redstart, Robin, Grasshopper Warbler, Sedge Warbler, Blackcap, Garden Warbler, Whitethroat, Willow Warbler, Chiffchaff, Wood Warbler, Goldcrest, Spotted Flycatcher, Pied Flycatcher, Hedge Sparrow, Meadow Pipit, Tree Pipit, Rock Pipit, Pied Wagtail, Grey Wagtail, Yellow Wagtail, Starling, Hawfinch, Greenfinch, Goldfinch, Siskin, Linnet, Twite, Redpoll, Bullfinch, Crossbill, Chaffinch, Corn Bunting, Yellowhammer, Reed Bunting, House Sparrow, Tree Sparrow.

Garganey, Little Ringed Plover, Dotterel, Wryneck and Lesser Whitethroat may also have nested.

Migratory and rare visitors: White-billed Diver, Great Northern Diver, Leach's Petrel, Greenland Whitefront,

Greylag, Pinkfooted Goose, Bean Goose, Barnacle Goose, Brent, Whooper, Velvet Scoter, Goldeneye, King Eider, Osprey, Curlew, Sandpiper, Green Sandpiper, Purple Sandpiper, Pectoral Sandpiper, Dowitcher, Lesser Yellowlegs, Buff-breasted Sandpiper, Red-necked Phalarope, Grey Phalarope, Glaucous Gull, Iceland Gull, Laughing Gull, Ivory Gull, Snowy Owl, Chough, Great Grey Shrike, Crested Tit, Water Pipit, Black-headed and Snow Buntings.

Chapter 15

Tayside Region

Angus

This county of 230,267 ha (568,750 acres) extends from the Braes of Angus and part of the Grampian highlands, with dotterels and eagles to the broad Strathmore and the Sidlaw Hills in the south. It borders the Firth of Tay, with the fertile Carse of Gowrie and the North Sea on the east. Pintail nest along the North and South Esks and green woodpeckers in their glens and in Glen Prosen. It has one colony of six pairs of little terns, while 200 common terns nest here and in neighbouring Kincardine. Occasional Sandwich and arctic terns also breed. Capercaillie nest in Glen Lethnot, Glen Esk and Fettercairn, Inshmaddie Forest, crossbills in Kinnaird Park, pochard at Duns Dish, Rossie Moor, shoveler at Duns Dish and Kinnordy and goosanders at Loch of Lintrathen (north). Peregrines have three eyries. Wigeon, gadwall and little grebe nest on lochs. Ptarmigan nest on Mount Keen and Braud Cairn, Tolmount-Glas Maol-Caenlochan, Ben Tirra and Clova (south Loch-nagar), Mount Battock, the Grampian–Aberdeenshire border, Broad Cairn, Carn Bannoch and Cairn of Claise, etc. Red-legged partridge have been introduced to Seafield Estate, Caller and Cortachy. There are black grouse, ravens, dotterel and eiders. Herring gulls nest on roofs in Dundee and Arbroath. Grey geese flock here in winter when 9360 greylags have been counted on the Kincardine border; flocks of velvet scoter and eider are then around. Autumn brings black terns, twenty-seven annual waders with the seventh largest Scottish flocks, including purple sandpipers on rocky parts; occasionally a rough-legged buzzard may overwinter, and the white-billed diver appears offshore. American dowitcher and Wilson's phalarope have been recent visitors. So has the scarlet rosefinch. Flocks of up to 160 little gulls gather in April and May in Taymouth off Broughty West Ferry, etc., and 250 in September. Many purple sandpipers, golden plover and turnstones winter on the rocky coast from Ferryden to Black Jack and from Ethiehaven to Carnoustie. A Kentish plover visited the mouth of Craigmill Burn in 1974.

Caenlochan: This National Nature Reserve on the Perth (Kirkmichael) and Aberdeen (Crathie and Braemar) border extends for 3640 ha (8991 acres) between Glen Clova (330774) and Glas Maol. Partly botanical, with nesting golden eagles and ptarmigan. A Nature Conservancy permit is required during late summer and autumn. Access is by the B955 from Kirriemuir to Glen Clova and Breadownie, then a path to Glen Doll and Glen Isla (Perthshire). There are nesting hen harriers, eagles, buzzards and dotterel above South Esk valley from Lochnagar range at Strathmore, and three hill paths across the glen to Deeside: (1) Capel Mounth, with Glen Doll at its west end, (2) Bachmagairn, and (3) to Braemar via Doll. Lower Clova has winter flocks of 200 twites. The Braes of Angus forest walk (NO285762) leads from the car park, Glen Doll Lodge Youth Hostel, via the B955 and by road 18 miles (29 km) northwest of Kirriemuir. The west part of Caenlochan is via the A93 Carnwell Road to Caenlochan Glen, or via Isla, Tulchan and Monega Hill and north paths from Glen Callater. There are also peregrine eyries, breeding ring ouzel, merlin, dunlin, raven, common gull, and in the Esk valley, breeding bullfinch and green woodpecker. Snow buntings are seen in summer.

Loch of Kinnordy, beside B951, 2 miles, 3·2 km, west of Kirriemuir. Drained to a waterfowl marsh with 80 ha reserve of RSPB.

Tay estuary : This shares with Fife large winter flocks of eider and tidal duck, waders, winter roosts of pinkfeet and greylags, especially 10 miles (16 km) from Broughty Ferry to Tayport (Fife), with eiders, and occasional Sandwich tern nesting at Barry Sands and Buddon Ness dunes, which were visited by bearded tits in the 1972 influx. The Dighty estuary at Monifieth, below Broughty Ferry (A930 from Dundee), has sanderling and other autumn waders, skuas (up to three pomerines, West Haven, July–October) and flocks of little gulls (250 at West Haven in September, 160 in May, and 158 at West Ferry, Broughty, in April and at Buddon Burn spring and autumn). Rafts of common and velvet scoters, mergansers, seaduck and divers are off Budden Ness in winter, as well as summer scoter flocks. Teal favour the upper estuary reed beds above Powgavie (Carse of Gowrie) and Invergowrie Bay. At Tay Bridge, Dundee (712574), the tide is 15 minutes later than at Leith, with 5·3 m springs, and at Tay River Bar 18 minutes later than at Leith with 5·2 m springs. Purple sandpipers, turnstones, rock pipits and eiders favour the shore rocks at Carnoustie, Easthaven and Usan. Lecturing in the YMCA at Dundee one year, I found a ready champion of its proximity to bird-watching in my chairman, then editor of the *Dundee Courier,* to which I contributed pre-war bird notes. It now has a flourishing bird club.

Arbroath Cliffs : Auchmithie, Gaylet Pot Cove, Prail Castle and Red Head have nesting kittiwakes, guillemots, razorbills, a few puffins, an old peregrine eyrie, cliff-nesting

house martins, fulmars and herring gulls. Red Head cliffs
lead into Lunan Bay, 8 miles (13 km) north of Arbroath on
the A92, with similar cliff birds, 100 velvet scoters in July,
autumn black terns from the beach, up to twenty arctic
skuas in August at Arbroath and an October peak in wader
flocks. Eiders nest on Boddin Point (north). The tide is 30
minutes earlier than at Leith.

Montrose Basin: The seventh largest wader flocks (16,000),
especially in February, and August gatherings of 160 moulting mute swans, plus 1000 winter greylags and pinkfeet
according to wildfowling disturbance, have long made this
a major bird haunt. Winter pintail, scaup and long-tailed
duck come here, 3000 wigeon in October, and among
autumn waders there are curlew sandpipers, grey plover,
spotted redshanks, knot, black and bar-tailed godwits,
especially at Scurdie Ness at the south entrance in
September, where moulting eider flocks gather. Waders
flock chiefly to the southern side (Mains of Usan). The tide
is 16 minutes earlier than at Leith, with 4·8 m springs.
About twenty-seven pairs of heron nest in North Dun
Wood, 4 miles (6 km) to the northwest. Duns Dish Loch, by
the South Esk, formerly had nesting wigeon and still has
pochard and shoveler, as well as wintering duck.

Scottish Wildlife Trust 760 ha (1800 acre) reserve. Over
10,000 terns concentrate here in late summer. Foreshore and
saltmarsh.

Loch of Lintrathan (285581): Reached by the B951 west of
Kirriemuir on the west border, this area has nesting great
crested grebes and tufted duck and up to 5000 mallard and
whoopers with a winter greylag roost. Its feeder, the Back
Water, is also interesting for birds. Great crested grebes nest

also on Balgavies (538509), 5 miles east of Forfar on the A932, which is visited by duck and a greylag roost, and on Forfar Loch, Glen Moy (445508). Black tern, tufted duck, whoopers, goosanders, greylag and pinkfoot also roost on Forfar Loch, and in September 1970 it was visited by Wilson's phalaropes. Great crested grebes also nest on Laird's Loch (occasionally with other birds) and Lochindore (which has a black-headed gullery) and long Rescobie Loch (510520), 3 miles (5 km) east of Forfar on the B9113 also has nesting great crested grebes, a greylag and pinkfoot roost, and visiting duck. Creighton is another southern winter duck water. Thriepley Loch (302383) also has nesting grebes and visiting tufted duck. Little gulls are passage migrants at these lochs and also at Rescobie Mill, a duck loch 10 miles (16 km) inland of Lunan Bay between the A932 and B9113 just beyond Balgavie. Loch Kinnordy (Kirriemuir) has a black-headed gullery, and Loch Balgavies (near Forfar), Craighton reservoir and Crombie Mill attract waterfowl. Autumn waders are good along the shore between Buddon Ness and Monifieth, Invergowrie to Kingoodie and Port Allen to Newburgh. See also Inchkeith, under Midlothian.

Balgavies Loch is a 74 acres, 29·9 ha reserve of the SWT beside the A932 road between Forfar and Friokeim. Extensive marshes together with nearby Rescobie Loch and Chapel Mains form an SSSI with nesting great crested grebe, sedge warbler and tufted duck. It is the winter haunt of six sorts of duck and a winter roost of pinkfoot geese.

Information
Recorder: G. M. Crighton, 23 Church Street, Brechin.
Society: Dundee Branch, Scottish Ornithologists' Club, Hon. Sec. Mrs A. Noltie, 14 Mentieth Street, Broughty Ferry, DD5 3EN.

Literature: Angus & South Kincardine Bird Report, *Angus Wildlife Review* (Dundee Museum).

Kinross

This small inland county of only 20,162 ha (49,812 acres) is a level plain enclosed by the Ochil Hills in the northwest, the Lomond Hills in the east and the Cleish Hills in the southwest. Loch Leven (not to be confused with Kinloch-leven on the west coast) makes the county one of the major bird touring centres, chiefly for its waterfowl and geese. It has the largest concentration of nesting duck in Britain. Fulmars nest 8 miles (13 km) inland on Benarty Crag, south

Pintail nest on Loch Leven and other waters

of Leven; herons nest at nearby East Brackley; pinkfeet also visit the River Leven and near the Great North Road, and rooks roost in winter at Barnhill, Powmill. Black and red grouse are on the Ochil foothills and Ledlanet Moor.

Loch Leven (160990) : This circular water, $8\frac{1}{2}$ miles (13·5 km) in circumference and about 1553 ha (5 square miles) in area, owes its immense waterfowl attraction to its unusual shallowness, especially on the eastern bank, with a prolific subaquatic flora providing their food. The total shore is 11 miles; there are seven islands and 51 ha (125 acres) of woodland. Public access is limited to three parts: (1) Burleigh Sands on the north shore, by the A911 from Milnathort to Lothries Bridge; (2) Kirkgate Park, below the A90 to Kinross (311702) on the west bank, with a ferry to Castle Island; (3) by the B9097, on the southern shore at Findale, below Vane Hill. The rest is a restricted national nature reserve, with a Nature Conservancy warden at Benarty, by Vane Farm. The southeast end is a 121 ha (298 acre) RSPB reserve at Vane Farm with a nature centre (closed Fridays and only open three days in winter). Controlled shooting is allowed during October–January. The largest island, St Serf's, 43 ha (105 acres), has Britain's biggest colony of tufted duck, over 600 nesting pairs, and 3000 winter visitors. There are also: 400–450 nesting mallard and 3000 in winter; twenty-five to forty breeding pairs and fifty winter gadwall; twenty–thirty breeding and 2000 winter wigeon; twenty pairs of breeding and 600 wintering shoveler; twenty pairs of breeding and 2000 wintering teal; fourteen breeding pairs of declining shelduck; mergansers in 1970; sometimes pochard and pintail; fifty pairs of common tern; 7500 pairs of increasing black-headed gulls; twenty-five pairs of mute swans, increasing to 600 in autumn; and nesting Canada geese, great crested grebes, coot, sedge warblers, reed buntings, sandpiper, oystercatcher, lapwing, curlew, ringed plover and occasional herring gulls. Short-eared owls, wheatears, stonechats, skylark, great spotted woodpecker, woodcock, willow warbler, tree sparrow, swallow and jackdaw are also on the list.

The area is equally important for autumn and winter visitors, with up to 8000–10,000 pinkfeet from late September to October, and again in spring, a winter roost of up to 5000 greylags on St Serf's sands, occasionally Greenland whitefronts, pale brents, barnacle, snow and

The Woodcock's breeding range has been extended by afforestation

Ross's geese (the latter two like the Canadas, escapees from duck zoos), and up to 400 whoopers, while its 10,000 duck include 600 pochard and twenty goosanders. Wigeon and pintail feed on barley stubble. Waders, especially when the water is low in autumn, exposing banks to the northeast of the island, include greenshank (which sometimes overwinter), curlew sandpiper, ruff, knot and grey plover. Autumn little gulls, black tern, visiting ring ouzel, barn owl and tree creeper, the osprey in August and an American wigeon once at the Leven mouth, as well as winter snow buntings, are also visitors.

Information
Recorder: Mrs B. H. Gray, Vane Farm Reserve, Kinross.
Literature: Allison, A. and Newton, I., Waterfowl at Loch Leven, *Proc. Royal Society of Ed.* (R), **74**, 568.
Campbell, R. G., Loch Leven, Kinross, *Wildfowl*, **21** (1970).

Perthshire
This centre of the country, varying from sixty highland Grampian mountains with eagles, dotterel, ptarmigan and diver lochs, down the Tay valley with Scotland's main population of great crested grebes, to estuarine geese and duck, is 673,963 ha (1,664,690 acres) in area. The countryside is well diversified, including Scotland's largest glen (the 32 miles (51 km) of Lyon) which lies below the 3984 feet (1196 m) of Ben Lawers (268739), whose southern slopes are a reserve and the Queen Elizabeth and other great forests, with hen harriers, capercaillie and black grouse. It has 12,955 ha (32,000 acres) of water, Scotland's longest river in the 120 mile (192 km) Tay, and seven lochs with great crested grebes, these and others with slavonians,

black-necks and ospreys. Even a breeding colony of
mandarins near Scone adds to the list. Nuthatches have
extended to Invergowrie and the north and capercaillie are
widespread: I found over a score of these great wood grouse
above Arbruchill Castle, at Clathnick and by the Melville
Monument above Comrie (771222). Osprey, pintail,
Scottish and common crossbills and spotted crake have also
nested at times.

Much of Flanders Moss with its lesser black-backed
gullery and a few herring gulls is in south Perthshire (see
under Stirlingshire).

Thirty-five pairs of golden eagle breed. There are three
nesting sites of redwings (north and south), one of snow
buntings, thirteen peregrine eyries, eighteen inland pairs
of ringed plovers, five pairs of black-throated divers, nine to
ten pairs of goldeneye, two or three sites of slavonian grebes
(Loch of Lowes). Also breeding are scoter (north), gadwall,
shelduck at Kingoodie, scaup, fieldfares (north), pied
flycatcher (Killiecrankie), Canada geese (Abercairney, in
the southwest, and Loch Mohalk), herons at Bridge of
Earn, Scottish crossbills (east) and forty pairs of introduced
red-legged partridge near Scone. Wood sandpiper and
Montagu's harrier have nested in the north. The major
Scottish greylag and pinkfeet flocks winter here, with
30,990 autumn greylags, at Comrie, Drumatherty Farm,
Spittalfield, Marshall's Farm, Dunning, at Auchterarder,
roosting at Glenfarg reservoir in the Ochils, Island Lochs,
Blairgowrie, Carsebrech, at head of Strathallan, Braco
(B8033), Monks Myre and Bloody Inches, lowlands of
Strathmore and Stormont Loch (with pinks in marsh fields
towards Marlee). A flock of 33,580 pinkfeet feeds on the
east and northeast harvest grain spills, visiting Dupplin
Loch ($56° 21'N$, $3° 34'W$) and Drummur, Wolfhill, above

Perth, Loch Matraick and Loch of Strathmore. Greylags roosting at Clunre and Blairg, Butterstone, Lowes and Craigleish, near Dunkeld, feed in the Isla valley. Escaped snow and blue geese sometimes mark these flocks and a few beans are seen in spring. Whoopers visit Loch Dochar in the east; autumn goosanders visit the Tay in Perth city, and nuthatches have been recorded at Invergowrie, and sixty curlew sandpipers where waders flock in the bay. Hoopoe, great grey shrike and bittern are also rarer visitors. Ptarmigan nest on the Grampians, Glas Maol and Cairnwell (east), above Loch Etricht (west), at the tops of Dalnaspidal, Dalnacardoch, Athol and Glen Shee, and at Schichallion, Carn Mairg, Talladh Bheithe Forest (north of Loch Rannoch) but are fewer in the south—Glen Lyon, Ben Lawers (via Lawers car park), Ben More-Stobian, Cruach Ardrain, Beinn Chabair (Callander), Ben Lui, Ben Oss and Beinn Dubhchraig (Tyndrum). The old pines of Glen Falloch, Tyndrum, Meggernie and Cairns (Glen Lyon) attract birds too.

Glen Lyon (732475): Thirty-two miles (51 km) long, with steeply wooded sides above the River Lyon's deep, rocky bed, Lyon is reached along the B846 from Loch Tummel or the by-road off the A827 by Loch Tay to Bridge of Lyon, to Loch Lyon, dammed at the top. Breeding blackcock have roadside leks between Bridge of Balgie and Loch Lyon, capers and crossbills are in Meggerine Wood (private Meggerine Castle), golden eagles nest and there are peregrines, ptarmigan (Carn Mairog, Meall nan Tarmachan, north of Loch Tay), ravens, etc. A field studies centre is at Garth (NN7574) reached by the B846 below Fortingal, and there are an information hut, car park and nature trail of the National Trust at 3984 feet (1196 m) Ben Lawers (636414) east of Killing on the A827 at Loch Tay.

The latter has several wooded islands at its eastern end; interesting birds including occasional wigeon and goosanders nest, also pied flycatchers (Drummond Hill, and Taymouth Castle, Kenmore). The latter (NO17423) has four forests trails in mixed woodland and larch, with capercaillie near the A82, 2 miles (3 km) west of Kenmore (NN765439) and on the north (1½ miles (2·4 km) west of Fortingal) and south sides of Drummond Hill.

Queen Elizabeth Forest: This covers 16,800 ha (60 square miles) around the Trossachs (495074) southwest of Perth, from Callander to the summits of Ben Lomond (3192 feet—958 m) and Venue (2386 feet—716 m) and the shores of lochs Lomond, Venachar, Drunkie and Ard and Chon with nesting haunts of mergansers, etc., by the B829 west of Aberfoyle. It includes Achray, Ard and Buchanan forests and has nesting black grouse, hen harrier, six peregrine eyries in the Trossachs, merlin, buzzard, sparrowhawk, long- and short-eared owls, woodcock, whinchat and redpoll, and is visited by eagles. Cobleland on the A81, 2 miles (3 km) south of Aberfoyle, has a camping site. The 1½ miles (2·4 km) Lake of Mentieth (584010) beside the A81 and the B8034 east of Aberfoyle is a winter roost for greylags, pinkfeet and gulls, is also visited by cormorants and whoopers, and has nesting great crested grebes, tufted duck, etc. In its private woods are capercaillie, herons and green woodpeckers. Lock Ard and nearby Achray and Rowardennan forests cover 19,028 ha (47,000 acres) west of Aberfoyle with forest walks at Cobleland (NS532987). Flanders Moss (550968) southeast of Mentieth off the B8034 (see under Stirlingshire) is 44 ha (110 acres) of Scottish Wildlife Trust reserve where greylags and pinkfeet roost, also duck and whoopers come here (and on Loch Rusk in the northeast). There is a black-headed gullery in the west. Much is still unclaimed and wet, other parts are afforested and are visited by hen harriers, great grey shrike, etc. Lake of Mentieth, once a major duck haunt, has declined from speedboat disturbance. The 48 ha (120 acre) Achray Forest (SSSI) includes lochs Venacher and Achray, with introduced greylags and visiting teal, tufted duck, goosander and whoopers. Buzzards breed there too. *Head Forester:* Queen Elizabeth Forest, via Aberfoyle.

Rannoch Moor (424578): This National Nature Reserve is on the south side of Loch Rannoch, 3 miles (5 km) from Kinloch Rannoch on the east (662588) on the B846, not to be confused with Rannoch Station on the west. The 5180 bleak and blasty hectares (12,799 acres) of bog on the Argyll border can also be approached from Kingshouse on the A82. It includes the Cairn Maog Schichallion, 3547 feet (1064 m) south of Kinloch, with ptarmigan. The Nature Conservancy reserve of 150 ha (3704 acres) in the northeast corner is mostly botanical. I have seen interesting birds on Loch Rannoch, Loch Ericht (northwest) and Loch Laidon (Argyll border towards Loch Ba). In June 1972 I found green sandpipers at 1300 feet (390 m) between Rannoch and Corrour, lapwings breeding at Corrour (1300 feet—390 m) and oystercatchers at Tulloch. Dunalaster reservoir and marshes, towards Tummel, have nesting snipe, redshank, greenshank, curlew, mallard, wigeon, teal, tufted duck, pochard and occasional goosander. They are visited by waders and duck. Black Woods on the south side of Loch Rannoch have nesting capercaillie and crossbills. Dunalaster Woods (B846) are interesting. To the east Strath Tummel Forest has four forest walks (NN863598–852602) with capercaillie at first light, or dusk. Four Ailean Forest trails from Queen's View (of Loch Tummel) car park are reached via Killiecrankie, 3 miles (5 km) north of Pitlochry, then 3 miles (5 km) west on the B8019. Capers nest at Pitlochry (941581), east of Glen Tummel on the A9 and A924. Glen Fircastle has black grouse, buzzards and green woodpeckers. A summer and winter chairlift at Glen Shee ascends Cairnwell Mountain. Ben Vrackie Mountain, and 20 ha (50 acres) of river oak and birch in the wooded Killiecrankie Pass lie just north of Pitlochry, with redstarts, wood warblers and green woodpeckers. Loch Kinnardochy by the B846, south of Tummel, is worth visiting. Aberfeldy (855491), east of Kenmore on the A827, has capers (Bolfraks) and grey wagtails nesting. Blair Atholl, north of Pitlochry, is near Ben y Gloe Forest. Dunkeld (027424), south of Pitlochry on the A9, has goosanders; Murthly Mill Dam (south), has waterfowl; a forest walk is at NO018422 and the National Trust Hermitage conifer wood has a trail with capercaillie, siskins, green woodpeckers, Scottish crossbills and redpolls. By the A923 Blairgowrie road, the Scottish Wildlife Trust's Loch of Lowes frequently has nesting ospreys, capercaillie, slavonian and great crested grebes, Canada geese, herons and winter greylags. Grebes and ospreys have nested also on nearby Craiglush. Blairgowrie has nesting great crested grebes and winter geese on White Loch, Marlee and Drumellie near the A923, another loch has nesting great crested and black-necked grebes, pintail and roosting greylags. Loch Clunie, further along the A923, also has nesting great crested grebes and a winter greylag roost. Kindrogen (051623) in Strathardle, 16 miles (26 km) north of Blairgowrie at Enochdhu, has a field studies centre with coniferous and deciduous woods in the Strath (NJ055630), winter greylags and a car park by the A924. Dunkeld, where the Tay enters the lowlands in the great sandstone vale of Strathmore, is a good bird-watching centre. Hawfinches and green woodpeckers nest in the Tayside woods at Scone Palace park, downriver. Strathbraan, or bran, which enters the Tay at Dunkeld, is a good bird haunt from the A822 at Rumbling Bridge, Trochrie, up to Amulree, with green and great spotted woodpeckers, tree creepers, redstarts, woodcock, siskins, black-headed gulls, curlew, golden plover, snipe, redshank, sandpipers, dippers, goosanders, black grouse, buzzard, corncrake, etc. Hen harriers and short-eared owls nest on certain moors.

Crieff (866215): has nesting golden eagle, ptarmigan and dotterel (2000 feet (600 m) on certain heights). Capercaillie are in the forests. Drummond Loch (west) has a greylag roost and Dapplin Pool, by the A9 towards Perth, a pinkfoot roost, these geese feeding between Methven and Crieff. In this Strathearn lowland, greylags roost at Innerdunning, Dalreoch, Netherfordum and Pitcairn Loch.

Taymouth (north bank) (see also under Angus): Five thousand pinkfeet and 2000 greylags feed on the Carse of Gowrie pastures, and roost on Mugdrum Island in the Firth. Passage migrants and winter passerines visit Invergowrie Bay and Inchyra reed beds.

Lochs: In addition to the waters mentioned, great crested grebes and other aquatic birds breed on lochs Balloch, Butterstone and Caresbreck by the railway near Blackford, by the A9 in the south, Pond of Drummond, Dupplin Loch, Monzievaird (Octertyre), Rae, Stave, Ordie and nearby Rutterston. Lochs Dochart (A85), Marlee, Murthly Mill Dam (with black-headed gulls, by the A9), Clunie

(Dunkeld), Glenfarg reservoir (A90) Blairgowrie Loch (southwest of Blairgowrie), Drumellie and Stormont are also good waters. Loch of Lowes, already mentioned, has several pairs of grasshopper warblers as well as nesting teal, tufted duck, summering water rail, green woodpecker, and goldeneye. It has a variety of winter duck as well as grebes and there are capercaillie north of Craiglush.

Information
Recorder: R. L. McMillan, 44 Durley Dene Crescent, Kintillo, Bridge of Earn.
Society: Perthshire Society of Natural Science.
Literature: Perthshire Bird Report.
Forestry Commission, *Queen Elizabeth Forest Guide* (HMSO, 1954).

Check list
Nesters: Black-throated Diver, Red-throated Diver, Great Crested Grebe, Slavonian Grebe, Black-necked Grebe, Little Grebe, Fulmar, Cormorant, Shag, Heron, Mallard, Teal, Gadwall, Wigeon, Pintail, Shoveler, (Mandarin), Scaup, Tufted Duck, Pochard, Scoter, Eider, Red-breasted Merganser, Goosander, Shelduck, (Greylag), Canada Goose, Mute Swan, Golden Eagle, Buzzard, Sparrowhawk, Hen Harrier, Osprey, Peregrine, Merlin, Kestrel, Red Grouse, Black Grouse, Ptarmigan, Capercaillie, Red-legged Partridge, Common Partridge, Quail, Pheasant, Water Rail, Corncrake, Spotted Crake, Moorhen, Coot, Oystercatcher, Lapwing, Ringed Plover, Golden Plover, Dotterel, Snipe, Woodcock, Curlew, Green Sandpiper, (Wood Sandpiper), Common Sandpiper, Redshank, Greenshank, Dunlin, (Great Black-backed Gull), Lesser Black-backed Gull, Herring Gull, Common Gull, Black-

headed Gull, Kittiwake, Common Tern, Arctic, Little, Roseate, Sandwich Tern, Razorbill, Guillemot, Puffin, Stockdove, Rockdove, Woodpigeon, Collared Dove, Cuckoo, Barn Owl, Long-eared Owl, Short-eared Owl, Tawny Owl, Swift, Kingfisher, Green Woodpecker, Great Spotted Woodpecker, Skylark, Swallow, House Martin, Sand Martin, Raven, Carrion Crow, Hoodie Crow, Rook, Jackdaw, Magpie, Jay, Great Tit, Blue Tit, Coal Tit, Long-tailed Tit, (Nuthatch), Tree Creeper, Wren, Dipper, Mistle Thrush, Fieldfare, Song Thrush, Redwing, Blackbird, Ring Ouzel, Wheatear, Stonechat, Whinchat, Redstart, Robin, Grasshopper Warbler, Sedge Warbler, Blackcap, Garden Warbler, Whitethroat, Willow Warbler, Chiffchaff, Wood Warbler, Goldcrest, Spotted Flycatcher, Pied Flycatcher, Hedge Sparrow, Meadow Pipit, Tree Pipit, Rock Pipit, Pied Wagtail, Grey Wagtail, Starling, Hawfinch, Greenfinch, Goldfinch, Siskin, Linnet, Twite, Redpoll, Bullfinch, Scottish Crossbill, Chaffinch, Corn Bunting, Yellowhammer, Reed Bunting, (Snow Bunting), House Sparrow, Tree Sparrow. Goshawk, Little Owl and Yellow Wagtail may also have nested.

Migratory and rarer visitors: Great Northern Diver, Greylag Goose, Pinkfoot Goose, Greenland Whitefronted Goose, Bean Goose, Brent Goose, Barnacle Goose, Velvet Scoter, Goldeneye, Whooper Swan, American Wigeon, Curlew Sandpiper, Spotted Redshank, Little Stint, Grey Plover, Bar-tailed Godwit, Black-tailed Godwit, Sanderling, Turnstone, Purple Sandpiper, Wilson's Phalarope, Little Auk, Arctic Skua, Great Skua, Pomarine Skua, Little Gull, Iceland Gull, Glaucous Gull, Black Tern, Bittern, Hoopoe, Great Grey Shrike, Waxwing, Crested Tit, Bearded Tit, Montagu's Harrier.

Western Isles

▲ North Rona

Butt of Lewis ✳
L. Stiapavat

Dell

✳ Flannans

Loch More Barvas

Loch Roag

Melbost Sands

LEWIS

Little Loch Roag

L. Branahuie

Stornaway

N O R

Husinsh Pt.

M I N C H

Shiants

Sound of Harris

HARRIS

← Rockall

Pabbay

← St. Kilda ▲ ✳

Griminish Point ✳

Newton Ferry

Haskeir

L. Scadavay

Loch Maddy

Balranald

NORTH UIST

L. Eport

▲ Monachs

L I T T L E

BENBECULA

M I N C H

L. Druidibeg

Vorran I.

SOUTH

L. Eynort

UIST

L. Hallam

L. Boisdale

Sound of Barra

Biruaslam

BARRA

Vatersay

Muldoanich

Lingay →

Sandray

Outer Heisker

Greanamul

Pabbay

Mingulay

Geirum Mor

Berneray

0	10	20	30	miles
10		40 km		

Chapter 16

Western Isles (Outer Hebrides)

The Island of Lewis and its extension Harris, and the Uists, 130 miles (208 km) from Barra Head to the Butt of Lewis, gale-swept from autumn to spring, stretch southwest–northeast. Separated from the Inner Hebrides by 12 miles (19 km) of the deep Minch, full of a concentration of common gulls in autumn when crossings reveal long-tailed skuas, Manx, sooty, Cory's and great shearwaters, Leach's petrels, gannets and other seabird movements; they lack the rich falls of Scandinavian passerines like the northeast isles. Isolated in the North Atlantic, St Kilda has the world's largest gannetry and Britain's tallest sea cliff and largest fulmar colony. Britain's major seabird colonies (especially gannets and puffins) are here. They are our major haunts of Greenland whitefronts and barnacles (2600 in spring). Occasionally small races of Canada geese appear which may be wild immigrants. Glaucous and Iceland gulls winter in Stornoway harbour, and its woods are the chief haunt of small passerines. Great seabird colonies, big autumn movements of shearwaters on northwest winds, summering turnstones, inland cormorant colonies, corncrakes, red-necked phalaropes, breeding Manx shearwaters and Leach's petrels, Irish dipper, Irish grouse, wild breeding greylags, twites nesting in Uist gorse bushes, occasional white wagtails and wintering Steller's eider, Lapland buntings and white-billed divers, are among many attractions. My memories of Lochmaddy still have black-throated divers flying humpbacked with duck-like quacks over the street rooftops between chimneys. Scotland suffers a confusion of duplicated place names. There are two Bernerays, one in the Sound of Harris and the other the southernmost of the string of eleven islets south of Barra, and two Pabbays in these areas. There are also two Borerays, one at St Kilda and the other in Sound of Harris. Another Oronsay is off North Uist, despite Colonsay's companion in the Inner Hebrides, while Barra Head is on the southern Berneray, not on Barra itself. Great skuas nest at Gress, North Tolsta and Loch Orasay. The Hebridean rock pipit of these Outer Isles is a darker-backed, paler buff-breasted coastal form of mountain water-pipit isolated after the last glacial period. The starlings are the Shetland race.

Benbecula (080853): The flattest of these islands, low, marshy, circular, 8 miles (13 km) across and full of lakelets and inlets, Benbecula is bridged to North and South Uists, where the channels dry out at low water. I failed to find any phalaropes here—only the typical Uist nesters: greylag, little grebe, moorhen, eider and shelduck (Cuinabunag on the west coast), Irish grouse, oystercatchers, snipe, dunlin, common gulls, rockdoves, sedge warblers, rock pipits and reed buntings. An occasional buzzard hunts overhead on its wide wings, and eagles nested formerly at Langness; but it has more migratory waders, occasionally Sabine's gull in winter, and here friends saw a white-winged black tern in full summer plumage late in May 1964. Loch Uskavagh and Bailivanish machair are visited by greylags and barnacles, occasionally whitefronts and whoopers, but less since the wartime airfield, now civilian and assuring speedy access from Glasgow and faster mail.

Barra (065800): This hilly island with a rocky coast of sea coves, 8 miles (13 km) by 2 to 5 miles (3–8 km) wide, lies to the south of South Uist. Access is by Loganair from Glasgow, or by boat from Mallaig to Castlebay (hotel) or from Oban, or by Uist fishermen. Here are nesting Hebridean wrens, fulmars, auks (guillemots, etc.), black- and red-throated divers, little terns and Irish dippers. Castlebay and North Bog moor are visited by duck, barnacle geese and a few brent and pinkfeet (Friday Island). Geese also visit Eriskay islet on the north and eleven more islets strung off the south coast, as well as the Sound (with 430 barnacles in March). Passerine migrations bring their 'falls'.

Berneray: This southernmost of the islets strung south of Barra, ending in Barra Head lighthouse, is beachless, duneless and without a valley. Its 600 feet (180 m) lighthouse cliff has nesting fulmars, 10,000 pairs of kittiwakes, shags, razorbills, guillemots (12 per cent bridled), puffins, storm petrels, a few arctic terns, snipe, rock and meadow pipits, great and lesser blackbacks, common gulls, oystercatchers, rockdoves, skylarks, wheat- ears, wrens, starlings and song thrushes. Barnacle geese winter from December. Sunday boats from Castle Bay, Barra.

Flannan Isles (073946; NA7246): These consist of seven uninhabited stacks in three groups, 17–20 miles (27–32 km) west of Lewis, with nesting Leach's petrels on Eilean Tighe, Eilean a'Ghobha, Eilean Mor, Roareim Soray, Sgeir Toman; storm petrels, fulmars, puffins, razorbills, guil- lemots, black guillemots, kittiwakes, greater black-backed and herring gulls, eiders, oystercatchers, shags, rock pipits and starlings. Lapland buntings are among visitors. Eilean Mor is 16 ha (39 acres) and has nesting puffins, guillemots, razorbills, fulmars, kittiwakes and shags. Eilean Tighe's Leach's petrels are at Geodh'an Truillich, also fulmars, puffins, razorbills, guillemots, kittiwakes, shags, eiders, inland herring and great black-backed gulls. Gannets began nesting here in 1969.

Harris (110895): The southern, more hilly, part of the island of Lewis is reached by sea from Skye (Uig) via Uist to Tarbert on the east (not to be confused with several mainland Tarberts). Morsgail Forest has nesting birds of interest. Other opportunities are at (Traigh Seilebost and Luskentyre estuaries in the west) (NG0798). Also nesting arctic skuas, black guillemots, kittiwakes (Husinsh point), and ptarmigan (Clisham of Harris). Grey wagtails have nested. Waders visit the northwest, winter flocks of wigeon and barnacles (from December) visit the islets, and sooty shearwater and spotted cuckoo have been recorded. Fifteen pairs of little tern nest in the Sound of Harris (south), which is visited by greylags, and also 600 barnacles from December to March (on islands of Shillay, Coppay, Ensay, Pabbay and Berneray), and flocks of up to 500 long-tailed duck. Black-throated divers, slavonian grebes and green-shanks also nest on Harris. A black-headed bunting visited Boreray in the Sound in 1970. Access is by boat from Leverburgh (Harris) to islands in the Sound, and from Lochmaddy (Uist).

Haskeir (Heiskir) (NF6182-5980): This rocky island northwest of North Uist (not to be confused with Outer Heskier, south of Barra) has nesting kittiwakes, auks, guillemots, razorbills and puffins (variable). Access is difficult.

Lewis ('The Lews') (139930): Largest and most northerly of the Outer Hebrides, 40 miles (64 km) long, the northern

extension of Harris, Lewis is reached via BEA to Stornoway
airport or boat from Mallaig and Kyle of Lochalsh. Mainly
flat peat bogs, indented with bays and very windy, it has
fifty pairs of arctic skuas, twelve pairs of great skuas, red-
and black-throated divers, greylags, merlin, peregrine,
golden eagle, whimbrel, greenshank nesting on most
moors, Irish dipper and grouse, Shetland starling, Hebridean wren, wigeon (Ness in the west), sandpiper, cliff
herons (Little Loch Roag, northwest), but apparently no
partridge or pheasants. Iceland and glaucous gulls winter in
Stornoway harbour where tides are 6 hours 20 minutes
earlier than at Glasgow with 4·3 m springs, and 4 hours later
than at Liverpool. Waders are also there. Apart from Glen
Valtos (Gallan Head), almost the only trees are Stornoway
Woods, with a 190 nest rookery (and roost), and nesting
great, coal, long-tailed and blue tits, tree creeper, robin,
mistle thrush, Hebridean song thrush, greenfinch,
chaffinch, willow warbler, chiffchaff, blackcap, goldcrest,
whitethroat, sedge warbler, spotted flycatcher, yellowhammer, long-eared owl, buzzard, tree sparrow, woodpigeon,
and collared dove. Melbost Sands in Broad Bay (northeast)
have nesting terns, passage waders and visiting duck, with
up to 500 longtails visiting the shallow bay and nearby Loch
Branaguie (October–May), as well as wigeon and whoopers, especially in southwest–northwest winds, and velvet
scoter off adjacent Eye Peninsula. The northern Butt of
Lewis (NB5166) to Borve, with nesting black guillemots,
kittiwakes and fulmars is also a sea watching point with
great and Cory's shearwaters. Kittiwakes also nest at Tolsta
Head (northeast) and Tiumpan Head (Eye Peninsula).
Port of Ness (east of the Butt) is another autumn sea watch
with passing gannets, Manx and sooty shearwaters, etc.
Skuas, red-throated divers, whimbrel and dunlin nest on

the moors. Grey wagtails have nested in the northeast. Loch
Stiapavat, near the Butt, has a black-headed gullery and
nesting coot and wigeon, visiting whoopers, duck, etc. Loch
Roag (southwest) has the Stack of Bearasay, only 200 yards
(180 m) long and 175 feet (53 m) at its highest, between
Old Hill island and the coast at the loch mouth. Steep cliffs
make the north and west impregnable, and only calm
weather without northwest winds makes possible the only
landing on the west side of the seapool gully of Stac an Tuill
on the more broken south coast. It has breeding Manx
shearwaters (possibly Leach's and storm petrels), fulmars,
shags, cormorants, black guillemots, herring gulls and rock
pipits. Pheasants have been introduced at Carloway and
Berneray island. Golden oriole and American white-rumped
sandpiper have also been recorded on Lewis in recent years.
In winter up to 500 longtail duck are with velvet scoter in
the north bay and up to fifteen great northern divers are
seen off the Breagh. Little auks, and 2600 barnacles are also
visitors, with mid-April marking the goose emigration. One
hundred and forty species were recorded by one observer in
1963–5 on Lewis. Heronries are at Balallan and Loch
Keose, on cliffs at Loch Roag and kittiwakes, etc. on
Scalpay island.

Mingulay: This little island lying south of Barra has a
valley, beach and dunes, and 700 feet (210 m) western
seabird cliffs at Bagh nah-Arineg and stacks of Anamull
with 3000 pairs of fulmar, 1200 of kittiwake, 3000 of
razorbill, 5000 guillemots (12 per cent bridled), and nesting
black guillemots, puffins, storm petrels, cormorants, greater
and lesser black-backed and herring gulls, peregrine,
rockdove, rock and meadow pipits, snipe, ringed plovers,
twite, skylarks, wheatears, wrens, starlings, song thrush,

oystercatcher, lapwing, hoodie, and visiting eagles and buzzards from Barra.

Monach Islands (645615): These are situated 6 miles (9 km) west of North Uist. The main islands, joined at low tide, are Ceann Ear and Ceann Iar, and the group includes the reef of Stackay, and Shillay, the most westerly, with a disused lighthouse. The islands are a National Nature Reserve of 578 ha (1425 acres), with only 337 ha (836 acres) exposed at high water, visited by 2000 barnacles and Greenland whitefronts in March. Most of the islands are uncultivated machair and dunes, without fulmars. Oystercatchers, arctic terns, twenty pairs of little terns, etc., nest in central fields, and many herring, common and lesser black-backed gulls in bracken thriving in goose-droppings.

North Rona (HW8132, 59° 7′ N, 5° 49′ W): The northern-most turf-covered island in the Outer Hebrides is a National Nature Reserve of 129 ha (320 acres) without restriction, 45 miles (56 km) northwest of Cape Wrath and northeast of the Butt of Lewis, whose passerine migration is shared. Windy, sheep-grazed green hills and cliffs with sixteen nesting species and six irregulars: Leach's petrels (village, south bay, July–August), storm petrels (walls), great skuas, 6000 pairs of puffins, razorbills, guillemots, black guillemots, 3000 pairs of kittiwakes, fulmars, peregrines, 1500 pairs of great blackbacks, 600 pairs of arctic tern, shags, eiders, oystercatchers, rock and meadow pipits, and starlings. Many turnstones summer, and 107 visiting species include red-breasted flycatcher, bullfinch and an eyebrow thrush in October 1964. Landing is in the east bay.

Pabbay: Situated in the Sound of Harris, Pabbay has a sheltered eastern bay, dunes and valley, but few bird cliffs: fulmars, shags, puffins, arctic terns, snipe, rock and meadow pipits, skylark, twite, wheatear, wren, starling, song thrush, oystercatcher, great black-backed and herring gulls. Nesters are also on Spuir Rock between Pabbay and Boreray, which had a black-headed bunting in July 1970. Barnacles winter here.

Rockall: This most westerly and remote isle is 191 miles (307 km) from St Kilda, 70 feet (21 m) high, and 250 feet (76 m) basal circumference. There are resting guillemots, kittiwakes and fulmars, but not nesting because storm waves top it. Also in summer come great and arctic skuas, puffins, storm petrels, Manx shearwaters, lesser black-backed gulls, and June–autumn passage of great and sooty shearwaters. Access is limited to privileged Navy helicopters, or to non-landing trips on trawlers from Fleetwood (Lancashire), etc. Gannets and fulmars were found to be abundant in a May visit on the Liverpool ship *London Craftsman*, when an exhausted swallow flew aboard. Long-tailed and pomerine skuas are more frequent here than at most sea-watches.

Shiant Islands (NG4197): In the North Minch southeast of Lewis, these islands have nesting puffins, fulmars, kittiwakes, guillemots and hoodies; shearwaters are apparently not proven. There is a passage of autumn shearwaters and 480 barnacles in April.

Sula Sgeir (HW6130, 59°6'N, 6°9'W): This is a National Nature Reserve situated 12 miles southwest of North Rona. There are 4000 nesting gannets, a few puffins, guillemots and Leach's petrels.

St Kilda (010900): The seven isles and stacks of this group form an 853 ha (2107 acre) National Trust and National Nature Reserve 45 miles (56 km) west of Griminish Point, North Uist, and 110 miles (176 km) from the mainland. Unrestricted access is by trawler, or National Trust volunteer working parties, or from the Army base via Shieldaig. Autumn–spring gales make it Britain's windiest place. There are many perpendicular precipices thrusting up sheer from the sea and seabird colonies, especially petrels, and the world's largest colony of 44,000 gannets is on Boreray and the Stacks, together with the largest and oldest British fulmar colony, and the greatest puffinry (probably over-estimated at '1 to 3 million'). Fulmars return in October–November, black guillemots on 20–23 March and puffins on 12 April, depending upon autumn moult and sufficient fish being available. There are at least 460 pairs of the larger St Kilda wren. The largest island, Hirta, 637 ha (1575 acres), rising to 1390 feet (417 m), 3 miles by 2 miles (5 by 3 km), has 11,000 pairs of kittiwakes, 10,000 of fulmars, eight pairs of great skuas, three pairs of whimbrel, peregrines, hen harriers, northern golden plover, ringed plover, greenshank, oystercatcher, eiders, storm petrels, great and lesser black-backed, herring and common gulls, ravens, hoodies, wheatears, rock and meadow pipits, Shetland starlings, twites, tree sparrows (east bay village), twenty to thirty pairs of Faroe snipe (village area), 20,000 guillemots (10 per cent bridled), black guillemots, puffins, and in 1972 red-necked phalaropes. Its 1164 feet (349 m) Carn Mor headland has nesting Manx shearwater, Leach's and storm petrels (and village walls), puffins (also in Village Bay and the Cambir), razorbills, guillemots, black guillemots, eiders, kittiwakes, rock pipits, wheatears, wrens, great skuas, etc., mostly in Mullach Bay below, with the

gulls (other than kitties) on the grassland of Glean Mor
above. Connachair, Britain's highest sea cliff, 1379 feet (318
m) in the northeast, harbours many fulmars, great skuas,
shearwaters, Leach's (on the buttress, Ard Uacherachd)
and storm petrels. There is a passage migration including
Lapland buntings, greylag and barnacle geese (Cambir),
300 Greenland whitefronts in April, ruff, black-tailed
godwit, dunlin, short-eared owl, and visits of snowy owl,
buzzard, snow buntings, American robin, evening grosbeak
and laughing gull, tawny pipit, rose-coloured starling,
rock thrush and Temminck's stint in June 1970. An
American yellow warbler was reported in 1977.

The other islands are Sanday, Soay, where Leach's petrel
and most puffins nest and barnacle geese are visitors, 600
feet (180 m) Dun with storm and Leach's petrels, puffins,
black guillemots, razorbills, shags, and, 4 miles (6 km) from
Hirta, and more accessible than the Dun, the gannets'
Boreray and its stacks. Boreray also has Leach's, fulmars and
puffins. Boreray Passage (3 miles—5 km) separates 600 feet
(180 m) Stac Lii, reached by a jump-landing ledge and
roped climb. Lesser Stac an Armin is Britain's tallest sea
stack, at 627 feet (188 m). Stac Lavenish stands nearby.

Uists: The third windiest part of Britain and one of the
wettest, with 240 rainy days a year, the Uists are two
almost treeless, mainly flat islands of peat bogs, machair,
poor farms whose dead sheep feed the hoodie crows (except
in the hilly east), with many sea lochs and inland lochans,
and a good north–south road linking the ports and islands
with causeways. Reached by air from Glasgow to Benbecula (see above) or Skye (Uig) (388638) to Lochmaddy
in the north (918687), or Oban and Mallaig to Lochbois-
dale in the south, the ports have hotels and guest houses

(Carnan, South Causeway, etc.). White sands mark its shores, and only 14° F (10° C) separate summer and winter temperatures. Red- and black-throated divers breed on hill lochs and mergansers, common gulls, mute swans and wild greylags breed on the lower lakes. Waders (red-necked phalaropes) and eagles are among the attractions; there are twelve pairs of merlins and all three islands echo the purring territorial songs of nesting dunlin with which the phalaropes consort, as well as harbouring common, little and arctic terns, redshank, black-headed gull, black guillemots (in the east at Petersport), and twite and Shetland starlings in holes in stony ground. Peregrine and hoodie crow nest on

Golden Eaglet, North Uist

the ground in heather. Sedge warblers are the commonest warblers, but there are few whitethroats or blackcaps. Stonechats, wheatears, Hebridean wrens, corn and reed buntings, tree and house sparrows are here, with greenfinches, curlew, coast-nesting rockdoves feeding in the fields, skylarks, swallows, house martins, nocturnally vociferous corncrakes, hen harriers gliding low, jade green shags, wing-spreading cormorants, mallard, tufted duck, snipe, blackbird, song thrush, robin, lapwing, Irish and very dark Hebridean red grouse, and the almost flapless flight of fulmars—these are all breeding. Wood and purple sandpipers are seen in summer, and black-tailed godwits in full plumage. The osprey has been here on May passage, like the spotted crake, while winter visitors range from great northern divers (which often tarry in summer plumage), to flocks of scaup, barnacle geese and Iceland gulls.

North Uist (895785): 17 miles (27 km) long and 3–13 miles (5–21 km) wide, North Uist is chiefly flat and more resembles Harris (from which it is separated by the 7 mile (12 km) Sound of Harris on the north) than more mountainous and Gaelic South Uist. One of the easiest golden eagle eyries I have photographed was hardly a grandmother's walk to a rocky ledge 500 feet (150 m), feeding its eaglets on rabbits, rats and grouse, occasionally greylag goslings. In use since 1946 it has an alternate eyrie. The first egg hatched at 4.30 p.m., 2 May, the other four days later. The female chick weighed four pounds by the 22nd, the male three and a half. Everytime I crossed the saddle I flushed a noisy pair of nesting greenshank. I saw eiders nesting at the large, inland lochs Huagavot, Vairugain and Fada in the hills above Newton Ferry road junction. Greenshank were also at a loch. I saw a pair of red-throated divers nesting on a little loch scarcely 100 yards square in the hills above Newton Ferry road junction. Blackthroats were on other lochs. In the absence of trees, hoodies, etc., nest in the heather. Herons nested on bare rock on the islets of Iosal and Duin, and at Loch Scadavar. I was interested to see a fulmar sitting on a nest on the old island tower at Loch Scolpaig, a goldeneye and a golden plover haunt near Teghairy Bay Head on the northeast. Red-necked phalaropes nest occasionally at another loch, which is a breeding site of gadwall. Goldeneye nest, too, whimbrel and coot have been seen with stonechats at another water; hen harriers and arctic skuas nest on the

Manx Shearwaters, fighting at nesting haunts, Western Isles

central plain, etc., while a roadside black-headed gullery is on Loch nan Smalag. Little terns nest at the coast, cormorants about $\frac{1}{2}$ mile (1 km) inland at Loch an Tomain. Cormorants, eiders, fulmars and puffins nest at Causamal Point. Grinnish Point is a good sea watch for passing auks and shearwaters, with nesting cormorants, arctic terns, greenshank, black guillemots and occasional whimbrel. Ard an Runair is another good sea watch with a northwest wind with 387 shearwaters an hour, including great, sooty and Cory's. Also Port nan Long at the end of the B893. Loch Iosal na Duin had a heronry. Whoopers linger like great northern divers into late May, longtail duck are winter visitors with some nesting claims near Vallay. Baird's sandpiper was recorded in September 1971, and the yellowhammer at Houghary in 1973. Eiders nest on Newton Ferry Moor, and dunlin, little and common terns and common gulls inland in fields and heather. Four hundred pomerine skuas were recorded in three days in May 1971. A green sandpiper's nest with four eggs was found in 1976.

Balranald (NF7070): This 607 ha (1500 acres) RSPB reserve, part restricted, by the A865 near Houghary (warden) in the northeast of North Uist, is mainly for duck and waders with occasional red-necked phalaropes among some forty breeding species. By no means the best place for phalaropes, it includes a marram-covered shore and the small offshore island of Causamul with little, arctic and common terns. It has fifty pairs of snipe, shoveler, gadwall, scaup, eider, merganser, shelduck, tufted duck, short-eared owl, cormorant, snipe, water rail, twite, dunlin, rock pipit, ringed plover, redshank, oystercatcher, etc.

Five thousand barnacles visit it on April–May passage,

summer turnstones, curlew sandpipers, little stints and spotted redshanks are seen, shearwaters and skuas pass offshore and a white-winged black tern was seen in 1974.

South Uist (080830): 22 miles (35 km) by 7 miles (11 km) with about 190 freshwater lochs and lochans, South Uist rises to 2085 feet (626 m) with nesting haunts of eagles, ring ouzels, hen harrier and red grouse. There are long, silvery western beaches, too, but mainly thin, acid 'machair' soil overlying white sand. Snipe, redshank and lapwing nest numerously in the fields. The farmyard cackle of wild greylags soon attracted my attention to their largest British colony of forty to seventy pairs at the partly restricted, wardened 1678 ha (4145 acres) National Nature Reserve of Loch Druidibeg (774397)—numerous peaty, island-strewn lochs hunted by hen harrier, little grebe and short-eared owl on the east side of the road just south of Grogarry House, Howmore. Many goslings hatch by mid May, and two or three pairs of eiders nest inland here. Some 300 greylags winter on the machair between Howmore and Eocha. I found red-throated divers nesting beyond the reserve, and both black- and red-throats at another loch, also red-throats with mergansers, short-eared owl, merlin, dunlin, common gull and red grouse at a roadside water south of the causeway. A few greylags nest on other waters, like Loch Bee (NF7743), with its regatta of mainly non-breeding mute swans, dunlins nesting on its marshy western shore, and a light-breasted brent among its May visitors. Greylags also nested on lochs Fada, an Phuirt-ruaidh by the road at Howmore, a'Mhachair (a haunt of common tern, tufted duck, oystercatchers and redshank) and at Stilligarry (a reserve extension with terns, dunlin, coot and little grebes). Grogarry House has house sparrows nesting in the garden bushes, blackbirds, spotted flycatchers, hedge sparrows, hoodies, tree sparrows, collared doves, corn buntings, house martins, and stonechats; a lesser grey shrike was seen here in May 1964. By the Skiport road skirting the reserve, a small plantation of pines, rhododendrons and junipers (among Uist's few trees) had long-eared owls nesting. Grogarry Lodge has a hostel annex. *Warden:* Stilligarry, Loch Boisdale.

Another of my reasons for visiting South Uist was its red-necked phalaropes which nest irregularly among the dunlin in the shallow, reedy bay of a loch, usually beginning to lay about 5 June. Like many migratory northern waders, they arrive mated, though a pair appearing on 9 June mated on that and the following day. They sometimes favour other lochs, too, and nine pairs were on South Uist in 1973. Hallan had arctic and common terns and black-headed gulls, ringed plover, teal, shoveler and tufted duck. I found phalaropes once on one boggy loch side, and dunlin on the other. Another water had gadwall and wigeon, and summering black-tailed godwits. Between Beinn Bheag and Loch Eynort I saw herons' nests in stunted rowans only a foot or two above the turfy, rocky islet close to the bank at Loch Nam Faeoileann. Cliff nests were also at Loch Boisdale. Sitting out a tide among the eiders and shelduck on Vorran Island off the west coast (turning at Market Stance) late in May I saw arctic skuas pursuing terns and whimbrel around all day, as well as non-breeding turnstones where oystercatchers and ringed plovers nested. There was another haunt of hen harrier, short-eared owl, ring ouzel and stonechat, Loch Eynort of short-eared owls, Howmore of common gulls and greylags. Ruidha Andvule promontory, 3 miles (5 km) south of Vorran, is a major haunt of eiders, etc., while elsewhere has had nesting eagles.

Alt Volagir wood is also interesting. Greenland whitefronts, greylags, barnacles, whoopers and velvet scoter are regular visitors, and a Steller's eider off Vorran attracted watchers from England in the 1972–5 winters; wood sandpiper is among autumn waders and rarities have been rustic bunting and the American shore (horned) lark *alpestris* in September 1953. Tides are half-an-hour later on west than on east coasts, with 4 m springs at Loch Skiport.

Information
Recorders: W. A. J. Cunningham, Aros, 10 Barony Square, Stornoway. (St Kilda) Dr I. Pennie, Varkasaig, Scourie, Sutherland.
Society: Western Isle Tourist Association, 21 South Beach Quay, Stornoway, Outer Hebrides.
Literature: Anderson, *et al.*, Flannan Isles, *Bird Study*, **8** (1961); *Scottish Birds* (1959).
Boyd, J. M. and Williamson, K., *Mosaic of Islands* (Edinburgh, 1963).
Boyd, J. M. and Williamson, K., *St Kilda Summer* (London, 1960).
Darling, Fraser, A Naturalist on Rona (Oxford, 1939).
Fisher, J., *Rockall* (London, 1956).
Hardy, E., Birdlife on Uist, *Birds Illustrated* (September 1965).
Knowlton, D. *The Naturalist in the Hebrides* (London, 1977).
Nature Conservancy Council, *Loch Druidibeg Nature Reserve* (Edinburgh, 1963).
Newton, I. and Kerbes, R. H., Breeding of Greylag Geese on the Outer Hebrides, 1974, *Journal of Animal Ecology*, **43** (1975).
Roberts, D. G., The Rockall Plateau, *Geographical Magazine*, XLVI, 6 (March 1974).

Roberts, R. and Atkinson, A., The Haskier Rocks of North Uist, *Scottish Naturalist,* **67** (1955).

Robinson, M. J. H., Breeding Birds of North Rona, *Scottish Birds,* **5**, 3 (1968).

Robson, M. and Wills, P., Birds of Bearsay (Lewis), *Scottish Birds,* **2**, 7 (1963).

Check list

Nesters: Black-throated Diver, Red-throated Diver, Little Grebe, (Slavonian Grebe), Fulmar, Manx Shearwater, Storm Petrel, Leach's Petrel, Gannet, Cormorant, Shag, Heron, Mallard, Teal, Gadwall, Wigeon, Shoveler, (Pintail), Scaup, Tufted Duck, (Goldeneye), Eider, (Scoter), Red-breasted Merganser, Shelduck, Greylag Goose, Mute Swan, Golden Eagle, Buzzard, Hen Harrier, Peregrine, Merlin, Kestrel, Irish Red Grouse, Water Rail, Corncrake, Moorhen, Coot, Oystercatcher, Lapwing, Ringed Plover, Golden Plover, Faroe Snipe, Curlew, Whimbrel, Sandpiper, Greenshank, Redshank, Dunlin, Red-necked Phalarope, Arctic Skua, Great Skua, Great Black-backed Gull, Lesser Black-backed Gull, Herring Gull, Common Gull, Black-headed Gull, Kittiwake, Common Tern, Arctic Tern, Little Tern, Razorbill, Guillemot, Black Guillemot, Puffin, Rockdove, Woodpigeon, Collared Dove, Cuckoo, Long-eared Owl, Short-eared Owl, (Swift), Skylark, Swallow, House Martin, (Sand Martin), Raven, Carrion Crow, Hoodie Crow, Rook, (Jackdaw), Great Tit, Blue Tit, (Coal Tit), Tree Creeper, Hebridean and St Kilda Wren, Irish Dipper, Mistle Thrush, Hebridean Song Thrush, Ring Ouzel, Blackbird, Wheatear, Hebridean Stonechat, Whinchat, (Redstart), Robin, Sedge Warbler, Garden Warbler, Whitethroat, Willow Warbler, Chiffchaff, Goldcrest, Spotted Flycatcher, Hedge Sparrow, Meadow Pipit,

Hebridean Rock Pipit, Pied and White Wagtails, Grey Wagtail, Shetland Starling, Greenfinch, Twite, Chaffinch, Corn Bunting, (Yellowhammer), Reed Bunting, House Sparrow, Tree Sparrow.

Garganey, Pochard, Spotted Crake, Blackcap, Wood Warbler, Redpoll, Bullfinch, Grasshopper Warbler, Linnet and Chough may have nested.

Migratory and rarer visitors: There is an autumn passage of Cory's, Great and Sooty Shearwaters, winter Great Northern and White-billed Divers, flocks of winter Long-tailed Duck and Velvet Scoter; also Steller's Eider come with autumn and spring passage of Barnacle Goose, Greenland Whitefronted Goose, a few Pinkfoot and Light-breasted Brent, as well as Whooper Swan, Gyr Falcon records increased with more bird watchers. The Osprey calls on spring passage. Migratory waders include Little Stint, Curlew Sandpiper, Spotted Redshank, Purple Sandpiper, Turnstone, Icelandic Black-tailed Godwit, White-rumped Sandpiper and Baird's Sandpiper. Glaucous Gull and Iceland Gull are regular winter visitors. White-winged Black Terns occasionally drift over. Snowy Owls are increasingly recorded and in recent years Great Spotted Cuckoo, Alpine Swift, Lesser Grey Shrike, Golden Oriole, Lapland Bunting, Rustic Bunting and Black-headed Bunting were also noted.

Chapter 17

Check List of Scottish Birds

E   Escaped   PV   Passage Visitor
I   Introduced   RB   Resident Breeder
MB   Migrant Breeder   V   Vagrant
                          WV   Winter Visitor

(Bracketed names are races of the same species)

Black-throated Diver	RB	Leach's Petrel	MB
Great Northern Diver		British Storm Petrel	MB
('Naark')	WV, RB	White Pelican	E
White-billed Diver	WV	Gannet ('Solan Goose')	MB
Red-throated Diver	RB	Cormorant	RB
Great Crested Grebe	RB	American Double-	
Red-necked Grebe	PV	crested Cormorant	E
Holbell's Grebe	V	Shag ('Scarf')	RB
Slavonian Grebe	RB	Magnificent Frigate Bird	V
Black-necked Grebe	RB	Grey Heron	RB
Little Grebe	RB	Purple Heron	V
Pied-billed Grebe	V	Little Egret	V
Black-browed Albatross	V	Great White Egret	V
Fulmar (large-billed,		Cattle Egret (Buff-	
auduboni)	RB	backed Heron)	E
Fulmar (small-billed,		Squacco Heron	V
glacialis)	WV	Night Heron	PV, E
Cory's Shearwater	PV	Little Bittern	V
Manx Shearwater	MB	American Bittern	V
Little Shearwater	V	Bittern	WV
Great Shearwater	PV	White Stork	V
Sooty Shearwater	PV	Black Stork	V
Wilson's Petrel	V	Glossy Ibis	V
Frigate Petrel	V	Spoonbill	PV

Greater Flamingo	E
Mallard	WV, RB
⌈ Teal	WV, RB
American Green-	
⌊ winged Teal	V, E
American Blue-	
winged Teal	E
Baikal Teal	V, E
Garganey	PV
Gadwall	RB
Wigeon	WV, RB
American Wigeon	
('Baldpate')	V, E
Pintail	WV, RB
Shoveler	WV. RB
Mandarin	B, E
Carolina Wood Duck	E
Scaup	WV, RB
Ferruginous Duck	V, E
Tufted Duck	WV, RB
Ring-necked Duck	E
Pochard	WV, RB
Red-crested Pochard	E
American Buffelhead	V
Goldeneye (Dowker)	WV, RB
Barrow's Goldeneye	E
Long-tailed Duck	WV
Velvet Scoter	WV
Common Scoter	WV, RB
Surf Scoter	V
Steller's Eider	V
Eider	RB
King Eider	V

American Ruddy Duck	E
Harlequin Duck	V, E
American Hooded	
Merganser	V
Red-breasted	
Merganser	RB
Goosander	RB
Smew	WV
Shelduck	RB
Ruddy Shelduck	E
Spur-winged Goose	E
⌈ Western Greylag	WV, RB, I
⌊ Eastern Greylag	E
⌈ Russian White-	
fronted Goose	WV
⌊ Greenland Whitefront	WV
Lesser White-	
fronted Goose	WV
⌈ Bean Goose	WV
⌊ Pink-footed Goose	WV
⌈ Lesser Snow (Blue)	
Goose	E
⌊ Great Snow (Blue) Goose	E
Ross's Snow Goose	E
Bar-headed Goose	E
Red-breasted Goose	E
⌈ Dark-breasted Brent	WV
⌊ Light-breasted Brent	WV
Barnacle Goose	WV. E
Canada Goose	I
Mute Swan	I
⌈ Whooper	WV
⌊ Trumpeter	E

⎡Bewick's Swan	WV	American Kestrel	V
⎣Whistling Swan	E	Red Grouse (Muirfowl)	RB, I
Black Swan	I, E	Ptarmigan	RB, I
Golden Eagle	RB	Black Grouse	RB, I
Spotted Eagle	V	Capercaillie	RB, I
Buzzard	RB	Red-legged Partridge	I
Rough-legged Buzzard	PV	Common Partridge	RB, I
Spotted Eagle	V	Quail	MB, V
Sparrowhawk	RB, PV	⎡Caucasian Pheasant	I
⎡Goshawk	PV, RB, E	⎢Chinese Ring-necked	
⎣American Goshawk	E	⎢ Pheasant	I
Red Kite	V	⎢Kirghiz (Mongolian)	
Black Kite	V	⎣Ring-necked Pheasant	I
White-tailed Sea Eagle	PV	Japanese Pheasant	I
Honey Buzzard	PV	Golden Pheasant	I
Marsh Harrier	PV	Reeve's Pheasant	I
Hen Harrier	MB	Common Crane	V
Montagu's Harrier	PV	Demoiselle Crane	E
Pallid (Pale)		⎡Water Rail	RB, WV
Harrier	V	⎣Iceland Water Rail	V
Osprey	PV, MB	Spotted Crake	PV
Hobby	PV	Sora Rail	
Peregrine	RB	(Carolina Crake)	V, E
⎡Gyr Falcon	WV, E	Little Crake	V
⎣Greenland Falcon	WV, E	Baillon's Crake	V
Lanner Falcon	E	Purple Gallinule	E
Saker Falcon	E	Corncrake	MB
⎡American Pigeon Hawk	V	Moorhen	RB
⎢Merlin	PV, RB	Coot	RB
⎣Iceland Merlin	WV	Great Bustard	V
Red-footed Falcon	PM	Eastern Little Bustard	V
Kestrel	RB	Houbara's Bustard	V
Lesser Kestrel	V	Oystercatcher	WV, RB

Sociable Plover   v
Lapwing   wv, rb
[Ringed Plover   pv, rb
Tundra (Arctic)
[Ringed Plover   pv
Little Ringed Plover   mb
American Killdeer   v
Kentish Plover   v
Grey Plover   wv
[Southern Golden Plover mb
Northern Golden
 Plover   mb, wv, pv
[American Lesser
  Golden Plover   v
Asiatic (Eastern)   v
  Golden Plover
Dotterel   mb
Black-winged Stilt   v
Turnstone   pv, wv
Long-billed Dowitcher   v
[Common Snipe   rb, wv
Faroe Snipe   rb, wv
American Snipe   v
Jack Snipe   pv
Great Snipe   pv
Woodcock   rb, wv
Curlew (Whaup)   wv, rb
Esquimaux Curlew   v
[Whimbrel   pv, mb
Hudsonian Whimbrel   v
[Black-tailed Godwit   pv
Icelandic Black-tailed
  Godwit   pv, rb

Bar-tailed Godwit   pv
Green Sandpiper   rb, pv
Wood Sandpiper   rb, pv
Marsh Sandpiper   pv
American Solitary
  Sandpiper   v
Common Sandpiper   mb
American Spotted
  Sandpiper   vb
Terek Sandpiper   v
[Redshank   rb
Iceland Redshank   wv
Spotted Redshank   pv
Greenshank   pv, mb
Lesser Yellowlegs   v
Greater Yellowlegs   v
American Stilt
  Sandpiper   v
Knot   wv
Purple Sandpiper   wv
Little Stint   pv
Temminck's Stint   rb, wv
[Southern Dunlin   pv, rb
Lapland (Northern)
  Dunlin   pv
Arctic Dunlin   wv
White-rumped
  Sandpiper   pv
Baird's Sandpiper   v
Pectoral Sandpiper   pv
Sharp-tailed Sandpiper   v
Least Sandpiper   v
Curlew Sandpiper   pv

Semi-palmated Sandpiper	V
Western Sandpiper	V
Sanderling	PV
Buff-breasted Sandpiper	PV
Upland Sandpiper	V
Broad-billed Sandpiper	V
Ruff	PV
Avocet	V
Grey Phalarope	PV
Red-necked Phalarope	MB
Wilson's Phalarope	PV
Stone Curlew	V
Cream-coloured Courser	V
Collared Pratincole	V
Black-winged Pratincole	V
Great Skua (Bonxie)	PV, RB
Pomerine Skua	PV
Arctic Skua	PV, RB
Long-tailed Skua	PV
Ivory Gull	WV
Great Black-backed Gull	RB
⎡Lesser Black-backed Gull	MB
Scandinavian Lesser Black-backed Gull	WV ⎦
Great Black-headed Gull	V
⎡Herring Gull	RB
Scandinavian Herring Gull	V ⎦
Common Gull (Maw)	RB

Glaucous Gull	WV
Iceland Gull	WV
Mediterranean Black-headed Gull	V
Bonaparte's Gull	V
Little Gull	PV
Black-headed Gull	WV, RB
Laughing Gull	V
Ring-billed Gull	V
Sabine's Gull	WV
Ross's Gull	WV
Kittiwake (Tarrock)	RB
Black Tern	PV
Whiskered Tern	V
White-winged Black Tern	V
Gull-billed Tern	V
Caspian Tern	PV
Sooty Tern	V
Common Tern	MB
Arctic Tern	MB
Roseate Tern	MB
Little Tern	MB
Sandwich Tern	MB
⎡Razorbill (Helligag)	RB
⎣Arctic Razorbill	WV
Little Auk	WV
⎡Southern Guillemot	RB
⎣Northern Guillemot	WV
Brunnich's Guillemot	V
Black Guillemot (Tystie)	RB
⎡Puffin	RB
⎣Arctic Puffin	WV

Pallas's Sand
  Grouse   v
Stockdove   RB

⌈ Rockdove (Blue Doo)   RB
⌊ Feral Pigeon   RB
Woodpigeon   RB
Turtle Dove   RB

⌈ Barbary Dove   E
⌊ Collared Turtle Dove RB
Rufous Turtle Dove   E
Cuckoo   M
Great Spotted Cuckoo v
American Yellow-
  billed Cuckoo   v
American Black-
  billed Cuckoo   v

⌈ White-breasted Barn-
   Owl   RB
| Dark-breasted Barn-
⌊ Owl   v
Snowy Owl   WV, RB
Scop's Owl   v
Little Owl   WV, RB
Eagle Owl   v
Tawny Owl   RB

⌈ Hawk Owl   v
⌊ American Hawk Owl   v
Tengmalm's Owl   v
Long-eared Owl   RB
Short-eared Owl
  ('Kattaface')   WV, RB
Nightjar   MB, PV
Needle-tailed Swift   v

Swift   MB
Alpine Swift   v
Kingfisher   RB
Bee Eater   v
Roller   PV
Hoopoe   PV
Green Woodpecker   RB

⌈ Great Spotted
   Woodpecker   RB
| Northern Great
⌊ Spotted Woodpecker WV
Lesser Spotted
  Woodpecker   RB
Wryneck   PV, MB

⌈ Short-toed Lark   v
| Eastern Short-toed
⌊ Lark   v
Bimaculated Lark   v
Crested Lark   v
Woodlark   PV

⌈ Skylark ('Laverock') RB
| Eastern (Siberian)
⌊ Skylark   v
White-winged Lark   v

⌈ Shorelark   WV
⌊ American Horned Lark v
Swallow   MB
Red-rumped Swallow v
House Martin   MB
Sand Martin   MB
Golden Oriole   MB, PV
Raven   RB
Nutcracker   v

Carrion Crow	RB	Dipper	RB
Hoodie (Grey) Crow	RB	Irish Dipper	RB
Rook	RB	Black-bellied	
Jackdaw	RB	Dipper	V
Continental Jackdaw	V	Bearded Tit	WV
Magpie	RB	White's (Golden	
Jay	RB	Mountain) Thrush	V
Chough	RB	Siberian Thrush	V
Great Tit	RB	Rock Thrush	E, V
Northern (Contin-		Mistle Thrush	RB
ental) Great Tit	WV	Fieldfare	RB, WV
Blue Tit	RB	Song Thrush	RB
Northern (Contin-		Hebridean Song	
ental) Blue Tit	WV	Thrush	RB
Coal (Cole) Tit	RB	Continental Song	
Continental Coal		Thrush	WV
Tit	WV	Redwing	RB, WV
Scottish Crested		Iceland Redwing	WV
Tit	RB	Dusky (Naumann's	
Marsh Tit	RB	Black-throated)	
Willow Tit	RB	Thrush	V
Long-tailed Tit	RB	American Robin	V
Northern Long-		Black-throated	
tailed Tit	V	Thrush	V
Nuthatch	RB	Eyebrowed Thrush	V
Tree Creeper	RB	Ring Ouzel	MB
Northern Tree		Blackbird	WV, RB
Creeper	V	Hermit Thrush	V
Wren ('Robbie')	RB	Grey-cheeked Thrush	V
Shetland Wren	RB	Wheatear	MB
Hebridean Wren	RB	Greenland Wheatear	PV
St Kilda Wren	RB	Black-eared Wheatear	
Fair Isle Wren	RB	(Western)	V

Western Desert Wheatear   V
Eastern Desert Wheatear   V
Black Wheatear   V
Pied Wheatear   V
Red-tailed Wheatear   V
Stonechat   RB
Asiatic Stonechat   V
Hebridean Stonechat   RB
Whinchat   MB
Red-flanked Bluetail   V
Redstart   MB
Black Redstart   RB, PV
Nightingale   PV
Eastern Nightingale   V
Thrush Nightingale (Sprosser)   PV
Red-spotted Bluethroat   MB, PV
White-spotted Bluethroat   V
Siberian Rubythroat   V
Robin   RB
Continental Robin   PV
River Warbler   V
Grasshopper Warbler   MB
Pallas's Grasshopper Warbler   V
Savi's Warbler   V
Lanceolated Warbler   V
Reed Warbler   MB, PV
Great Reed Warbler   V

Blyth's Reed Warbler   V
Marsh Warbler   V
Sedge Warbler   MB
Aquatic Warbler   V
Thick-billed (Reed) Warbler   V
Paddyfield Warbler   V
Melodious Warbler   V
Icterine Warbler   V
Olivaceous Warbler   V
Booted Warbler   V
Blackcap   MB
Barred Warbler   PV
Garden Warbler   MB
Whitethroat   MB
Lesser Whitethroat   MB, PV
Siberian Lesser Whitethroat   V
Sardinian Warbler   V
Subalpine Warbler   PV
Willow Warbler   MB
Northern Willow Warbler   PV
Chiffchaff   MB
Siberian Chiffchaff   WV
Scandinavian Chiffchaff   PV
Greenish Warbler   PV
Wood Warbler   MB
Arctic Warbler   PV
Bonelli's Warbler   V
Dusky Warbler   V
Radde's (Bush) Warbler   V

Yellow-browed Warbler   PV
Eversmann's Warbler   V
Pallas's (Leaf) Warbler   V
⌈Goldcrest   RB, WV
⌊Continental Goldcrest   WV
Firecrest   WV
Spotted Flycatcher   MB
Pied Flycatcher   MB
Red-breasted Flycatcher PV
Collared Flycatcher   V
⌈Hedge Sparrow
    (Dunnock)   RB
│Continental Hedge
│   Sparrow   V
│Hebridean Hedge
⌊   Sparrow   RB
Alpine Accentor   V
Richard's Pipit   PV
Tawny Pipit   V
Meadow Pipit   RB
Tree Pipit   MB
Pechora Pipit   V
Olive-backed Pipit   V
Red-throated Pipit   V
⌈Water Pipit   WV
│Rock Pipit (Tang
│   Sparrow)   RB
│Hebridean Rock Pipit   RB
│Scandinavian Rock Pipit   V
│American (Greenland)
⌊   Water Pipit   V
⌈White Wagtail   PV, MB
⌊Pied Wagtail   RB

Grey Wagtail   RB
Citrine (Yellow-headed)
    Wagtail   PV
⌈Blue-headed Yellow
│   Wagtail   PV
│Yellow Wagtail   MB
│Grey-headed Yellow
│   Wagtail   PV
│Black-headed Yellow
│   Wagtail   V
⌊Syke's Wagtail   V
Waxwing   WV
Great Grey Shrike   WV
Lesser Grey Shrike   PV
Isabelline Shrike   V
Woodchat   PV
Red-backed Shrike   V
Red-tailed Shrike   V
Steppe Shrike   V
⌈Starling (Stukie)   WV, RB
⌊Shetland Starling   RB
Rose-coloured Starling
    (Pastor)   V
American
    Ovenbird   V
Hawfinch   RB
Greenfinch   RB
Goldfinch   RB
Siskin   WV, RB
Serin   E
⌈Linnet   RB
│Continental
⌊   Linnet   V

Twite ('Hill Lintie')   RB
Hebridean Twite   RB
Scandinavian Twite   WV
Redpoll (Lesser)   RB
Mealy Redpoll   WV
Greenland Redpoll   WV
Arctic (Hornemann's)
  Redpoll   WV
Bullfinch   RB
Northern Bullfinch   E, PV
Trumpeter Bullfinch   V
Scarlet Rosefinch
  (Grosbeak)   PV
Pine Grosbeak   V
Continental
  Crossbill   WV, MB
Scottish Crossbill   RB
Parrot Crossbill   V
Two-barred (White-
  winged) Crossbill V
Chaffinch   RB
Continental Chaffinch   V
Brambling   WV, MB
Bobolink   E
American Red-winged
  'Blackbird'   E
Baltimore Oriole   V
Chestnut Bunting   V or E
Corn Bunting   RB
Yellowhammer
  ('Yorlin')   RB
Continental
  Yellowhammer   V

Cretzschmar's Bunting   V
Black-headed Bunting   V
Pine Bunting   V
Red-headed Bunting   E
Yellow-breasted
  Bunting   V
Ortolan   PV
Cirl Bunting   V
Rustic Bunting   V
Little Bunting   V
Reed Bunting   RB
Pallas Reed Bunting   V
Lapland Bunting   WV
Snow Bunting   RB, WV
Icelandic Snow
  Bunting   WV
Indigo Bunting   E
Lazuli Bunting   E
Blue 'Grosbeak'   V
Evening 'Grosbeak'   E
Black-headed
  'Grosbeak'   E
Painted Bunting   E
American Song
  Sparrow   V
White-crowned
  Sparrow   V
White-throated
  Sparrow   V
Slate-coloured Junco   V
Black and White
  'Warbler' (USA)   V
Myrtle Warbler   V

Tennessee 'Warbler'	v	House Sparrow	
Yellow Warbler	v	(Spuerg)	RB
Cape May Warbler	v	Tree Sparrow	RB

Rappell's Warbler was claimed in 1977, in Shetland.
(Nineteenth century records of American Red-tailed Hawk
and Ruby-crowned Kinglet are not considered authentic.)

Index